Hopkins Against History

17 February 1997

For Deanne Bredvell

Good memories of reading a set of new poets together.

Hopkins Against History

Eugene Hollahan

Eugene Hollahan

CREIGHTON UNIVERSITY PRESS
Omaha, Nebraska
Association of Jesuit University Presses

Editorial
Creighton University Press
2500 California Plaza
Omaha, Nebraska 68178

Marketing andDistribution
Fordham University Press
University Box L
Bronx, New York 10458

ISBN: 1-881871-12-6 (cloth)
1-881871-13-4 (paper)

Printed in the United States of America

For

Brian Walsh Hollahan

"The music of his mind"

and

Capt. Mark Ransom Hollahan, USMC

"Yes. Why do we all, seeing of a soldier, bless him?"

(1)   . . . the full weight on the modern artist of what I have called 'the burden of the past' pressed first upon the poet; and it was in England especially that the problem became dramatized . . .

Bate vii

(2)   History gives the consciousness of what we are and what we have.

Droysen 74

(3)   The historical consciousness has enabled modern man to hold the entire past of humanity present within himself.

Wilhelm Dilthey, in Treitler 173

(4)   What is untrue history? Nothing and worse than nothing.

Hopkins, *Correspondence* 146

CONTENTS

ACKNOWLEDGMENTS

Many of the ideas in this book were first tested in articles and reviews in the following journals: *PMLA, Nineteenth-Century Fiction, Studies in Philology, Texas Studies in Literature and Language, Comparative Literature Studies, Studies in the Novel, Modern Fiction Studies,* and *Novel: A Forum of Fiction.* These exploratory essays are cited where appropriate in the course of my present argument. An earlier version of Chapter 3 appeared in *Texas Studies in Literature and Language.* I offer sincere thanks to the editors of these journals.

Versions of chapters 2, 3, and 4 have been presented at conferences sponsored by the Modern Language Association of America, the Interdisciplinary Nineteenth-Century Studies Association, the American Literature Association, the Christianity and Literature Association, the John Henry Newman Centenary Conference, and the International Hopkins Association. In every case, I have benefitted by having my hypotheses diligently contested.

In *Crisis-Consciousness and the Novel* (1992), I teased out the complex development of a crisis-trope, centering upon the word *crisis* itself, that to no small degree shapes modern thought and feeling. I became acutely aware that writers of many kinds position themselves in intricate and at times awkward positions in relation to history. In the case of Hopkins, I discovered an agonized Victorian crisis-consciousness in the form of a poet's peculiarly antithetical consciousness of ideological historiography.

Following out the implications of this discovery, I have been encouraged by scholars and critics who showed me the hazards but also the rewards of historicizing an author from an earlier period. These writers are identified in my introduction and are cited wherever appropriate in "Hopkins Against History." Specifically, I am indebted for intellectual guidance and personal encouragement to Jerome Bump, former editor of *Texas Studies in Literature and Language*. Likewise, to Hans Kellner, Harold Bloom, many members of the English Institute at Harvard University, and a large camaraderie of Hopkins scholars around the world. Peter Milward, S.J., at Sophia University in Tokyo, showed me how to defamiliarize Hopkins's most familiar poems so as to see them afresh. To Jerome McGann I owe a debt of thanks for his multivolumed historical judgment of literary work. Hayden White alerted me to the cogency of regarding both historiology (what has happened) and historiography (traces of what has happened) as problematical and worthy of study. "Hopkins Against History" owes much to the advice and example of these scholars. The faults are all mine.

Three colleagues in the Department of English at Georgia State University provided assistance. Janet Gabler-Hover, Paul H. Schmidt, and Murray Brown read early drafts and provided me with corrective good sense and humane encouragement. The Department of English, the College of Arts and Sciences, and the University Research Fund provided several kinds of assistance, including financial support, during the period of research and writing.

Acknowledgment is hereby made to Oxford University Press for permission to excerpt materials from *The Poetical Works of Gerard Manley Hopkins*, ed. Norman H. MacKenzie (Clarendon, 1990).

In *Hopkins Against History*, I employ the latest *MLA* style of documentation. Accordingly, I provide one "Works Cited" list at the end of the book.

PREFACE

(1)   Here is a writer emancipated from time and tradition.
                                                     Anon., *Month* (1912)

(2)   . . . it is dreadful to explain these things in cold blood.
                                            Hopkins, *Letters* 113-14

(3)   O, once explained, how clear it all is!
                                            Hopkins, *Letters* 274

I must begin, as I will end, under the rod of a chastening precept. "When a man writes a preface he tries only to say an antithesis, and never thinks of the truth." This famous pronouncement by Charles James Fox must sober and steel any writer who would prepare the ground for a presumed audience of readers.

In 1989, a global community of readers commemorated Gerard Manley Hopkins during the centenary of the poet's death. They produced an outpouring of writings and other expressive forms, critical as well as adulatory. Anyone who wishes can look at the exhibition catalogue *Hopkins Lives* to enjoy at least a glimpse of the Hopkins enterprise down to 1989. Following 1989, one plausibly expected a kind of hiatus, a leveling off or settling down of interest in Hopkins.

Now, however, the critical enterprise that might have seemed settled for a time has been reopened and revitalized to a degree that promises to be even more productive than the previous era. Witness the essay collection *Gerard Manley Hopkins and Critical Discourse* (Hollahan). In 1991, a new biography of the Victorian poet-priest appeared from the pen of Robert Bernard Martin, and, in 1992, Norman White published another biography. Shortly before, in 1990, *The Poetical Works of Gerard Manley Hopkins*, edited by Norman MacKenzie, had appeared from Clarendon Press. For a new generation to come, this annotated edition of 179 poems and fragments, arranged chronologically, provides for a new readership for the remarkable man whom MacKenzie refers to as GMH.

John Updike remarked that Richard Ellmann's multifaceted work on James Joyce represents one of the wonders of modern literary history (130). No less impressive and fruitful, although taking different discursive forms, has been Norman MacKenzie's thirty years of work in the service of Hopkins studies, culminating in his 1990 edition of the poems. By presenting all of the poems and fragments in chronological order, the new edition invites a fresh look at numerous historical issues bearing upon Hopkins.

In several respects, MacKenzie's new edition lays the groundwork for any study of Hopkins's poetic development. The chronological arrangement, however problematical (see my chapter 2), effectively constitutes, so to speak, a first draft of any sustained commentary. That is, the poems are in some very real senses their own best commentary. In addition, MacKenzie's critical apparatus—glosses of words by the thousands, early and late versions of a dozen or so poems, variant readings of numerous draft versions, serious attention given to the first half of Hopkins's neglected work, drafts (fair-copies, significant transcripts), abundant background materials, cross-references to MacKenzie's own two-volume *Hopkins Poetic Facsimiles*, histories and descriptions of the various albums where the poems were precariously stored against oblivion, explanations of prosodic notations, and abundant historical information—these and other features assure that this edition is probably as near a definitive edition as would be possible at the present time.

In order to insert "Hopkins Against History" into the new cycle of Hopkins studies following upon MacKenzie's 1990 edition, I will exclusively cite it. Sadly, perhaps, such exclusive reliance upon this edition results in the bracketing and setting aside of familiar versions of specific poems which we have come to admire in anthologies and earlier editions, most notably the popular fourth edition. In citing MacKenzie's new edition, I present Hopkins's arbitrary and at times vexing diacritical marks and paratextual marks, his attempts to control all future readings of his poems. Witness one of the Sonnets of Desolation, where an antithetical Hopkins fights the deity Himself:

Not, I'll not, carrion comfort, Despair, not feast on thee;
Not untwist—slack they may be—these last strands of man
In me ór, most weary, cry *I can no more*. I can;
Can something, hope, wish day come, not choose not to be.
But ah, but O thou terrible, why wouldst thou rude on me
Thy $\left\{\begin{array}{l}\text{wring-world}\\\text{wring-earth}\end{array}\right\}$ right foot rock? lay a lionlimb against me? scan
With darksome devouring eyes my bruisèd bones? and fan,
O in turns of tempest, me heaped there; me frantic to avoïd thee and
     flee?
Why? That my chaff might fly; my grain lie, sheer and clear.
Nay in all that toil, that coil, since (seems) I kissed the rod,
Hand rather, my heart lo! lapped strength, stóle joy, would laugh,
     cheer.
Cheer whóm though? The héro whose héaven-handling flúng me,
     fóot tród
Me? or mé that fóught him? O whích one? is it éach one? That night,
     that yéar
Of now done darkness I wretch lay wrestling with (my God!) my God.

                                    (*Poetical* 183; #159)

In order to comprehend such strenuous efforts to control readerly response, we should remind ourselves that Hopkins's contemporary Robert
Browning used the dramatic monologue form to give the diligent reader
almost complete control of the poem (Woolford 71-5). Hopkins's peculiar
diacritics, I think, represent a desire to oppose or evade not only the exigencies of time to come but also the written inscriptions of times past that
we think of as historiography.

The biographer Norman White thinks that no entirely coherent pattern
can be convincingly imposed on Hopkins's life.

> Hopkins's powerful and original temperament, a strange mixture
> of innocence and expertise, of old prejudices and clear-sighted ob-
> servations, worked against his achieving happiness and success. It
> constantly expressed itself in enthusiasms and antipathies rather
> than calm appraisals. He adored or hated his environments; his re-
> actions to place and to the lack of a settled home are centrally
> important to Hopkins and his poetry. He sometimes despaired at his
> apparent inability to control himself and his destiny. His solutions
> were typically impractical and extreme. He attempted to simplify
> his problems and evade his demons by complete submission to

his problems and evade his demons by complete submission to ancient comprehensive ideological systems; he became a Roman Catholic and then a Jesuit. His university and personal education had taken him into a subtle and confused modern English world more suited to experiment and individual response than to the judgements of an imposed doctrinal framework. Within the religious discipline his problems were sometimes crushed but never worked out, and they continued to surface to the end of his life. In poems Hopkins wrote in Wales richly vigorous personal responses to experience were squeezed into a moral grid, the results attempting to be conclusions of universal value. After his leaving Wales the possibility of an audience diminished; the mood of the poetry darkened as the opportunity for unified self-exploration increased. Sometimes he sought a land of Lost Content in Victorian poems whose sentiments are difficult for modern readers. Finally in Ireland a new power and kind of originality were forced into his poems of self-examination by his diminished loyalties and many dimensions of isolation. (vii-viii)

The conflicted Hopkins described by White, riddled with "antipathies," is to no small degree the Hopkins central to "Hopkins Against History."

Certain disturbing epithets occur regularly in discussions of Hopkins: preposterous, obscure, exclusive, dense, difficult, uncertain, self-effacing, puzzling, adamant, extreme, outlandish, eccentric, bizarre, grotesque, perverse, hybrid, violent, wayward, peripheral, and odd. These and other such opinions appear, for example, in a review of MacKenzie's edition and Martin's biography. The reviewer aptly subsumes all such labels for Hopkins under one term: *unbordered*. Accordingly: "With his distrust of self-pity, his stiff reticence, and his self-effacement, Hopkins can seem an enchanting but oddly unbordered soul—someone not easily boxed within the foursquare confines of a book" (Leithauser 114).

Leithauser praises MacKenzie's arrangement of Hopkins's oeuvre in chronological order of composition for its accommodating both readerly refreshment and historical reappraisal. Even so, he also notes that Hopkins is hard to pin down in history because this self-styled "Time's eunuch," over the length of his brief lifetime (1844-1889), enacted a temporal tug-of-war between earth and heaven, a struggle between the evanescent and the eternal (116-17).

Leithauser labels Hopkins a "radical prosodist" and then asks in admiring wonder: "Where in the world did this singular prosodist come from?" (116). His question is precisely the question we might well ask about a poet whose small body of work enriched the metrical resources of the language of Shakespeare, Milton, and Wordsworth. I intend to follow out some of the implications of Leithauser's question by historicizing Hopkins in ways consistent not only with the most stimulating thought of our own day but also with his own unbordered and perhaps unborderable genius. My hypothesis will be quite simple. Hopkins, I will propose, is not just a "singular prosodist" or even a "radical prosodist." He is, in my own terminology, an ontological prosodist, a poet who tries, by means of a distinctive sprung-rhythm metric, to evade both the nightmare of history and certain ideological distortions of Victorian historiography. In doing so, he captures ontological essences (inscapes) of things and persons, thereby enriching Victorian crisis-consciousness and consciousness in general.

My historicizing efforts require that I follow subterranean and circuitous routes, at times with only the slenderest Ariadne's thread, while interpreting some of the most obvious elements of Hopkins's life and works. I refer to elements such as his refusal to follow up on an early success, his invention of sprung rhythm, his single use of the words *Falcon* and *Buckle*, his refusal to arrange and publish his poems, his reliance upon the sonnet form, his composition of a shipwreck poem, his leaving much work in the form of fragments, his unschooled gestures toward musicology, and even his total avoidance, in his poetry, of the Victorian keyword *history*.

The great development in nineteenth-century English versification was the rejection of strict accentual syllabics in favor of accentualism. Hopkins invented sprung rhythm—overstressing which allows recognition of English-language accentualism—in order to cope with and to represent his tortuous sense of time (Fussell 71; 60). The Hopkins I myself will represent made his main contribution to Victorian consciousness by employing a sprung-rhythm prosody not only to escape the constraints of historical time but also to body forth his own version of historical time. A commonplace of Victorian culture is that life in Victorian England meant, in effect and broadly speaking, following the dictates of a "new universe of time." Hopkins's invention of sprung rhythm may have been his means of responding to, perhaps his means of rebuking, the principle of disciplined time operative at all levels of life, including the writing of history and the writing of poetry. At every step of my journey, I am guided by Joseph Brodsky's definition of *prosody*: "prosody, which is simply a repository of time within language" (357).

To historicize a poet usually means to provide a rounded picture in some detail (Levinson 14). I am constructing a fairly detailed "Hopkins

Against History," but it is perhaps not surprising that I discover "antithesis" at the heart of my subject. Speaking of the critical activity that began with the 1965 Yale Symposium on Literary Criticism, one historian describes the phenomenon thus: "Tensions between antithetical approaches are fundamental to the critical enterprise" (Miller, *Theory* 1). In no small measure because they are inherent in Hopkins's own utterances, many of the numerous antitheses characterizing recent criticism enter into my own speculations about Hopkins.[1]

Humphrey Carpenter thinks that we need a good biography of Hopkins because "he had a romantically difficult relationship with his art" (xvi). Both Martin and White testify abundantly to Hopkins's strangely unbalanced and exotic personality that finds expression in difficult, intense poetry. We also need to augment existing historical interpretations of Hopkins's life and art at least in part because he had a romantically *antithetical* relationship with writings from the past or about the past. Hopkins was a Christian author, but, as Mircea Eliade thinks, the book-based Christian religion "entered History in order to abolish it" (Desmond 92). Perhaps by resisting history, as I think he attempts in numerous ways to do, he is simply doing his Christian duty.

My own critical attitude, particularly in chapter 2, might be mistaken for a futile grousing about a Hopkins that might have been but never was. Nothing could be further from my conscious intention. My effort to glimpse Hopkins shadow-boxing with historiographers, including in chapter 2 my speculations regarding the poetical career Hopkins might have had, is entirely a heuristic effort to understand the obscure silence Hopkins elected for himself.

About my title, "Hopkins Against History," I must say a cautionary word at the outset. Prudence and common sense teach us that for any individual not to be of his own time and place would be a patent absurdity or logical impossibility. When I argue that Hopkins lived and wrote "against history," I mean simply that numerous features and elements of Victorian culture that alarmed or offended Hopkins seem to coalesce in an antithetical response to written representations of history. For convenience, in many contexts I will stipulate for *history* when (as each such context should make clear) I am referring to *historiography*. Any sensitive individual living the nightmare of modern history might understandably respond by means of peculiar strategies, defensive gestures, or desperate ploys. Among literary figures we think, for example, of Baudelaire and Joyce. A writer's consciousness of historiographical discourses can result in a writing "in" history, a writing "after" history, a writing "out of" history, or a writing "from" history. In special cases, such as Montaigne, there may also occur a writing "against" history (Hampton 134-97). Montaigne experienced a crisis in his reading of history, in response to ideological distortions of history. He modified his reading of the past into a relatively more private activity, an activity centering on an "interiorized ethical model" (195). Something approximately like Montaigne's revisionary gesture toward history is the phenomenon I will propose as being Hopkins's reaction "against history," specifically against an ideological historian like Henry Thomas Buckle or against the Victorian literary history that by reifying his genius could deaden his life and work.

My goal is in part to understand Hopkins's contributions to Victorian consciousness, such contributions accruing to posterity despite, but perhaps to some degree because of, Hopkins's "consciousness of the triumph of time" (Bump, *Hopkins* [ix]; 52). Nothing will be lost, and something valuable may be gained, if we attempt to historicize Hopkins in ways consistent not only with the thinking of our own day but also with his own past-burdened genius.[2]

At every stage, I conjecture cause-and-effect relations. Yet I know as well as anyone how tenuous such hypotheses may finally prove. I realize how any poet is part of a given reality, a historical moment, but how difficult it is to establish irrefutable connections. One of Hopkins's historical critics puts the problem this way:

[As] little as the study of language serves to elucidate Hopkins's trials of religious allegiance or the sacramental nature of his poetry, the theological and pastoral campaigns of his spiritual mentors cast equally scant light on the medium of his poetic activity or the transformations that he wrought in it. (Plotkin 60)

Historicizing Hopkins requires one's hazarding numerous guesses about the dark sources of literary art, with no guarantee of results. Even so, armed with Hume's healthy skepticism, one proceeds.

I must anticipate objections to one of my procedures. From start to finish, I employ quotations from a variety of sources as theme-setting epigraphs to every chapter and interchapter, as well as to the book as a whole. My purpose is not only to permit such passages to do some of my work but more so to present a physically and formally *overdetermined* appearance, something equivalent to Hopkins's own overburdened, overdetermined appearance by reason of the diacritical marks disfiguring his verses. Even as I recognize that Hopkins very likely grasped the Viconian principle that "meaning is diacritical" (Said, *Beginnings* 196), I feel compelled to construe these burdensome diacritics—clearly aspects of design within the author's control—as representing an ineluctable expression of Hopkins's historiographically tormented spirit. To interpret one's own writing for future readers is, in a sense, to function as a historiographer. At a purely formal level, and at the risk of committing the fallacy of imitative form, I use my epigraphs to approximate both the overdetermining effects of Hopkins's diacritical marks and also his consciousness of his own Victorian predicament.

Jane Austen reputedly said of her most complex heroine Emma Woodhouse: "I am going to take a heroine whom no one but myself will much like" (Austen-Leigh 157). How many readers will like the antithetical Hopkinsian consciousness I take for my subject? A word such as *like*, even in one of Austen's famous ironical senses, seems too bland for the imaginative effort Hopkins requires of anyone who would inquire into his life, mind, and art. Many readers will reject out of hand my version of Hopkins the unbordered soul struggling against history but in the process producing poems in a poetic rhythm of lasting value. I predict, though, that some readers will respect and perhaps grudgingly admire the antithetically heroic Hopkins I propose, even if they ultimately modify a precept from Hopkins himself by admiring but conjecturing otherwise.

27 February 1993
Port Royal, South Carolina

Introduction

The Shaped Negation:
A Model for an Antithetical History

(1)   Wordsworth's poetry is a mimetic denial of history so vigorous, full, and detailed that denial, the shaped negation, becomes the positive fact.

Liu 48

(2)   It is this language of taboo, this antithetical use of the precursor's primal words, that must serve as the basis for an antithetical criticism.

Bloom 66

(3)   . . . the old civilisation and order must be destroyed . . . all the history that is preserved in standing monuments.

Hopkins, *Letters* 27-8

(4)   . . . what I mean [about sprung rhythm] is clearest in an antithesis.

Hopkins, *Correspondence* 22

David Hume grumbled that historical research was a "dark industry" (Breisach 286), but historians since Hume have tried to brighten the work place that includes everything that ever happened down to this very moment. Many researchers pursuing the noble dream of objectivity are shocked to discover that in assembling and construing facts they are "nailing jelly to the wall" (Novick 1-17). Even more disturbing, some historians confront the possibility that to do their work they must "get the story crooked" by resorting to metaphors and other tropes (Kellner vii-xi).

In our dealings with authors from earlier periods, we should "always historicize" if we wish to attain true understanding of their utterances. On the other hand, to historicize an author can mean many contradictory things, none of them easy to access or apply. History can mean not only everything that has happened since the creation but also everything that has been written or recorded about whatever has happened. History thus includes both a historiology and a historiography, though nowadays the latter term applies equally to both activities (Novick 8 n. 6). At a time like the present when we are undergoing a crisis of historical consciousness (Breisach xi), we might understandably elect to defer the task. Happily, the intellectual ferment marking the current crisis makes the challenge hard to resist.

How are we to historicize Gerard Manley Hopkins, an ontological prosodist who seems to disregard and to escape familiar historical categories? Living in a century when things and persons were being increasingly degraded, Hopkins invented inscapes which preserved and defended the unique essence of particular persons and things. And, living in a century when levelling processes such as mindless conformity threatened to regularize and enslave things and persons by making them alike, Hopkins in effect urged poets to adopt a sprung rhythm that would open up new individuating possibilities for English prosody and for English culture generally. So insistent was Hopkins concerning his theories that we have spent most of our critical energies on the sprung rhythm and Catholic theology he sometimes shrilly, sometimes arrogantly, always intelligently urged. Given that his poems were not published until 1918, fully twenty-nine years after his death, historical questions were from the outset ignored. Issues generally focused on metrical issues and philosophical issues, including vexing theological questions.

The last word of Hopkins's last poem is that most unpoetical—but arguably most historiographical—of all English words, *explanation*. In "To R. B." a dying Hopkins elucidated for his friend and eventual first editor Robert Bridges, by means of the most complete gestation image he would ever use, a biological analogy for the dynamics of poetic process.

He laments the sad state of his own barren poetical genius. We encounter here one of Hopkins's most radically historicist poems.

To R.B.

The fine delight that fathers thought; the strong
Spur, live and lancing like the blowpipe flame,
Breathes once and, quenchèd faster than it came,

Leaves yet the mind a mother of immortal song.
Nine months she then, nay years, nine years she long   5
Within her wears, bears, cares and combs the same:

The widow of an insight lost she lives, with aim
Now known and hand at work now never wrong.
Sweet fire the sire of muse, my soul needs this;

I want the one rapture of an inspiration.   10
O then if in my lagging lines you miss
The roll, the rise, the carol, the creation,
My winter world, that scarcely breathes that bliss
Now, yields you, with some sighs, our explanation.

                                    (*Poetical* 204; #179)

The movement from a vernal "fine delight" to a wintry "explanation" effectively measures one aspect of Hopkins's strange poetical career or non-career which gestures toward but effectively negates any tropological progress from metaphor to irony. The declension from the spiritualized "inspiration" to the awkwardly chiming, rational-sounding "explanation" condenses a sad tale indeed. The disappointed Hopkins thus ends one of the most ecstatic of poets' lives by pathetically offering not a bang but a whimper, a lame apology, an explanation, "the poorest substitute for a poetic text" (Said, *Beginnings* 274). Somewhat like Hamlet to Horatio, Hopkins implicitly pleads for Bridges to supply an explanation of his friend's noncareer. Bridges obliged his tormented friend in many ways, chiefly by preserving, editing, and posthumously publishing Hopkins's poems in 1918, thereby enabling the phenomenon of a literary achievement we are increasingly learning to appreciate.[1]

The writing of literary history involves a conflict of two interests, the need to describe the past and the need to explain it (Perkins). By choosing *explanation* as his final word, Hopkins left the ball squarely in the historian's court. Subsequent to 1918, many of Hopkins's readers labored to provide explanations of many kinds, from many critical and philosophical angles. My own critical model incorporates elements from diverse sources, including attempts to place Hopkins in one historical context or another.

We already have an emerging picture of Hopkins in his Victorian setting. In very general terms, Wendell Johnson pioneered the ongoing effort. Subsequently, Alison Sulloway placed Hopkins in his historical moment by examining Hopkins in relation to a distinctive Victorian temper composed of Oxford University, John Ruskin, Victorian calamitarianism, and the ideal of the Victorian gentleman. Sulloway claimed that "Hopkins adopted the materials of Victorian England and of Europe's past wherever he found them pertinent, and used them effectively wherever he could, in and out of the pulpit" (195). From another angle, Todd Bender interpreted Hopkins within the history of poetical reputations in England and within the classical tradition. Bender argues thus: "Far from being divorced from all tradition, the peculiar style of Hopkins is largely the result of a fortuitous confluence of tradition which led him to push forward at a precocious rate in directions already formed in Victorian art" (168). Zaniello has placed Hopkins in a scientific context: "I offer Hopkins as an extraordinary witness to the Age of Darwin, a Victorian intellectual who did understand many of the momentous changes in the science, philosophy, and theology of his time" (xiv). Walter Ong's work on Hopkins and the modern self deals with ontological, and hence ahistorical, themes; nevertheless, Ong offers an account of "Hopkins's sensibility, the new experience of time and self," emerging in Victorian England (53). Cary Plotkin places Hopkins in a frame of reference shaped by Victorian philology. Plotkin speaks for all these historians in his conclusion: "This calls for a change in perspective—ours" (11).

As a group, these historicizing critics both clear the ground and establish a ground for my examination of Hopkins's response not to history but to historiography. They also call attention to the inevitability of one's losing sight of Hopkins himself in the process of devoting necessarily long stretches of attention to various large contexts. Repeatedly we wonder, what has become of our poet? Given this ineluctable liability, one severe test for the literary historian is to elaborate a context at some length without too eagerly referring ahead to the poetry being contextualized. One can only hope to muster the necessary patience and negative capability.

Hopkins's poems can be construed as aesthetic artifacts preserving human experiences which are thus made available for reenactment by future generations quite apart from any specific historical considerations. This aesthetic principle throws each reader back into the recesses of his own innermost soul and self. However, Hopkins's best poems, like all poetry of genuine merit, coalesce many levels of experience (Martin 232). Hopkins's complex, guardedly disputatious, at times devious, antithetical reactions to reality as history and to history as historiography are by no means his least interesting utterances. No one has seriously attempted to historicize Hopkins in terms of the poet's own view of historiography. Prompted by my own discovery of a clue in Hopkins's most famous sonnet "The Windhover"—a clue in full view from the very beginning, so to speak—I intend to examine this other Hopkins.

To historicize a poet can mean many things. Certain well established procedures of historical criticism and literary history bear upon the problem. Historicism is a series of concepts and practices focused upon the cultural and social context within which literature appears. By general agreement, historicism concerns itself with issues raised by a work's paradoxical status as a timeless aesthetic object but one which is also a time-specific product of historical forces. In its extreme forms highly methodological and systematic, historicism initiates a four-pronged examination of a literary work: the historical context, the work as an aesthetic artifact, the impact of the work in its own sociocultural world, and its significance for readers in subsequent, seriously different, places and times.

Four broad critical procedures inform historicism. First, a Hegelian method endeavors to place the work within a transcendental continuity of historical process. Second, a naturalistic and sociological method follows St. Beuve and Taine by placing the work within contemporary social meanings and values. Third, a nationalistic effort places the work within a context of folk customs and political practices peculiar to a single country. Fourth, an aesthetic method regards the work in its artistic mode, as an artifact shaped by historical forces, dialectically able to affect its contextual world by embodying meaning and value for its own day and time but also able to carry into the future a power to shape and interpret later historical moments (Holman and Harmon 239-40).

Frequently, in reading Hopkins we sense that he existed oddly out of the loop of Victorian forms of power. In our own day, New Historicism refines and specializes historicist methods of interpretation, in particular with reference to cultural notions of ideology, discursive form, and the circulation of power within a culture. Two ideas in particular seem relevant to Hopkins: first, "history must disclose and reconstruct the conditions of consciousness and action" (Veeser 217), and, second, "representation 'makes things happen'" (165). Other assumptions prove instructive:

every expressive act embeds itself in material practices, every oppositional critique uses the very tools it condemns, and literary and non-literary
texts circulate inseparably. Even so, no single discourse expresses a total
or absolute truth. My critical model draws upon Greenblatt's definition
of a work of art: "the product of a negotiation between a creator or class
of creators, equipped with a complex, commonly shared repertoire of
conventions, and the articulations and practices of society" (Veeser 12).
In order to historicize a Victorian poet, we may need to examine the circulation of materials and discourses so as to locate specific sites of exchange and negotiation between discursive forms and forms of consciousness (13). My antithetical model of Hopkins is in some senses a representation of an oppositional poet playing desperate power games against
dominant forms of Victorian historiography.

In several respects, I follow Greenblatt by regarding a literary utterance as a nexus of cultural powers in circulation and conflict. Even so,
at one crucial point I diverge. Greenblatt would have us believe that
Shakespeare could "borrow comfortably" from Harsnett's work on exor-
cism (176). We are asked to believe that *King Lear* is essentially a "reit-
eration" of Harsnett's book (177). Hopkins, as radically as any English
poet, reacts against existing forms of discourse in such wise that his
formal utterances do in fact constitute fields of force where orthodox and
subversive impulses collide. By contrast, though, the Hopkins I represent
agonizes continually in response to Victorian and earlier forms of discourse. He never enjoys a moment's comfort, and he assuredly never
merely reiterates.

MacKenzie's 1990 edition represents Hopkins from several historical
angles. He attempts to establish the history of the manuscript albums
where Hopkins's poems are preserved (xxv). With the help of technical
experts and earlier Hopkins editors, he attempts to trace the evolution of
Hopkins's peculiar handwriting styles (xxvi). He attempts to arrange the
179 fragments and poems chronologically according to the dates of composition. In "Chronological Arrangement" (lix-lxiv), he divides Hopkins's
writing career into distinct phases and points the reader toward future
work to be done: "The chronology of each period in Hopkins's creativity
may call for special investigative procedures" (lx). Thus, for example, the
sonnets of 1877 (including "Spring," "The Windhover," "The Caged Skylark," and "Hurrahing in Harvest") can be construed as a sequence
marked by increasing metrical complexity (lxi). Concerning specific
poems, MacKenzie employs familiar backgrounding procedures and
materials while expressing the belief that "deeper study of the historical
records" leads to increased understanding of the factual basis of a poem

like "Margaret Clitheroe" (xlvii). At the same time, MacKenzie recognizes that the objective veracity and historical congruence he seeks to establish between poem and genetic circumstance will not always be forthcoming, in part because of Hopkins's peculiar "self-built lexicon" (xxviii), his inconstant attention to his own manuscripts, his "otherworldly neglect" of practical matters, and his distractedness or absent-mindedness. All such behavior erases much of the record (lii-lv). Fortunately, MacKenzie is adept at detecting nuances of "historical poignancy" (lxxiv) occurring at certain Hopkinsian intersections of fact and fiction.

Hopkins's poems are distinct from each other in many respects, but they are also linked by numerous echoes, repetitions, and abiding concerns. In addition, his letters, essays, notebooks, and devotional exercises contextualize but destabilize the poetry. Individual poems tend to become buried, annihilated, or overwhelmed by the interconnections between historical events and processes. Numerous elements of Hopkins's actual life—the Jesuit order, Oxford education, reading (in Scotus, Ignatius, Suárez, Greek philosophy, sacred scripture, Catholic liturgy), Paterian and Ruskinian aesthetics—these and other elements threaten to proliferate so as to "dissolve Hopkins into what influenced him, to make his work no more than a 'product' of its time" (Miller, *Theory* 71).

The reviewer Leithauser complained (wrongly, I think) that Martin's biography of Hopkins failed to confront two crucial elements of Hopkins's genius: the spiritual and the psychoanalytical (116). The antithetical model I will use includes these elements. Hopkins, after all, in addition to his technical innovations via sprung rhythm, was also both an adept at spiritual metaphor and an interestingly conflicted human being.

Perhaps more so than any other English poet, Hopkins is a poet of metaphor (Brooke-Rose 313-15). Metaphor can be construed in a variety of ways: as a means of drawing writer and reader intimately nearer each other, as a disruption or disfigurement of language, as an ethos builder, as a basis for religion, as a bridge between life and art, as a fundamental linguistic competence, as a mode of cognitive feeling, and even as literal statement. It can also be seen as offering an alternative to the world of facticity and history as ordinarily understood. In discussions of metaphor, we encounter such antithetical formulations as "new world," "new meaning," "second world," and "new order" (Sacks). We should be reminded here of Pope's image of the metaphorical powers of the true poet: "Where a new world leaps out at his command" (*Essay on Criticism*, II, 285). In short, metaphor itself can be understood as an antithetical mode of expression.

Concerning sprung rhythm, Hopkins himself would urge that "what I mean is clearest in an antithesis" (*Correspondence* 22). How does metaphor bear upon my argument that Hopkins responds antithetically to history? Metaphor is the metaphorist's ad hoc attempt to reject the actual world by transcending actuality in certain ways that recall consciousness of the spirit in western culture. In this sense, as Karsten Harries explains, metaphor is sometimes understood as a gesture toward a spiritual alternative to the ordinary world.

In "Metaphor and Transcendence," Harries tries to debunk an aesthetic view offered by modern criticism, a view of metaphor as an utterance which essentially lets a "new world" emerge. He would replace this ontological view with another view, less threatening perhaps, which holds that in order to do their proper work poets need only, and in fact are able only, to represent a reality we already know. As it were, a Heideggerian poetry of earth, nature, and God (87). Ironically, he contributes to my model by exhibiting the very argument he wishes to refute. Inadvertently, Harries convinces us that the radical of presentation in poetry is indeed metaphor but that metaphor offers us "something altogether new" in the aesthetic mode of "a second world" (79).

Metaphor, as a weapon "directed against reality," will take leave from familiar reality and allow us to "forget the world" (78). Fundamentally a strategy for "derealization" expressive of the "spirit's empty constructions" (81), poetic metaphor provides an "escape from reality" (79-80). Wishing to debunk the "refusal of reality that is inseparable from the aesthetic project," Harries attempts to deny that "the poet's metaphors promise a plenitude that temporal existence has to withhold" (81). Harries's effort to refute the notion of metaphor's representing an "aesthetic refusal of reality" (84) or a "vacation from reality" (86) ironically leaves his reader even more convinced than before that poetic metaphor expresses in part a Nietzschean "rancor against time" (81).[2]

The reviewer's second complaint was that Robert Martin displays ignorance of any psychoanalytical dimension to Hopkins's personal history. The reviewer is mistaken on this point, given that Martin offers psychoanalytical diagnoses throughout. In general, to the degree that psychoanalytic theory can be generalized to explicate literature as a form of consciousness, it affords insights into the responses a poet makes to the historical world viewed as the psyche projected outward and writ large (Holland 1-30). Alan Liu even argues that an antithetical response to historiography can express a poet's own deepest affirmations (Liu 32).

An antithetical response might represent the defense mechanism we think of as denial, essentially a means of excluding from consciousness certain threatening perceptions of outer reality. Whereas repression defends against dangers within, denial acts against perceptions of dangers without (Holland 53). Essentially a form of displacement, denial represents a defense mechanism equal to repression, reversal, reaction formation, undoing, projection, introjection, regression, splitting, symbolization, sublimation, and rationalization. What a poet leaves out of a poem, for example, may express a profound denial (57-8). Any literary form, by its abrupt appearance in time and space, enacts a process of erasure. In a chiasmic process of doing and undoing, or of denial by exaggeration, at one level of experience it brings out of the void a short-lived image of experience, one which quickly then vanishes again back into the void.

Denial by exaggeration is a specific and familiar response which caricatures some threatening force to the point of absurdity (109). We should perhaps think here of Hopkins's extreme metrical experiments in an ambitious poem such as "That Nature is a Heraclitean Fire."

That Nature is a Heraclitean Fire and of the
comfort of the Resurrection

Cloud-puffball, torn tufts, tossed pillows | flaunt forth, then chevy on
    an air-
Built thoroughfare: heaven-roysterers, in gay-gangs | they throng;
    they glitter in marches.
Down roughcast, down dazzling whitewash, | wherever an elm arches,
Shivelights and shadowtackle in long | lashes lace, lance, and pair.
Delightfully the bright wind boisterous | ropes, wrestles, beats earth
    bare   5
Of yestertempest's creases; in pool and rutpeel parches
Squandering ooze to squeezed | dough, crúst, dust; stánches, stárches
Squadroned masks and manmarks | treadmire toil there
Fóotfretted in it. Million-fuelèd, | nature's bonfire burns on.
But quench her bonniest, dearest | to her, her clearest-selvèd spar   10
Mán, how fást his firedint, | his mark on mind, is gone!
Bóth áre in àn únfathomàble, áll is in an ̃enórmous dárk
Drowned. O pity and indig | nation! Manshape, that shone
Sheer off, disseveral, a star, | death blots black out; nor mark
    Is ány of him àt áll so stárk   15

But vastness blurs and time ˈ beats level. Enough! the Resurrection,
A héart's-clarion! Awáy grief's gásping, ˈ joyless days, dejection.
          Across my foundering deck shone
A beacon, an eternal beam. ˈ Flesh fade, and mortal trash

Fáll to the residuary worm; ˈ world's wildfire, leave but ash: 20
          In a flash, at a trumpet crash,
I am all at once what Christ is, ˈ since he was what I am, and
This Jack, jóke, poor pótsherd, ˈ patch, matchwood, immortal
    diamond,
                Is immortal diamond.

(Poetical 197-98; #174)

Ostensibly about nature and God, this poem, revealing Hopkins's most
explicit self-image ("poor potsherd"), may employ stylistic exaggeration
in order to deny existential complexity such as sexuality (Holland 112)
or the stress characteristic of adult life in general (126).

Holland explains the rationale of antithetical denial in terms of fierce
absolutes:

> One must either accept the world or reject it wholly. Both these
> defenses the psychoanalyst would call forms of denial: denying the
> existence of forbidden things by seeing only what they are not; de-
> nying compromise or imperfection. (129)

In literature, any defense mechanism such as denial can appear under the
guise of meaning or form, most interestingly and pleasurably the latter
(189).

No matter how subtle, an antithetical response to the stresses common
to human history may express hostility to certain traces of historiography:
"The very form of the poem, in acting out a denial, may gratify an aggressive wish to annihilate those [persons or forces] guilty of the offend-
ing sight" (131). Form itself, then, may be a central defense or denial,
and denial may function at every level, being embodied even in specific
words like *ended* and *finished* (144). Denial can be associated with a
strategy such as the wish to resist a mythic pattern by means of distancing, parody, or affect block. Likewise, some poems manifest denial
by attempting to obtain reassurance through a deliberately adopted disillu-
sionment (290-1).

One feature of Harold Bloom's speculations concerning the anxiety of
influence is a definition of his key term *antithetical* (65-6). In rhetoric,

antithesis refers to the juxtaposition of contrasting ideas in parallel or balanced words, phrases, and structures. Extending and modifying this meaning, Nietzsche and Yeats separately described a kind of person who defines himself in terms of his own opposite human type. Freud defined antithesis in dream-work at the level of the word itself; accordingly, dream-work includes the linking of opposite words in new compound words that create complex new meanings. Freud, of course, clinically describes a compulsion neurosis, but, as Edward Said has noted, Freud also used a 1910 essay, "The Antithetical Meaning of Primal Words," to characterize antithesis as a pervasive phenomenon of language itself (Said, *World* 75). In his turn, Bloom adapts Freud's observation so as to explain how a poet confronts the past in the form of an opposite type of poet, a precursor, in order to "clear a mental space for himself." Thus: "It is this language of taboo, this antithetical use of the precursor's primal words, that must serve as the basis for an antithetical criticism" (66). We may reasonably posit for poetry itself a "critical and antithetical role" vis-à-vis orthodox historical consciousness (McGann, *Social* viii). I further generalize from Bloom so as to conjecture an image of Hopkins standing in an antithetical relation not so much to a precursor poet such as Milton or Wordsworth or Longfellow as to history itself, more specifically to some imagined Victorian historiographer.

Biographically, I follow William Empson's advice: "One is not tied to the author's biography [but any] student of literature ought to be trying all the time to empathize with the author (and of course the assumptions and conventions by which the author felt himself bound)" (vii-viii). To reiterate: the reviewer Leithauser complained that Martin's *Gerard Manley Hopkins: A Very Private Life* seems deficient on two counts, namely, in avoiding scrutiny of the psychological and spiritual dimensions of Hopkins's brief life. Perhaps inevitably thin on the spiritual side, Martin's account of the poet's life in fact stays close to such information as is verifiable. Martin offers numerous observations and speculations about the forces churning within. His biography contributes in no small way to my model, as the following summary will demonstrate.

Martin's Hopkins is in many ways a conflicted personality, at once rebellious, unmannerly, oedipal, complicated, aggressive, tormented, finicky, and hostile. He enjoys the paranoid pleasure of being "hunted." Beginning with a young Hopkins who hated his middle name "Manley" and who was habitually "rebelling against" his father Manley Hopkins (5), Martin represents a Hopkins who "needed constantly to assert to himself, and probably to others, that he was cut out for heroic conflict" (176). Hopkins's rich if immature psyche expressed itself in a "legalistic aggressiveness" that thrived on the idea of repression, so that "when there was no repression, it became necessary to invent it" (153). Hopkins's "defensive fears" and "hunted reaction" betray psychic conflicts (308).

Hopkins would become a maestro at representing personal torment but also at assuaging, at least momentarily or fictively, his own personal torment.

> My own heart let me more have pity on; let
> Me live to my sad self hereafter kind,
> Charitable; not live this tormented mind
> With this tormented mind tormenting yet.
> I cast for comfort I can no more get   5
> By groping round my comfortless than blind
> Eyes in their dark can day or thirst can find
> Thirst's all-in-all in all a world of wet.
> Soul, self; come, poor Jackself, I do advise
> You, jaded, lét be; call off thoughts awhile   10
> Elsewhere; leave comfort root-room; let joy size
> At God knows when to God knows what; whose smile
> 'S not wrung, see you; unforeseentimes rather—as skies
> Betweenpie mountains—lights a lovely mile.

(*Poetical* 186; #163)

The clinical truism that only conflicted persons are capable of producing serious art applies to Martin's representation of Hopkins. The poet loved the Roman Catholic church, but he also reviled it for its abundant "bad taste" (292). Of this Jesuit priest, one of the most perceptive nature poets, Martin writes: "He was both in love with the phenomenal world and aflame with fear of it." The sexuality that could have linked him in familiar ways with the life of his own time and with the biological history of the human species had to be suppressed and "refined almost out of existence" (77).

An oedipal struggle characterized Hopkins's relations with his father (146). It translated into a generalized rebelliousness (155), appearing in social intercourse as inconsiderateness and bad manners (138). A complicated personality to anyone who knew him up close (150), he spent his brief forty-four years in painful awareness of the "*sordidness* of things" (118), and he repeatedly acted out a depressive pattern of guilt, contrition, and forgiveness (99) as one settled response to such awareness. Like many artists given to attitudinizing his tastes and personal preferences (194), Hopkins regularly expressed hostility toward his father (68) while at the same time chasing after some substitute father-figure, such as Jowett, Liddon, Pusey, or Newman (44).

Martin shows how Hopkins was inwardly divided on the question of literary fame. Like Heraclitus, who motivates one of his greatest poems, Hopkins at times regarded signs of historical permanence as delusive masks (30), but he also yearned for the historical permanence that would come from literary fame: "Hopkins wanted both heavenly and earthly recognition, and who is to blame him?" (279).

Hopkins began his writing career with "The Escorial," where he provided explanatory notes referring to historical sources and artistic intentions. He ended his career with the sonnet "To R. B." with its problematical closing trope *explanation*. In between these two symbolic gestures, he devoted no small part of his energies to explaining to his correspondents such unfamiliar matters as the arcane lingo and undergraduate customs at Oxford. He took considerable pleasure in explaining the cant and ritual typical of the Jesuit novitiate (27). By contrast, though, so Martin thinks, Hopkins's diary seems intended to erase or simply omit most signs of social life as ordinarily understood (69). Likewise, his journals offer almost nothing about the great crises of his life and little direct reference to his presumedly deepest feelings (161).

Such paradoxes, gaps, or simply mixed feelings carry over to Hopkins's general orientation to history and the past itself. He read Villari's and Rio's histories of Savonarola, but only George Eliot's "pagan" novel *Romola* deeply moved him (78). He hated to see the "eradication of the past" at Oxford (56), but his conversion to Roman Catholicism involved him in one of the most antithetical movements in English history, in effect a turning back of the clock or wiping clean of the slate (42). He longed for old historical linkages (62), but he embraced Roman Catholic doctrines, such as the Real Presence of Christ in the eucharist, which effectively erase history or at least both affirm and deny history (41). History becomes for Hopkins not a fact but an interpretation or enabling trope, even if in his poems he eschews the Victorian keyword *history*. By contrast, we recall Newman's sixth discourse in *Idea of a University*, where Newman explains that his *beau ideal* of the perfected intellect would become, among other things, "almost prophetic from its knowledge of history."

Hopkins's antithetical turmoil centers, as Martin argues, upon the poet's father, himself a poet, Manley Hopkins. Two more dissimilar men can hardly be imagined than the silent, secretive, hunted Jesuit priest and his father, a successful business man, head of a large family, founder of an actuarial firm even today still in existence, the Consul-General for Hawaii, author of handbooks on the law of averages and on maritime insurance, as well as the author of three volumes of poetry. What son would not be daunted by such energy, success, and all-around competence? This was the man that "Gerard was rebelling against" (5).

Martin's oedipal Hopkins is matched by that described by Norman White, who thinks that Hopkins expressed a personal "antagonism" in championing Duns Scotus over the Jesuits' approved theologian Thomas Aquinas, a quirky antagonism that led to Hopkins's failing his examination in dogmatic theology and effectively shutting off one sort of priestly career (283-4). Given the psychoanalytic tensions that seem to play themselves out in Hopkins's reactions to the writings of historiographers, we can safely imagine that the conflicts came to a head in the infamous "Red" letter Hopkins wrote to Bridges in 1872. We see here Hopkins at his antithetically most explicit and most courageous. Logomachy being an inseparable part of discourse about the things that really matter (Abrams, *Mirror* 4), Hopkins's lifelong logomachy with life-as-historiography, inwardly repressed at times, finds expression in this impassioned utterance.

> I am afraid some great revolution is not far off. Horrible to say, in a manner I am a Communist. Their ideal bating some things is nobler than that professed by any secular statesman I know of (I must own I live in bat-light and shoot at a venture). Besides it is just—I do not mean the means of getting to it are. But it is a dreadful thing for the greatest and most necessary part of a very rich nation to live a hard life without dignity, knowledge, comforts, delight, or hopes in the midst of plenty—which plenty they make. *They profess that they do not care what they wreck and burn, the old civilisation and order must be destroyed. This is a dreadful look out but what has the old civilisation done for them?* As it at present stands in England it is itself in great measure founded on wrecking. But they got none of the spoils, they came in for nothing but harm from it then and thereafter. England has grown hugely wealthy but this wealth has not reached the working classes; I expect it has made their condition worse. Besides this iniquitous order the old civilisation embodies another order mostly old and what is new in direct entail from the old, the old religion, learning, law, art, etc and all the history that is preserved in standing monu-

ments. But as the working classes have not been educated they know next to nothing of all this and cannot be expected to care if they destroy it. The more I look the more black and deservedly black the future looks, so I will write no more. (*Letters* 27-8; Martin 217-18; emphasis added)

Hopkins's dismay over the condition of England, fused here with his own private griefs, momentarily epitomizes his stance toward the past (Martin 218). For an antithetical statement from a major Victorian poet equal to this one, we might have to turn to George Meredith's poems sympathetic to the Russian revolution (Hollahan, *Crisis-Consciousness* 100-7). After reading Hopkins's letter, we can better understand why some of his readers find in his poetry clear evidence of an "incomprehensible alien world" that must be avoided or erased (MacKenzie, "Introduction" lxvii).[3]

Hopkins does violence to the protocols of literary decorum at various levels of linguistic practice (Plotkin 2). He tends toward such extremes of expression as to deny ordinary uses of language. Geoffrey Hartmann notes that Hopkins's ways with words "evoke the tendency of semantic distinctions to fall back into a phonemic ground of identity," a sort of "dark, rich nothing" characteristic of a presumed chthonic ground of being (Miller, *Theory* 125). At the most radical levels, then, and in numerous ways, Hopkins denies or otherwise reacts against conventional discourse, including discourses of history.

Hopkins had good reason to feel paranoid about his civilization. According to the Catholic Emancipation Act of 1829, for an Englishman to become a Jesuit was to commit a misdemeanor serious enough to result in banishment for life (White 189). As my title suggests, I plan to argue that the "hunted" Hopkins rarely let down his guard with respect to English life as reified by various historicisms. He thus represents an instructive if problematical subject for a study of Victorian crisis-consciousness. By contrast, Matthew Arnold seems never to have suffered any anxiety on this score: "Arnold enjoyed a tall and successful aloofness from the historicizing spirit of his times" (Wimsatt and Brooks 442). In another sharp contrast with Hopkins, at a crucial time in Walter Pater's intellectual development the aesthetician read the historian Ernst Renan and was thereby able to "relax into historicism" (Carolyn Williams 47 n. 4). In many respects, the famous Pater influenced the obscure Hopkins. As Martin puts it, "Pater openly voiced doubts that bubbled up in Hopkins" (131). Pater's hard-won aesthetic historicism, culminating in *Marius the Epicurean*, provides a perspective from which to describe the stance of his student and sometime disciple. Hopkins, chiasmically as it were, reverses the polarity of Pater's viewpoint. As I will propose in five separate chapters, Hopkins operates not like Pater in terms of an aesthetic historicism but instead in terms of an antihistoricist aesthetic.[4]

Given the violent ruptures in Hopkins's life and art, "Hopkins Against History" might threaten to become merely an omnium gatherum of unrelated essays. Happily, though, we can recuperate the scattered fragments of Hopkins and his attendant Victorian debris under the aegis of his reactions to Victorian historiography. The resultant interpretation should contribute to our increasingly capacious sense of the entire Hopkins oeuvre.

Norman MacKenzie followed Hopkins into "many unfrequented corners" of arcane lore. He resorted to Scotland Yard's high-tech Infra-red Image Convertor in order to decipher overlays of handwriting by Hopkins and Bridges (*Poetical* vii-viii). In my own ways, I also play the detective, but my *modus operandi* will be quite different. In chapter 1, "'air, pride, plume, here / Buckle!': Hopkins Against Henry Thomas Buckle," I will focus on Hopkins's practice of placing within individual poems, as well as in his career and oeuvre as a whole, certain obvious clues to his historical critique. He resorts to what Flieger calls the "Clue in Full View" (941-42). The most vexing crux in Hopkins is an enigmatic utterance at the climax of "The Windhover": "air, pride, plume, here / Buckle!" What could "Buckle" mean in this context? Does it mean, as has been suggested, discipline or fight or fall? Clash, clasp, or collapse (*Poetical* 383-3)? But what of English history? Could it be that a proper name is cleverly disguised by the word's positioning at the beginning of a line of verse?

If we focus historically on the "Buckle" crux, we discover that this great poem of 1877 is in effect a critique of a Victorian ideology (secularism, relativism, humanism) embodied in a famous Victorian book sure to be perceived by Hopkins as proclaiming a dangerous world-view. Had Hopkins published "The Windhover" during his lifetime, readers could have recognized a topical referent. In 1857-61, Henry Thomas Buckle published a revolutionary book, *The History of Civilization in England*, which permanently changed the way history is understood and written. In "The Windhover," Hopkins engages with Buckle's discourse as an embodiment of a skeptical Victorian frame of mind. By construing "The Windhover" as an aesthetic discourse belittling and displacing Buckle's historical discourse, we can begin to understand the discursive roots of Hopkins's antithetical views. "The Windhover" and other poems may prove to be embedded in history in unsuspected ways. "The Windhover" invites our appreciation on two new counts, both for its specific conversation with Buckle's philosophy and more generally for Hopkins's thereby-focused engagement with Victorian historical consciousness.

Hopkins always denied any obscurity in his poetical methods. Was he obliged to point out to his handful of readers that the capitalized noun *Buckle* in a manuscript poem referred to one of the most famous English-men of their day, a writer whom "everybody reads"? In chapter 2, "'to succeed by failure': Hopkins Against the Tradition for Lyrical Assort-ments," I propose that Hopkins's bold anti-Buckleian gesture in "The Windhover" serves as a paradigm case and reaches to his entire oeuvre. He rejects literary history outright by the simple strategy of holding his poems back from publication. Thereby, he holds himself away from the main flow of literary culture and the mainstream of Victorian conscious-ness. Recent investigations by Neil Fraistat make it clear how important it has been for poets to assemble and arrange assortments of poems into collections for publication. In context of tradition, audience, contemporary rivalries, and other dynamics of literary culture, a poet's ordering of a lyric assortment enables a crucial stage in self-fashioning. Hopkins re-fused to carry out such a crucial aesthetic task. Set against the long his-tory of lyric assortments from Ovid onward, as well as the post-1918 history of his own collected poems, this great refusal offers an instructive example. As conventionally understood, the event that triggered Hop-kins's negative decision was the editorial rejection of *The Wreck of the Deutschland*, later placed first by Bridges as a "dragon in the gate" of the first edition. Yet Hopkins himself, from the deepest recesses of his per-sonality and genius, blocked any public access to his mind and art. Plac-ing this self-curtailing poet against the tradition for lyrical assortments helps us to see Hopkins enacting a personally costly but, given his ulti-mate triumph after 1918, historically valuable gesture against history.

Paradoxically, at his most literary Hopkins appears to function at his most antithetically historical. In chapter 3, "Hopkins Against Longfellow: Antithetical Bondings between 'The Wreck of the Hesperus' and *The Wreck of the Deutschland*," we encounter another enlightening episode in Hopkins's development. No odd couple equals for oddness the radical innovator Gerard Manley Hopkins and the arch-conservative Henry Wads-worth Longfellow. Both were important nineteenth-century poets, yet one was vastly popular whereas the other never saw the body of his writings in print. We might not expect to find a dynamic relation between "The Wreck of the Hesperus" (1840), a popular but minor poem in ballad form, and Hopkins's earth-scorching ode *The Wreck of the Deutschland* (1876). Yet external and internal evidence suggests that Longfellow's recitation-day chestnut rendering an event in American history enters into the psychogenesis and composition of Hopkins's experiment in sprung rhythm. Hopkins is on record as believing that no poem can be entirely original but must necessarily incorporate something "old or borrowed." From his father Manley Hopkins, he derived an interest in shipwrecks and an interest in Longfellow. His own lifelong awareness of contemporary literature kept him alert to the reputation of the popular American moralist-in-verse. When he came to write his own ambitious poem occasioned by an actual shipwreck, he drew upon many literary models and traditions. Among these sources was a national ballad, "The Wreck of the Hesperus." Harold Bloom's theory of the anxiety of influence enables an antithetical interpretation of this historical connection. Hopkins found in Longfellow's national ballad much skillfully done (to be imitated); much imperfectly done (to be amended); much left undone (to be executed by a new poetics). Longfellow's old-fashioned poem is, so to speak, a grounded "ship in distress" awaiting the flood-tide of Hopkins's religious ecstasy and new versification.[5]

In chapter 4, "Hopkins Against Frederick II: 'The Windhover,' *De Arte Venandi cum Avibus*, and Modern Consciousness," I am compelled to take another circuitous route in order to glimpse Hopkins's reactions to history. The Ariadne's thread I must follow here leads from the sonnet already examined in chapter 1 to another skeptical historiographer, this one not a contemporary like Buckle but one ostensibly buried in the distant past. The development of the sonnet form has been well documented by scholars such as Walter Mönch and S. K. Heninger. Aided by Paul Oppenheimer's speculations centering the origins of modern consciousness in the invention of the sonnet form, we now can hypothesize anew the historical consciousness embodied in "The Windhover." Why did such a daring poem take an old-fashioned poetical form? Why is it about a falcon? Modern consciousness begins with Giacomo da Lentino's invention, between the years 1225-1230, of the silently-read, inward-turning, problem-solving, logical-seeming sonnet. Giacomo's master, the Holy Roman Emperor Frederick II of Hohenstaufen (1194-1250), polymathic first modern ruler and arguably the first modern man, encouraged Giacomo's literary experimentation and himself composed sonnets. Frederick the skeptic also composed a classic historical account of falconry, *De Arte Venandi cum Avibus* (*The Art of Hunting with Birds*) (c. 1245). Examining Hopkins's celebrated "dapple-dawn-drawn Falcon" alongside Frederick's encyclopaedic falcon ("bird life [expresses] attractive manifestations of the processes of nature") leads me to conjecture another episode in Hopkins's intricate response to, in this case a reenactment of, historiography. Like the revolutionary Frederick, Hopkins may have perceived in the sonnet's fusion with falconry a distinctive consciousness which repeats but critiques a Frederickian dialectic of passion and action, of subversion and containment. He rejects Frederick's skeptical philosophy even as he uses Frederick's subject matter within the form invented by Giacomo.

Hopkins's struggle with history includes his occasional appeal or escape to music. Another expression of his antihistoricist aesthetic unfolds in chapter 5, "'most secret catgut of the mind': Hopkins, Music, and the Erasure of History." There, I depict a Hopkins who turns toward music as a means of escaping or erasing history. Happily, this is a Hopkins who, in a number of poems about music, stoutly rejects any possibility that the musical tone will expunge poetical words about the human condition.

Four of these five chapters focus on specific issues and a handful of Hopkins's poems. In order to redress what may seem to be a Wartonian "unwieldy excrescence of a disproportionate episode," I also examine all of the 179 poems and fragments arranged by MacKenzie. My method in this ancillary effort is to adopt Ihab Hassan's device of the "interchapter." I place four interchapters between the main chapters, inquiring whether the poems exhibit either historical materials or antithetical sentiments. One theme emerging in the interchapters is that Hopkins's first poem, "The Escorial," based on a famous book of Spanish history, evidently establishes historiographical principles that complicate his development and oeuvre. Other themes emerging in the interchapters have to do with Hopkins's numerous fragments and his avoidance of the Victorian key-word *history*.

Both Martin and White depict a Hopkins who was easily distracted, one whose eye could be caught by some topic subsidiary to this main interest and who would then take off after a new prey. The four inter-chapters are intended to read not so much as organic stages in a single unified narrative but as episodes, each with its own center of interest, that mimic a fragmented artist's life. At the risk of committing the fallacy of imitative form, they function as shifters intended to alter readerly perspectives quite abruptly, introducing "disciplined discontinuities" that, as McGann thinks, can discursively "rhyme with" the complexities of my subject, the antithetical poet Hopkins (*Social* ix).[6]

Scientists practice either little science or big science (Price). We can safely imagine that in studying historiography we shall encounter big forms of history and little forms. History can be quite large, with its century after century of human experience and its volume after volume of information, analysis, and explanation. My antithetical model includes an

assumption that Hopkins as a sonneteer practices little history. In chapter
1, for example, I urge that Hopkins's little sonnets belittle monumental
forms of Victorian historiography such as Buckle's *History of Civilization
in England*. He would have on his side one principle of modern epistemology, to the effect that no sense-datum can convincingly be kept going,
kept present to the mind, for more than two or three minutes at one time
(Duran 21). As it were, the length of a sonnet.

Hopkins also expresses a radical opinion of his Victorian contemporaries' historicist enterprise simply by refusing to use their keyword
history in any of his poems. In making this little refusal, Hopkins induces
a sort of Nietzschean "untimeliness" (GoGwilt 480). He is thus almost
unique among English poets. I will take up this *refus du style* in interchapter 3.

The Hopkins I am representing embodies the existential human person
who is both object and subject of historiography, one who is simultaneously an inhabitant of the present, an emigrant from the past, and an im-
migrant into the future. To return to the question asked by the reviewer
of Martin's biography: where did this radical prosodist come from?
Hopkins is not easy to get a purchase on, not least because he did not
bequeath to us an autobiography on the order of Ruskin's, Newman's,
Benjamin Hayden's, or Blanco White's. The complexities we face in setting out to historicize Hopkins can be perceived by our referring to
Cockshut's study of Victorian autobiography. There, Hopkins finds no
place as an autobiographer, but his poetry proves essential to Cockshut
when he would thematize his own argument (177; 211; 215).

The disappearance of God bears upon Victorian crisis-consciousness.
One of the chief ways Victorians experienced this crisis was by the emer-
gence of the historical sense in and of itself (Miller, *Disappearance* 12).
Hopkins was not exempt from the painful ordeal:

> Hopkins, who seems so different from other nineteenth-century
> writers who suffered the absence of God, in reality ends in a simi-
> lar place. Like so many of his contemporaries he believes in God,
> but is unable to reach him. Deserted by his nature, he is left with
> a blind violence of will toward a God who keeps himself absent.
> (359)

Following Miller's logic, to speak of Hopkins's historical sense as antithetical is almost a perfect redundancy or truism.

My model would not be complete without one further idea—this one
from Wilhelm Dilthey—that perhaps best expresses my own informing

trope: "The historical consciousness has enabled modern man to hold the entire past of humanity present within himself" (Treitler 173). For "modern man" read "antithetical Hopkins." Here is where "Hopkins Against History" must begin, with an oppositional poet who takes too much upon himself but in his fierce attempt to achieve an ontologically stable self produces writings of permanent value.

"air, pride, plume, here / Buckle!":
Hopkins Against Henry Thomas Buckle

(1)   . . . a text that on its surface bore the least possible affilia-
        tion with history in the everyday sense: a poem, that is, as
        smooth of history as an effaced coin.

                                                              Liu 638

(2)   . . . above all, there has been a controversy over the
        meaning—or, indeed, meanings—of "here / Buckle!" Is it
        a noun or a verb?

                                                              Pick 9

(3)   . . . this must be worked out in connection with Buckle's
        task.

                                                          Droysen 89

(4)   . . . Buckle exploded like an inflated wind-bag.

                                                      St. Aubyn 183

"'Everybody nowadays reads Buckle,' she objected. 'There is no God
you see.'" Thus, in the 1860s, when the pious, patriotic Gerard Manley
Hopkins was approaching manhood, a Russian journalist satirized a society woman for pretending to keep abreast of the latest skeptical book
from England. This anecdote is cited in Lambert's *Sons Against Fathers,*
a history of Russian radicalism and revolution (Hanham xxiv). The refer-

ence is to Henry Thomas Buckle's *The History of Civilization in England* (1857-1861), one of the sensational books of the century, translated into numerous languages, and influential down to the first World War, by which time it had been assimilated into the emergent human sciences. Here we encounter in Hopkins's experiences with Victorian historiography not some cloudy generalities but a specific quantum of hard data.

Twenty years after Buckle first appeared, Hopkins inscribed into his greatest sonnet, "The Windhover," arguably the most worrisome trope in nineteenth-century poetry ("Brute beauty and valour and act, oh, air, pride, plume, here / Buckle!"). What does Hopkins's "Buckle" mean? Hopkins is said to be representing an event, a description, a command, a bird's flight pattern, a transcendence, a collapse, an epiphany. What, though, of English history? Without adducing concrete evidence that Hopkins carefully studied Buckle's famous book, but assuming that no educated Englishman in the 1870s could avoid exposure to Buckle's large and loud Victorian reputation, I wish to suggest that, in addition to accomplishing numerous other effects by using the capitalized word "Buckle," he is also responding to a set of Victorian values—somewhere between a mentality and an ideology—embodied in the writings of this famous historian. In a sense, Hopkins would thus be echoing Matthew Arnold's famous objection, in *Culture and Anarchy* (1869), that Buckle lacked both sweetness and light.

> A fanaticism . . . deforms and vulgarizes the well-known work, in some respects so remarkable, of the late Mr. Buckle. Such a fanaticism carries its own mark with it, in lacking sweetness; and its own penalty, in that, lacking sweetness, it comes in the end to lack light too.

For Arnold, then, and very likely for Hopkins, Buckle lacked subtleties of consciousness essential to survival in the emergent modern world.

Hopkins always denied that his poetry was in any sense obscure, but MacKenzie provides special information—linguistic, theological, biographical, scientific—toward the "solution of the many obscurities which stimulate some readers and merely confuse others" ("Introduction" xxvi). Is it not the case that two famous cruxes in "The Windhover" focus on Victorian historical consciousness? Does not the capitalized noun *Falcon* (as I will argue in chapter 4) link the brilliant fourteen-liner to the art of falconry and its *duecento* connection with the invention of the sonnet form? Likewise, does not the capitalized word *Buckle* link "The Windhover" to Henry Thomas Buckle? Hopkins may thus have wittily posed for his presumed Victorian readers an intellectual challenge to interpret a clue in full view (Flieger 941). Even if the poem continues to require further interpretation, this link should now become part of our own critical consciousness of the historical ordeal that faced the beleaguered Victorian individual.

"The Windhover" was written early in 1877 as Hopkins prepared for his ordination as a Jesuit priest later that same year. Let us remind ourselves what this celebrated poem looks like, as marked by his arbitrary, peculiar diacritics (slurs, outriders, unconventional stress marks) now collated in Norman MacKenzie's new complete edition.

The Windhover:

to Christ our Lord

I caught this mõrning morning's mînion, king-
 dom of daylight's dauphin, dapple-dáwn-drawn Falcon, in his
  riding
Of the rólling level úndernéath him steady aír, and stríding

Hígh there, how he rung upon the rein of a wimpling wing

In his ēcstasy! then off, off forth on swing,   5
 As a skate's heel sweeps smooth on a bow-bend: the hurl and

  gliding
Rebuffed the bíg wínd. My heart in hiding
Stirred for a bird,—the achieve of, the mãstery of the thing!

Brute beauty and valour and act, oh, air, pride, plūme, here
 Buckle! AND the fire that breaks from thee then, a billion 10
Tímes told lovelier, more dangerous, O my chevalier!

 No wõnder of it: shéer plód makes plóugh down sillion

Shíne, and blue-bleak embers, ah my dear,
 Fall, gáll themsélves, and gásh gõld-vermílion.

(*Poetical* 144; #120)

Thus it appears, in all its oddness, like a shaggy beast crusted over with time's untimely accretions. Its dynamized verbal material represents a linguistic mode that resists narrative summation and thereby opposes history itself.

"The Windhover" is probably the most explicated short poem in the English language (Pick 1). Almost every word poses a problem. The difficulty with "Buckle" has been summed up as follows:

Above all, there has been controversy over the meaning—or, indeed, meanings—of "here / Buckle!" Is it a noun or a verb? If a verb, then is it indicative or imperative? Or optative? Most commentators have taken it as the pivotal word in the poem and Schoder remarks that "here all must part company." However, another critic suggests that the important word is not "Buckle" but "here!" In that case, where? In the bird? In the poet's "heart in hiding"? Still another contends that the poem would be just as clear if the word "Buckle" were dropped completely. (Pick 9)

In the sense I am proposing, the crux in "Buckle" has indeed, from the beginning, been dropped or entirely missed.

Buckle's controversial book embodies a large complex of quasi-scientific Victorian attitudes (secularism, relativism, humanism, skepticism) that would vex and challenge Hopkins. Henry Adams recorded a vivid impression of *History of Civilization in England*:

"Those of us who read Buckle's first volume when it appeared in 1857, and almost immediately afterwards, in 1859, read the *Origin of Species* and felt the violent impulse which Darwin gave the study of natural laws, never doubted that historians would follow until they exhausted every possible hypothesis to create a science of history." (Breisach 289)

Darwin praised Buckle as a source of knowledge and truth and as "the very best writer of the English language that ever lived" (Hanham [v]). Everybody from George Eliot to John Ruskin to the man in the street was reading Buckle, so that no reader—had Hopkins had readers—would have missed a blatant poetic allusion to this famous author. Yet Hopkins never published his poems; no contemporary reader would have the chance to construe the "Buckle" reference. To complicate matters subsequently, Hopkins's discursive strategies have directed attention instead to ahistorical matters such as metrics, ontology, and abstract theology.

Humphry House edited Hopkins's notebooks in 1937; later, he cited an important reference to Buckle by Charles Dickens (173). House was the one critic sure to remark upon—if only to dismiss—the coincidence of "Buckle!" and Buckle. He did not, and no other Hopkins critic has ever made the connection. Surely one of the strangest oversights in literary history, explicable in part by Bridges's having held back Hopkins's poems until 1918. By that time, in part because of the disruptive effects of the first World War, Buckle's celebrity had passed even though his ideas were assimilated into the human sciences.

In "The Windhover," pyrotechnics of imagery, inscape, and sprung rhythm dictate that history take a back seat. Yet any attempt to understand Hopkins's opinions of Victorian historiography might with some reason begin with an examination of Buckle's career as a historian. Buckle embodies a skeptical Victorian frame of mind, bristling with hypotheses and opinions, flashing with intellectual fireworks (Hanham x). Precisely the kind of cultural mindset and reputation Hopkins would find both threatening and challenging. We witness quite directly in this confrontation some intimate relations between poetry and history in the form of historiographical discourse.

Like George Henry Lewes, Buckle aspired to advance modern thought on a variety of fronts. He would produce only one book, but that book is a wonder to behold. Appearing at about the same time as Mill's *On Liberty* (1859), *History of Civilization in England* is likewise a history and manifesto of English liberty. An uncompleted introduction to a proposed multivolume project, as edited by Robertson in 1904 it consists of twenty chapters or 900 pages of fine print, including 3,395 authorial footnotes and Buckle's own analytical table of contents, together with his list of more than 1,000 authors cited.[1]

Reading historiographically means to read backwards, so perhaps the best way to read Buckle is to begin at his conclusion. A poet like Hopkins who celebrates individual differences as being "counter, original, spare, strange" ("Pied Beauty") would surely bristle at Buckle's famous last word: *regularity* ("one glorious principle of universal and undeviating regularity"). Buckle's summing up, a key to his wide Victorian appeal, is worth noticing at some length. In urging that superstitious men give up their "base and grovelling conceptions" of an omniscient deity and join the march of progress, he expresses one potent strain of Victorian opinion.

> The whole scope and tendency of modern thought *force upon our minds conceptions of regularity and of law* to which [superstitions] are diametrically opposed. Even those who cling to them do so from the influence of tradition, rather than from complete and unswerving belief. That child-like and unhesitating faith with which the doctrine of interposition was once received, is succeeded by a

cold and lifeless assent, very different from the enthusiasm of former times. Soon, too, this will vanish, and *men will cease to be ter-*
rified by phantoms which their own ignorance has reared. . . . The
handwriting is on the wall; the fiat has gone forth; the ancient empire shall be subverted . . . and new life being breathed into the
confused and chaotic mass, it shall be clearly seen that from the
beginning there has been no discrepancy, no incongruity, no disor-
der, no interruption, no interference; but that all the events which
surround us, even to the furthest limits of the material creation, are
but different parts of a *single scheme which is permeated by one*
glorious principle of universal and undeviating regularity. (901-2;
emphases added)

Buckle's kind of evolutionary optimism held sway for a considerable time
in Hopkins's England and would certainly threaten Hopkins's own value
system. Let us keep in mind, though, that Hopkins, as was so often the
case, was of two minds about the principle of regularity. He wished to
impose order upon his own unruly emotions and upon the sordid and un-
predictable life of his times (White 186), but in "On the Origins of
Beauty" he thought otherwise: "And variety [individual inscapes] is opposed to regularity, is it not" (*Journal* 89).

Buckle insists that only the natural sciences can uncover the mental
and physical laws governing human actions. He invokes statistical data
to demonstrate that regularity is the keynote of human behavior. Humans
are affected by four physical agents: climate, food, and soil (which determine the accumulation of material wealth), and nature in general (which
determines the accumulation and distribution of thought by stimulating
understanding and imagination). Europe enjoys moderate conditions
which permit the exercise of judgment; by contrast, India experiences
violent extremes of nature and thus exhibits excessively tormented imagination (chaps. 1-3).

Buckle gives voice to numerous Victorian aspirations and delusions.
For example, progress depends solely upon improved material circumstances within which human genius can find expression. Progress may be
moral or intellectual, but moral change is so gradual that only intellectual
change brings measurable progress. Religion and violent behavior impede
progress, but the march of intellect makes people less intolerant and warlike. Reactionary institutions such as religion, literature, and government
(legislation) have retarded progress. Superstitions have made even the
writing of reliable history an insurmountable problem (chaps. 4-6).

At this point, Buckle changes his strategy. Adapting his scientific plat-form, he surveys, country by country, the intellectual development of England, France, Spain, and Scotland. England was to have been the focus of Buckle's proposed multi-volume work because England is the modern nation where skepticism first developed. England kept church and state from interfering with the general advancement of knowledge (chap. 7). By contrast, France tolerated the "protective spirit" of interference by church and state longer than did England, so France lagged behind (chaps. 8-14). Catholic Spain almost entirely resisted the benefits of skep-ticism, science, and progress; hence, it stays mired in ignorant servility (chap. 15). Buckle's five concluding chapters depict the intellectual his-tory of Scotland. His continuing importance can be measured by John Clive's including the closing chapters, as *On Scotland and the Scotch In-tellect*, in the series Classics of British Historical Literature (Hanham).

Hopkins's reaction to Buckle would be colored by his affection for Oxford University. Buckle's scientific history reduced humans to mere automata and so provided Oxford historians with a rallying point for their insistence on free will (James Thompson 2:310-11). By contrast, W. E. H. Lecky became Buckle's disciple by aspiring to render the inner life of a people (2:334); likewise, the Romanian historian Xenopol emulated Buckle. Thompson notes: "Capable critics regarded his work as a magnif-icent attempt to show deductively the effects of material causes on human civilization" (2:446). Buckle influenced the young men of his generation (2:445), a fact sure to cause Hopkins no small degree of alarm.

Buckle displays a wide range of historical knowledge, raises interest-ing questions about effects of climate and physical environment on nation-al character, and maintains a persuasive explanatory style. His argument that behavior "at large" was to some extent regular, uniform, and thus predictable still proves quite convincing (Turner 317). *History of Civil-ization in England* abundantly illustrates Peter Gay's opinion that his-torical writing must combine science and art: "Style is the art of the historian's science" (217). Plotkin rightly thinks that if we are to establish Hopkins's background we may need to include elements of disciplines such as Victorian philology that are not in the main line of development (11), but in fact Buckle occupies a central position in the human sci-ences.[2]

If we are to connect Hopkins's "The Windhover" with the Victorian world-view epitomized in Buckle's influential book, we must establish specific points where they might plausibly make contact. The most obvi-ous starting points would be Buckle's opinions on issues like skepticism, religion, poetry, the Society of Jesus, and nature—such issues being admittedly central to Hopkins's own concerns—ending perhaps with Buckle's last word, *regularity*.

A panic set in when some of the Victorian reading public encountered Buckle's laws governing human behavior (Buckle 15; Robertson's note). If the arrogant young Hopkins himself might not panic, yet Buckle's notorious skepticism would surely cause some alarm to an intense intellectual who would embrace one of the most conservative forms of Christianity. In Buckle's own program, the "law of a progressive scepticism" (295) is essential for all enlightenment and progress. In effect a radical *novum organum*, skepticism earns Buckle's approval as an "abomination to the ignorant," a gadfly to superstition and entrenched opinion, and as rousing "even sluggish understandings" to inquire after the truth. Progressive skepticism promotes religious tolerance, intellectual inquiry, and progress itself (190).

England was one of the countries where skepticism first openly appeared, and there it enabled the discovery of "constantly-progressive knowledge." Buckle recounts the rise and growth of skepticism and religious tolerance as owing in no small part to Chillingworth's 1637 classic *The Religion of Protestants*, where "all authority in matters of religion is openly set at defiance" (196-97). By Buckle's own day and age, theological matters had "ceased to be supreme" (200). In every department of English life, including sciences such as geology (243 n. 218), skeptics challenged old ideas and thus enabled many advancements in knowledge. Buckle even contemptuously described Hopkins's beloved Oxford University as a "refuge of superstition" which stubbornly resisted skeptical questioning (197).

Buckle's general resistance to organized religion coalesces intensively from time to time around specific issues. *History of Civilization in England* was sure to provoke strong if ambivalent responses from Hopkins by reason of Buckle's treatment of the Society of Jesus, where the historian's anti-clericalism comes to a head. With unabashed approval, Buckle recounts how meddlesome Jesuits were expelled from France in 1762 on the grounds of belonging to the past and obstructing scientific improvements (484-85). He approves of the Jesuits' being suppressed in Spain in 1867 by Charles III. But Buckle complicates the matter by expressing an exaggerated appreciation of the Jesuits in their original purpose and function.

> The Jesuits, for at least fifty years after their institution, rendered immense services to civilization, partly by tempering with a secular element the more superstitious views of their great predecessors,

the Dominicans and Franciscans, and partly by organizing a system of education far superior to any yet seen in Europe. In no university could there be found a scheme of instruction so comprehensive as theirs; and certainly nowhere was displayed such skill in the management of youth or such insight into the general operations of the human mind. It must in justice be added that this illustrious society, notwithstanding its eager and often unprincipled ambition, was during a considerable period the steady friend of science as well as of literature; and that it allowed to its members a freedom and boldness of speculation which had never been permitted by any other monastic order. (479)[3]

As ecclesiastical authority waned, the Jesuits sought to preserve their power by resisting the very knowledge they had earlier fostered. Politically, in recounting the history of France, Buckle approvingly cites the suppression of the Jesuits as one of the proximate causes of the French Revolution. Philosophically, he places the decline of the Jesuits in context of the historical debate over free will and predestination or determinism (487).

On the subject of literature in general, where Hopkins himself would have strong and increasingly knowledgeable opinions, Buckle utters some of his most forceful views. On the whole, he denigrates literature. Along with religion and legislation, literature is more affected by the "condition of mankind," relative to the advancement of knowledge, than affecting it (163). Literature is dismissed at one point as merely the "form in which the knowledge of a country is registered." Indeed, writers of exceptional genius leave the common people so far behind or below as to accomplish little practical good. Accordingly, given that literature in itself is but a "trifling matter," what counts is the condition or frame of mind of the people who read it (151-2). Hopkins, of course, in his self-contemptuous moments, would share Buckle's dismissive attitude toward literature. He pretended to think little of his own poems and hoped rather to accomplish something worthwhile and lasting not in poetry but, like Buckle, in some large piece of scholarship. On the other hand, in another mood he would have shared Robertson's objection to Buckle's argument: "[*As the 'condition of mankind' has been shown to be determined by knowledge, and knowledge *comes as literature* (by Buckle's definition), this formula must be regarded as inexact.—ED.]" (163). Ironically, Hopkins could not fail to grasp that Buckle's social program in effect rebuked Hopkins himself by rebuking any author who withheld his writing from the general population.

On the specific issue of poetry, Buckle expresses attitudes that Hopkins might well share, but he also pronounces judgments that could stir up ambivalent feelings in Hopkins as being similar to his own conflicted attitudes toward his literary career, ambiguously avocation or vocation. Buckle's explicit view of poetry aligns it closely with science.

> There is in poetry a divine and a prophetic power, and an insight into the turn and aspect of things, which if properly used would make it the ally of science instead of the enemy. By the poet, nature is contemplated on the side of the emotions; by the man of science, on the side of understanding. But the emotions are as much a part of us as the understanding; they are as truthful; they are as likely to be right. Though their view is different, it is not capricious. They obey fixed laws; they follow an orderly and uniform course; they run in sequences; they have their logic and method of inference. Poetry, therefore, is a part of philosophy, simply because the emotions are a part of the mind. If a man of science despises their teaching, so much the worse for him. (846)

Given Hopkins's commitment to poetry, psychology, and scientific inquiry (Zaniello 130-45), he might well share parts of Buckle's complex opinion.

Buckle's view of nature might both console and challenge Hopkins when the historian connects it with imagination. Buckle is at his most confident in explaining how physical laws having to do with climate, soil, and food exert profound influence upon individuals and societies (22-68). Wealth, health, intellectual development, and democratic freedom—characteristics of advanced European culture—are said to result in large part from ideal conditions of climate, soil, and food. Buckle's presentation is of a piece with midcentury naturalism and determinism of the more benign, if excessively Eurocentered, sort. His overall presentation of numerous statistics (ratios of wage, rent, profit, interest) intended to illustrate the human struggle to survive would surely move Hopkins as much as anyone existing within a normal range of intellect and sympathy.

A curious turn in Buckle's argument occurs when he generalizes from a vivid contrast between Europe and the more extreme conditions obtaining in India. Buckle connects violent extremes in nature with potentially dangerous results of the imagination, including literary imagination (68-84). Setting up a stark contrast between imagination and understanding, he urges that imagination responds to natural violence in ways that terrorize the mind into a "dangerous licence" of fearful superstition: "To

follow out the consequences of this great antagonism, it would be necessary to indicate how the infinite, the imaginative, the synthetic, and the
deductive, are all connected; and are opposed, on the other hand, by the
finite, the sceptical, the analytic, and the inductive" (84). Given that
"everywhere the hand of nature is upon us," even in Europe an oversensi-
tive or nervous temperament (e.g., Hopkins?) could plausibly find nature
over-stimulating, even terrifying. The imagery of fearful mountains and
"cliffs of fall" in one of Hopkins's Sonnets of Desolation can illustrate
this emotional linkage between extremes of nature and imagination.

> No worst, there is none. Pitched past pitch of grief,
> More pangs will, schooled at forepangs, wilder wring.
> Comforter, where, where is your comforting?
> Mary, mother of us, where is your relief?
> My cries heave, herds-long; huddle in a main, a chief-   5
> Woe, wórld-sorrow; on an áge-old ánvil wínce and síng—
> Then lull, then leave off. Fury had shrieked 'No ling-
> Ering! Let me be fell: force I must be brief.'
> O the mind, mind has mountains; cliffs of all
> Frightful, sheer,   ⎰ not man's fathoming. Hold them cheap   10
>   ⎱ no-man-fathomed.
> May who ne'er hung there. Nor does long our small
> Durance deal with that steep or deep. Here! creep,
> Wretch, under a comfort serves in a whirlwind: all
> Life death does end and each day dies with sleep.

(Poetical 182; #157)

The wrenching Buckleian images of fearful mind-mountains and terrifying cliffs, as Norman White observes, have come to be regarded as classic tropes for mental torment (396).

We are trying to imagine how Hopkins would respond to and evaluate
the wide sweep of liberal Victorian opinions articulated by Buckle, so we
must have recourse to the poet's conflicted view of life and history in
general. Hopkins's complex efforts both to approach and to avoid history
exemplify Marx's famous remark in the *Eighteenth Brumaire of Louis
Napoleon*:

> Men make their own history, but they do not make it just as they
> please; they do not make it under circumstances chosen by them-
> selves, but under circumstances directly encountered, given and

transmitted from the past. The tradition of all the dead generations weighs like a nightmare on the brain of the living.

Henry Thomas Buckle brought together not only massive data from the past but also many controversial strands of advanced English thought—belief in progress, emphasis on statistical numbers, hatred of superstition, nationalism, skepticism, and physical influences on human character. Buckle could have been exactly what the contentious but smoldering Hopkins needed in order to enable his poems, including his greatest sonnet. The two men will come to seem almost like collaborators.[4]

Scientific history such as Buckle's describes endless supersession, leaving no place for the mind to rest (Kemp 161). Yet even against the skeptical Victorian consciousness concentrated in *History of Civilization in England*, "The Windhover" holds its own. Hopkins's poem bravely and intelligently, if obliquely, confronts Buckle's project. By a daring paradox, Hopkins amends Buckle's restless history and soothes our historical anxieties by writing one of the most agitated poems in the English language. Readers continually wonder: is "Buckle!" a noun or a verb? If "Buckle!" indeed alludes to Henry Thomas Buckle, we have access to materials for a more satisfactory, if intricate, solution. Hopkins's exclamation may in fact be read one way as a verb which rebukes Buckle's factually objective enterprise in *History of Civilization in England*. My argument in this case would run as follows.

One type of poet yearns after a condition of pure immediacy or unmediated being. Seamus Heaney provides an explicit statement of this aspiration: "I ate the day / Deliberately, that its tang / Might quicken me all into verb, pure verb." Heaney, of course, is a decidedly Hopkinsian poet (Buttel). The notion of the irreducibility of the verb *per se* has been elucidated by Foucault (*Order* 92-6). He distinguishes mere words from propositions, which bestow upon any vocal sign its "supreme linguistic possibility" (92). In the evolution of language, it is chiefly the verb which induced or initiated language proper (93). Foucault strips the verb of its accretions, its nouns and adjectives, so we can see the verb in its constitutive purity. He relates this process to Hopkins's own day and age:

And throughout the nineteenth century, language was to be examined in its enigmatic nature as *verb*: in that region where it is nearest to being, most capable of naming it, of transmitting or giving effulgence to its fundamental meaning, of rendering it absolutely manifest. (96)

Hopkins perhaps converts Buckle's substantive surname into a verb enacting not only a natural process but something very like process *per se.*
Thus he rebukes Buckle's influential program, with its reifying statistical
collection of things.

Buckle's mode of presentation was an evolutionary narrative that, as
Hopkins would perceive, is logically problematical. As Breisach comments: "Buckle shared with Comte the inconsistency of offering positivist
methods in combination with a speculative pan-psychic overall development that did not satisfy positivist criteria of truth-finding" (275). Even
so, despite such logical objections, Buckle had entered into an important
historical debate. He initiated the movement which attributes utmost importance to overwhelming statistics in the form of large numbers as a
source of historical insights (337). Looking ahead to Hopkins, we note
that as late as 1885, a scant four years before his death, he composed a
paper on statistics (*Letters* 292).

His own polymathic and sorely resented father, of course, had made
a career based upon his genuine expertise as an average-adjuster, an actuarial expert who published *A Handbook of Averages* in the same year that
Buckle's famous book appeared. Buckle's enthusiastic reliance upon averages and statistics might stir up long-festering resentments. The Victorian
mania for statistics itself owes something to the development of actuarial
insurance (St. Aubyn 171). Given Manley Hopkins's commercial success
in maritime insurance, this circumstance carries no small interest for the
historical researcher who can entertain psychoanalytical explanations of
human behavior. Hopkins's conflicted attitude toward his actuarialist
father is part of his anxiety of influence, as I propose in chapter 3.

Hopkins disagrees with Buckle but pays the courageous historian a
compliment by doing so via a great poem. Such generosity contrasts with
Ruskin's petty sniping. Ruskin sneers at Buckle's godlessness (29:59); he
sneers at the "omniscient Mr. Buckle" (28:157); and, he describes the
Rialto in Venice thus: "indecently dirty—that is modern progress, and
Mr. Buckle's civilization" (24: 233). Ruskin goes to considerable trouble
to revile his famous contemporary: "I think the impudence of the modern
Cockney mind is more shown in its attempt to write history than in
anything else: Mr. Buckle's *History of Civilization*! Why a cock sparrow
bred in Tower Ditch might as well think it could write the History of the
Tower" (22:500). The sonneteer Hopkins, picking his way through Victorian debris, indeed might well side with the cock sparrow as the best of
all possible historians.

If Hopkins's poems had been published during his own lifetime, they
might have been held up to contempt: "Had they appeared when they

were written, it seems probable, the stammering, urgent poems by Hopkins would have been greeted with the sort of ridicule from which even Browning was not exempt" (Adams, *Land* 450). More to my immediate point, however, if "The Windhover" had appeared in the 1870s or 1880s, readers would not have failed to read "Buckle," even cleverly disguised as the first word in a line of verse, as in fact a reference to the famous H. T. Buckle. "The Windhover" is, we remember, the poem where Hopkins began a line of verse with a lower-case letter: "King / dom." We should be prepared to see "Buckle" as a proper name.

How many readers since 1918 must have wondered if "Buckle" might refer to the controversial but assimilated historian? We can safely assume that Hopkins's post-1918 readers, hankering after theological certainties, would in every such case suppress a reference to a historiographical philosophy which had once been controversial and even scandalous. As Alan Liu says in another connection, they would have rejected such an interpretation of "Buckle" as a "trivialization of the universal" (465).

Buckle writ history large, but *literary* history "permits us to write history small" (Brown, "Contemplating" 18). Literature itself also permits us to write historiography small. Let us for the moment bracket other interpretations of "The Windhover." Let us hypothesize that the poem constitutes a critique of Buckle as embodying a liberal or skeptical Victorian consciousness. Even upon a first reading it appears that Hopkins's best poem responds variously to several of Buckle's assertions. The title itself grounds the speaker's experience in the natural world that is Buckleian man's dialectical other half, even if the epigraph "to Christ our Lord" gives back to religion what Buckle reserves for nature and pure reason. Hopkins did not add the epigraph until seven years after he composed the poem. If we regard this paratextual addition as a nervous afterthought—and pointless coming from a priest—we can reasonably assume that Hopkins originally intended to meet Buckle entirely on Buckle's own naturalistic grounds. A principle espoused by Kenneth Burke seems to be at work here: "it is of the essence in antagonism, as in antithesis, that the Champion and his Enemy be profoundly complicitous" (Liu 142).

Hopkins's anti-Buckleian sonnet amounts to a heroic *refus du style*. In the body of the poem, from the subjective and transitory opening—"I caught"—to the concluding aesthetic subjectivity of the final image—"gash gold-vermilion"—Hopkins offers both a realization of and also an alternative to Buckle's assemblage of facts and his "great doctrine of averages." Throughout the octave, binary opposites extend his opening gambit. The first line is perfectly regular ten-syllable iambic pentameter line; the second line not only begins with the broken form "dom" but also metrically breaks open this running-rhythm regularity with sixteen syllables of a potent sprung rhythm: "dom of daylight's dauphin, dapple-dawn-drawn Falcon, in his riding."

The falcon image elaborated in the octave invokes nature, but the aristocratic anti-Buckleian analogies "minion" and "dauphin" rapidly convert nature to culture. These aristocratic figurations, together with "rein" and "heel," invoke processes of the imagination itself, and the excitable sprung-rhythm metrics of lines 2-8 bring to mind Buckle's description of the loss of emotional control under extremes of natural excitation. What Buckle fears, though, Hopkins embraces, intensifies, and flaunts. Buckle's trademark, a solid specificity of detail, is honored but is then converted to figurative, impalpable essence ("achieve" and "mastery"). Throughout the octave, Hopkins seems to undercut one of Buckle's champions, the struggling worker, not only by signifiers like "minion" and "dauphin" but also by a lavish expenditure of sound and sense.[5]

Still upon a first reading, the first triplet of the sestet presents not only the keyword "Buckle" but more of H. T. Buckle's key motifs: brute nature, valor, significant action, climate (air), and human pride. Hopkins uses the hyperbolic *billion* as if to satirize Buckle's huge collections of statistical numbers. Derek Price thinks that statistics should not be accorded more confidence than "half an order of magnitude" (153). Hopkins's own boyish enthusiasm for aggregates, such as stars and clouds, would be tempered by a healthy skepticism toward statistics. Neither *billion* nor *buckle* is a word regularly used by Victorian poets. Except for Robert Browning, who uses *buckle* twice, none of Hopkins's contemporary poets ever uses either term in a poem. Hopkins uses each word only this one memorable time. By beginning his tenth line with "Buckle!" and ending it with "billion," he links the two words for a time and an eternity. It might not be too much to suggest that the satirical effect of Hopkins's "Buckle's billions" would equal, and perhaps anticipate, the effects of Eugene O'Neill's lampooning title *Marco's Millions*.

Buckle's theme of the risk involved in the march of progress is echoed in Hopkins's surprising adjective *dangerous*. We are reminded of a maxim from Bacon: "reason doth buckle and bowe the Minde . . . [whereas poetry] doth raise and erect the mind" (*Proficience and Advancement of Learning*, Book II, paragraph 43). Hopkins would side with Bacon against Buckle.

The second triplet of the sestet threatens to become quite intricately pro-Buckleian. It undercuts the "minion" and "dauphin" of the octave with depictions of a plodding ploughman (economic struggle; wages) and a sillion (soil; furrow; homely labor). But it is rather more anti-Buckleian:

given that a skeptic habitually wonders about things that others take to be settled, Hopkins's very language ("No wonder of it") obviates such skeptical questionings. On the whole, even a cursory reading establishes several obvious, if loosely connected, engagements with the Victorian beliefs and consciousness embodied in *History of Civilization in England.*

Subsequent readings of "The Windhover" complicate Hopkins's oblique way of confronting Buckle. Question after question urges itself upon us. A hawk embodies the natural drama inherent in the Darwinian struggle for survival or, so to speak, the dynamics of the food chain. However, if this hawk is a trained falcon (a likelihood I raise in chapter 4), it then embodies even more so a complicated cultural ceremony designed to transcend such materialistic considerations as the food chain.

"The Windhover" is universally regarded as a rush of sprung rhythm sound effects, of boyish enthusiasm. As such, it would rebuke Buckle's presumably sober narrative, even if we recall that Buckle himself was criticized by his own admirers for "enthusiastic declamation" (Robertson viii). Hopkins, it would appear, both denies and affirms Buckle.

Another complication bears upon Buckle's principle of regularity. Hopkins quickly undermines the iambic regularity of his first line; hence, he would seem to be refuting regularity. Nevertheless, the poem as a whole establishes that the falcon ("beauty and valour and act") is paralleled and equalled by the humble plough and ember. Hence, we end with patterns of natural and cultural repetition or regularity. The "air" associated metonymically with pride and plume we may construe as Buckle's own confident discursive voice that overrides all opposition. When the falcon's "hurl and gliding / Rebuffed the big wind," we might well think of Buckle. After all: "Buckle exploded like an inflated wind-bag." Thus, in 1885, some eight years after "The Windhover," Grant Allen described in *Charles Darwin* one of the effects of Darwin's own evolutionary thesis on Buckle's reputation (St. Aubyn 183).

Hopkins himself had written undergraduate essays on science—"Distinguish Exactly between Deduction, Induction, Analogy, and Example" and "The Tests of a Progressive Science" (Zaniello 130-4). He probably understood the principles of science as well as or even better than Buckle understood them. Yet he might well have decided that the scientized and regularized world envisioned by Buckle meant that the existential human person would very likely vanish or, as Hardison puts it, disappear through the skylight (285-348). To Buckle's vision of human life, Hopkins would more than likely oppose something resembling Duns Scotus's *species specialissima* (Christ 143) or simply the individual struggling to save his soul.

At crux after crux, Hopkins complicates his judgment of the Victorian crisis-consciousness represented and triggered by Buckle. If the falcon is a minion and a dauphin, then the falcon is, figuratively at least, a human being. However, if the falcon equates with the plough, then a human can be a mere machine, thereby provoking Orwellian nightmares not inappropriate to a mordant view of Buckle's philosophy. Then, too, an ember, likewise figuratively a human being, can "gall" itself or, so to speak, live and die, sacrifice itself, for the sake of an idea or even an aesthetic effect ("gold-vermilion"). Even at the level of rhyme scheme, Hopkins critiques the historian. Buckle attributed a mysterious power to numbers themselves (St. Aubyn 25). Hopkins's extravagantly statistical *billion* follows a Buckleian path to a homely *sillion* (arable ground or furrow) but eventuates in one of the most purely aesthetic images in English poetry ("gash gold-vermilion"). To Buckle's great statistical machine of a world, Hopkins would oppose something like Bonaventure's famous world-image: "a great coal radiant with light" (Gilson 230). If climactic order determines meaning, Buckle's mystique of numbers has been judged and dismissed by Hopkins's version of Pater's self-consuming hard, gemlike flame.

Buckle helped to initiate the human sciences. Hopkins perhaps anticipates Edmund Husserl and T. S. Kuhn in rejecting any belief in a steady, progressive accumulation of scientific knowledge. Like Jürgen Habermas, too, he acknowledges the lonely suffering of individuals who escape the steering inherent in programmatic social science (*Legitimation* 120). Hopkins anticipates Foucault's subtle pronouncement on such quasi-sciences: "Western culture has constituted under the name of man, a being who, by one and the same interplay of reasons, must be a positive domain of *knowledge* and [hence] cannot be an object of *science*" (*Order* 366-7).

Had Hopkins in fact carefully studied Buckle, he could easily have liked *History of Civilization in England* for the same reason that James Russell Lowell liked it, i.e., he found in it so much to disagree with (St. Aubyn 31). Almost every word in "The Windhover" potentially witnesses to Hopkins's judgment of Buckle. "The Windhover" shows that Hopkins grasped the principle which Habermas calls the connection between objective knowledge and human interests (*Knowledge* 301-17). Hopkins would agree with J. A. Froude, whose 1864 essay "The Science of History" rejects Buckle on the grounds that free will and moral choice meant that the only human law is "self-interest" and that only an "old-fashioned moral—or, if you please, imaginative point-of-view" can adequately describe human life (1:16). Froude's collective title for his volume where "The Science of History" appears—*Short Studies on Great Subjects*—

perfectly characterizes Hopkins's sonnet as a response to the large Buck-leian strain in Victorian historiography.

Consciousness of a skeptical strain in historicism itself returns us to the realm of the aesthetic (Carolyn Williams 284). On the question of the value of skepticism, newly reopened in our own day by Derrida, the aes-thetician Pater proves useful in any effort to connect Hopkins and Buckle at the level of discursive form. Pater was an essayist and a lifelong skep-tic; the essay itself enacts a mode of skepticism. The essay form necessi-tates a version of truth at once personal and elusive; essayistic inquiry has no specific end in sight but only endless intellectual process. By contrast, the treatise form to which Buckle committed his inquiry does not lend itself to skepticism, being an ambitious array of premises and conclusions adding up to an all-sufficient scholarly explanation. Likewise, but in a different mode, an oracular poem like "The Windhover," provocative but enigmatic, avoids skepticism in favor of enthusiastic intuitions (Iser 17-19). Formally considered, then, only in the most oblique fashion should either Buckle or Hopkins be regarded as either skeptical or anti-skeptical. Nevertheless, we can assume that Hopkins's intense poem formally re-bukes Buckle's generically inappropriate pronouncement of a skeptical program in *History of Civilization in England*. Hopkins thus proves him-self in numerous respects a subtle master of the "pervasive and Protean role of allusion in the poetry of all sophisticated ages" (Wimsatt and Brooks 217).

After "The Windhover" in 1877, Hopkins's poems exhibit numerous signs of an abiding concern with aspects of Buckle's project. His most admired poems show acute powers of observation at the service of a luxuriant, wild, at times terrorized and terrorizing, imagination. Some ex-amples: "Pied Beauty" (against regularity); "The Caged Skylark" (the body as constraint); "Hurrahing in Harvest" (celebrating nature's fecun-dity); "The Loss of the Eurydice" (rationalizing natural disasters); and, "Duns Scotus's Oxford" (honoring medieval scholasticism), the last of which singlehandedly attempts to refute Buckle at the level of Catholic theology.

Tówery city and branchy betwéen tówers;
Cuckoo-echoing, bell-swarmèd, lark-charmèd, rook-racked,

    river-rounded;
The dapple-eared lily below thee; that country and town did

Ónce encounter in, here coped and poisèd powers;

Thou hast a base and brickish skirt there, sour   5
That neighbour-nature thy grey beauty is grounded
Bést in; graceless growth, thou hast confounded
Rúral rural keeping—folk, flocks, and flowers.

Yet ah! this air I gather and I release
He lived on; these weeds and waters, these walls are what   10

He haunted who of all men most sways my spirits to peace;

Of realty the rarest-veinèd unraveller; a not
Rívalled insight, be rival Italy or Greece;

Who fíred Fránce for Máry withóut spót.

(*Poetical* 156; #129)

Other examples: "The Bugler's First Communion" (soldierly piety);
"Felix Randal" (compassion for laborers); "'I wake and feel the fell of
dark, not day'" (flesh as "dull dough"); "'No worst, there is none'" (terrifying landscapes); "'Yes. Why do we all, seeing of a soldier, bless him?'"
(Christ as military leader); "To his Watch" (man's time-telling task);
"Harry Ploughman" (the soil, the soil!); "Tom's Garland" (revolution
from below); "St. Alphonsus Rodriguez" (unquestioning religious piety).
One poem, "The Blessed Virgin compared to the air we Breathe" (spiritualized environment), even more so than the sonnet on Duns Scotus,
refutes Buckle's scientific version of atmospherics.

> Wild air, world-mothering air,
> Nestling me everywhere,
> That each eyelash or hair
> Girdles; goes home betwixt
> The fleeciest, frailest-flixed   5
> Snowflake; that's fairly mixed
> With, riddles, and is rife
> In every least thing's life;
> This needful, never spent,
> And nursing element;   10
> My more than meat and drink,
> My meal at every wink;
> This air, which, by life's law,
> My lung must draw and draw

Now but to breathe its praise,   15
Minds me in many ways
Of her who nót only
Gave God's infinity
Dwindled to infancy
Welcome in womb and breast,   20
Birth, milk, and all the rest
But mothers each new grace
That does now reach our race—
Mary Immaculate,
Merely a woman, yet   25
Whose presence, power is
Great as no goddess's
Was deemèd, dreamèd; who
This one work has to do—
Let all God's glory through,   30
God's glory which would go
Through her and from her flow
Off, and no way but so.

(*Poetical* 173; #151)

Ironically, Hopkins's last word *explanation* invites the attention of a discursive historian like Buckle himself to rationalize this linguistically ambitious, linguistically difficult poet.

We know that poets exploit sources in order to achieve power, most particularly power over the very sources themselves (Hawkins 481; Kellner 301). What do we find in the case of Hopkins and Buckle? We still have "Buckle" potentially meaning many things but no one thing exclusively. In 1895, when Hopkins had been dead for six years, Robertson took up the cudgels for Buckle in *Buckle and His Critics*. Among the adversaries of the new historiography championed by Buckle around the time of *On Liberty* and *Origin of Species*, we find the imposing names of Ruskin, Froude, Carlyle, and Lord Acton.[6] Now it seems that Hopkins should be listed as one of Buckle's critics, as an antithetical poet who responded via poetical discourse to the discursive power of Buckle's revolutionary treatise.

Despite the difficulties, such a conjecturally abstruse intertextual bonding between "The Windhover" and Buckle registers more hopefully than some other conjectural linkages between poetry and history. Roland Barthes complains that the opposition between history and poetry is not

even bridgeable but rather is an opposition of mutually exclusive contexts:

> It seems that this is a difficulty pertaining to our times: there is as
> yet only one possible choice, and this choice can bear only on two
> equally extreme methods: either to posit a reality which is entirely
> permeable to history, and ideologize; or, conversely, to posit a real-
> ity which is *ultimately* impenetrable, irreducible, and, in this case,
> poetize. In a word, I do not yet see a synthesis between ideology
> and poetry (by poetry I understand, in a very general way, the
> search for the inalienable meaning of things). (*Mythologies* 158-59)

Poetry and history may in fact never touch, but Hopkins could not easily
accept such a conclusion. Nor should we.

Oscar Wilde wrote that we have a duty to rewrite history. Hopkins
very likely believed that poetry must attempt to confront history, and, in
the present instance, to confront historiography. Our responsibility is to
see that criticism witnesses to this central confrontation. Buckle the pious
skeptic remains alive in the human sciences he helped to foster. He also
remains alive in Hopkins's great poem ostensibly about a man and a bird.
When we read "The Windhover" we reexperience Hopkins's awakening
from and to the nightmare of Victorian and modern crisis-consciousness.
Hopkins pays homage to Buckle; he radically critiques and corrects
Buckle; he preserves Buckle in one of the greatest English sonnets. Yet,
we know that Buckle himself began by questioning whether there was in
fact a "Possibility of History" (*Miscellaneous* 1: 200-7). There would be
some justice in our thinking that Hopkins answers such a radical query
in the negative. Could it be that he replaces a narration with a lyrical
effusion so as to obliterate both history and time? What if, figuratively
so to speak, Hopkins induces a slightly asymmetrical chiasmus by responding to Buckle's history of poetry with a sprung-rhythm version of
the poetry of history?

History and language exist in a most curious and compelling relation.
Foucault has remarked upon this fact, at once a stumbling block to understanding and a pathway to understanding: "the whole backwash of history
to which words lend their glow at the instant they are pronounced"
(*Order* 315). *Buckle* is only a word, but a word can serve as a shield and
a weapon (Allan and Burridge). Hopkins makes *Buckle* not only a shield
and a weapon against the nightmare of history but something more, something as yet teasingly indefinable in any absolute sense. From Barthes's
grim perspective, we can see the risk and cost to Hopkins of attempting

the poetical life during the decades when "Buckle!" was the rallying cry of an irresistible but decidedly unpoetical discursive power.

Both Buckle and Lord Acton aspired to write a history of liberty; hence, the "Catholic Acton and the Deist Buckle should be read together" (Hanham xxxvi). Likewise, we should read the skeptic Buckle and the Catholic believer Hopkins together. Hopkins's intertextual dig at Buckle guarantees that we will.

Interchapter 1

"Where springs not fail":
History and Antithesis in Poems #1-45 (1860-64)

(1)   I have desired to go
                         Where springs not fail,
                 To fields where flies no sharp and sided hail
                 And a few lilies blow.
                                                 (*Poetical* 29; #20)

(2)   This soft, loose material ["The Escorial"] is a strange be-
           ginning for a poet whose later utterance was to go the
           limits of tension and austerity.
                                                 McChesney 2

In four interchapters, I intend to focus on two main goals. First, to survey
Hopkins's poems for signs of historical interest or antithetical emotions.
Second, to determine the historiographical implications of Hopkins's first
poem, "The Escorial." *En passant*, various other issues will arise along
with an increasingly capacious sense of the overall oeuvre. The very
abruptness and fragmentation induced by the four interchapters enable us
better to perceive how "broken up" Hopkins was but also how heroically
he labored to pull his life and work together.

Hopkins began his poetical career as a prizewinning sixteen-year-old
poet and as a historical poet. "The Escorial," written very likely with con-

44

siderable aid from his father, won the Highgate School poetry prize for
1860. For such a young ephebe a splendid virtuoso piece, its 125 lines
provide architectural description, nature description (a violent torrent),
listing and appreciation of numerous art treasures once exhibited at the
Escorial, and moralizing narration, undergirded by twenty-four footnotes
provided by Hopkins himself. One of his primary sources was the third
volume of W. H. Prescott's *History of the Reign of Philip II*, the theme
of which is Philip's efforts to establish and maintain Spanish and Catholic
supremacy in Europe (Darnell 121). Hopkins's fourteen Spenserian stanzas closely follow Prescott's facts and rather conventionally judgmental
sentiments. All too predictably, it might seem, Catholic Spain appears
austere to the point of harshness. The first three stanzas effectively illustrate Hopkins's descriptive thought-style in the poem as a whole.

1

There is a massy pile above the waste
Amongst Castilian barrens mountain-bound;
A sombre length of grey; four towers placed
At corners flank the stretching compass round;
A pious work with threefold purpose crown'd—   5
A cloister'd convent first, the proudest home
Of those who strove God's gospel to confound
With barren rigour and a frigid gloom—
Hard by a royal palace, and a royal tomb.

2

They tell its story thus; amidst the heat   10
Of battle once upon St. Laurence' day
Philip took oath, while glory or defeat
Hung in the swaying of the fierce melée,
'So I am victor now, I swear to pay
The richest gift St. Laurence ever bore,   15
When chiefs and monarchs came their gifts to lay
Upon his altar, and with rarest store
To deck and make most lordly evermore.'

3

For that staunch saint still prais'd his Master's name
While his crack'd flesh lay hissing on the grate;   20
Then fail'd the tongue; the poor collapsing frame,
Hung like a wreck that flames not billows beat—
So, grown fantastic in his piety,
Philip, supposing that the gift most meet,
The sculptur'd image of such faith would be,   25
Uprais'd an emblem of that fiery constancy.

Together the poem and the explanatory footnotes add up to an impressive
youthful performance. The twenty-four explanatory notes invite us to leap
ahead to Hopkins's last poem, in 1889, with its pathetic appeal to critical
explanation. We can hardly avoid wondering if the explanatory strain inherent in historical poetry like "The Escorial" might not have subsequently developed, under different circumstances, into a larger element
in Hopkins's poetical growth?

Hopkins's commencing his public poetical career as a historical poet
using a historical source should be closely scrutinized. William Hickling
Prescott (1796-1859), the first important American historian and the most
famous, merited a biography by George Ticknor in 1864. As recently as
1969, a scholarly biography by C. H. Gardiner offers ten reasons why
Prescott was crucial to the development of modern historiography. In between Ticknor and Gardiner, other scholars have added to our understanding and appreciation of the New England brahmin Prescott. In 1905,
Harry Thurston Peck produced a critical biography placing Prescott at the
head of American historians (180). In 1975, Darnell published a critical
account of Prescott's work for the Twayne series on American authors.
One other book deserves mention here: a 1943 Prescott reader edited by
Charvat and Kraus has kept representative selections of Prescott's writings, including a highly wrought passage about the Escorial, before a
wide reading public.

Surprisingly, the early poems following "The Escorial," from "*Promê-
theus Desmotês*" (#2) to "'All as that moth call'd Underwing, alighted'"
(#45), manifest little in the usual way of historical research or interest and
almost nothing that seems logically to follow from his first poem.
Admittedly, some things of biographical and even genuinely literary interest do appear, including academic exercises, Miltonic and Keatsian
imitations, nature descriptions, nature meditations, biblical redactions,
pseudo-Jacobean drama, nature studies, natural history, and so on, a good

deal of it in fragments or unfinished versions. Yet not even Hopkins's gesture at Browning's type of dramatic monologue in "Pilate" (#10) seems historical in ways comparable to his first performance. Only "St. Dorothea" (#42), drawing upon the *Acta Sanctorum*, even approximately takes us back to the blatant historicality and other memorable effects of "The Escorial." Witness the dramatized Browningesque version of "St. Dorothea."

> That a quince I pore upon?
> O no it is the sizing moon. 20
> Now her mallow-row is gone
> In tufts of evening sky.—So soon?
> Sphered so fast, sweet soul?—We see
> Fruit nor flower nor Dorothy.
>
> How to name it, blessed it! 25
> Suiting its grace with *him* or *her*?
> Dorothea—or was your writ
> Ser´vèd by´ méssenger´?
> Your parley was not done and there!
> You went into the partless air. 30
>
> It waned into the world of light,
> Yet made its market here as well:
> My eyes hold yet the rinds and bright
> Remainder of a miracle.
> O this is bringing! Tears may swarm 35
> Indeed while such a wonder's warm.
>
> Ah dip in blood the palmtree pen
> And wordy warrants are flawed through.
> More will wear this wand and then
> The warpèd world we shall undo. 40
> Proconsul!—Is Sapricius near?—
> I find another Christian here.

(*Poetical* 59; #42)

Anyone might reasonably be tempted at this point to dismiss "The Escorial" on the grounds that the historical element in Hopkins's first poem would be owing entirely to the announced topic for the Highgate competition of 1860. On the other hand, these early exercises do betray a variety of potently antithetical attitudes. In reading them, we can see how Robert Martin or Norman White or any biographer could extrapolate psychological motifs that add up to an emotionally complicated Hopkins. The Miltonic exercise "Il Mystico" (#3) pugnaciously announces that Hopkins's spirit, or at least the speaker's spirit, is one of the "pure souls" entirely alien to the materialistic secular world. "A Vision of the Mermaids" (#6) offers an escape into unnatural natural history, but at the end its sad Prufrockian closure ("oft I watch but see those Mermaids now no more") amounts to a rejection of man by nature. Its speaker is reluctantly thrown back upon the exigencies of historical consciousness. This poem, with its vivid siren song sung by the mermaids, will figure in my consideration, in chapter 5, of Hopkins's sporadic attempts to use music as a means to erase or otherwise obviate history. Other poems which cursorily or implicitly rail against one aspect or another of human existence include "Spring and Death" (#8), with its delicate protest against natural mutability and human transitoriness, as well as "A soliloquy of one of the spies left in the wilderness" (#12), which expresses a stern disapproval of Anglicanism.

Hopkins's early work implies in curious formal ways a variety of radically antithetical opinions. It may not be too much to urge that "New Readings" (#18) uses metaphysical wit to recast, and hence to reject, standard Anglican readings of scriptural passages. Similarly, "Heaven-Haven" (#20) uses a delicate lyricism to express a deep wish for an escape from ordinary human life; we get a clear if brief glimpse of Hopkins's habit of emotional and intellectual denial. The fragment "Why should their foolish bands, their hopeless hearses" (#22) rejects and even reviles contemporary human life in terms of an aesthetic critique of burial customs. "Epigrams" (#32) satirically critiques various kinds of social behavior, not excluding modern poetry ("Our swans are now of such remorseless quill, / Themselves live singing and their hearers kill"). Most antithetically, perhaps, "A Voice from the World" (#38) attempts to rewrite Christina Rossetti's admired poem "The Convent Threshold."

Scanning the first forty-five poems in the 1990 edition within the context of my main hypotheses, I am left with three strong impressions. First, as Miller notes in *Disappearance of God*, Hopkins's early poetry depicts a world where God is not only unattainable but terrifyingly invisible (74-5). Second, the young Hopkins seems to work at his best whenever some historical or antithetical motive offers itself. Third, in light of the relative meagerness of any historical materials in the early poems from "Aeschylus" to "'All as that moth call'd Underwing, alighted,'"

Hopkins's first poem, "The Escorial," looms more and more portentously as a crux in the poet's attitude toward history and, by extension, toward life. In my opinion, it becomes, long before the *Wreck of the Deutschland*, another "dragon in the gate" blocking but paradoxically providing access to a true understanding of Hopkins's consciousness and genius.

I must pause here for a moment over Miller's observation about the disappearance of God in order to seek for some formal explanation. In chapter 2, "'to succeed by failure': Hopkins Against the Tradition for Lyrical Assortments," I will suggest that Hopkins's entire noncareer comes under Rajan's category of the literary "unfinished." Without a doubt, any survey of the first forty-five poems must take note of the numerous unfinished pieces and fragments. Admittedly, fragmentary relics are inevitable features of any poet's apprenticeship and ongoing technical experience and experiment. In Hopkins's case, as in the development of other poets, we sometimes can see how a phrase, a rhythm, or trope occurring here and there in the fragments ultimately finds a place in some finished poem. Even so, MacKenzie's having placed such fragments in chronological order requires our granting to them, at least hypothetically, a status of importance nearly equal to the finished pieces.

The usual explanation is familiar enough for Hopkins's having foundered so often that numerically more than half of his output takes the form of fragments: "Eschewing what he called 'Parnassian'—a true poet's competent second-best, a poeticizing without inspiration—he preferred to leave yet another fragment rather than carry through a piece of work about which he was not wholly 'in earnest'" (Gardner, "Introduction" xix). Yet this explanation does not answer every question. Accordingly, we must find a means of generalizing about the fragments, and to do so we may need to invoke some theory of the fragment *per se*. The work of Thomas MacFarland or Marjorie Levinson on romantic fragments might prove helpful here, but we have access to a deeper and more cogent theory in Lucien Goldmann's structuralist work on Pascal, taken together with Northrop Frye's interpreting the fragment itself as a genre crucial to the processes of literary self-fashioning.

Goldmann believed that in order to understand the presumed relations between reality and concept we should first attempt to identify the "pure linguistic forms" taken by any utterance we would understand. One of Goldmann's test cases was Pascal's understanding of the "nature of the fragment" in relation to the structure of what was to become the famous Pascalian wager (suppose there were a God, what then?). Goldmann reasons thus:

You are familiar with all that was written about the "true outline"
of the *Pensées* until a structuralist analyst showed not only that the
fragment as a literary form was necessary to Pascal but that—and
this is far more important—he used it intentionally and that it was
a Cartesian perspective that had prevented considering *fragments as
ends in themselves.* For Pascal's message is that Man is great in
that he searches for absolute values but small in that, without ever
ceasing to search, he knows that he can never approach these
values. The only form to express this context is, of course, one
which does not prove the contrary: which doesn't show either a
man who has abandoned the search or one who has approached the
goal. The fragment is such a form . . . for Pascal's faith is a wager
that is a total commitment to God, with the permanent possibility
of its not being kept—an uncertain certitude. The text itself must
then show both aspects of total commitment and of the refusal of
such commitment by him who bets in the void. We can see why
the form in which Pascal cast his "wager" is a necessary one and
perfectly adapted to its content. (107; emphases added)

Goldmann's interpretation of the fragment as an expressive form, whether
or not we fully agree with its Pascalian implications, can assist us in our
attempt to interpret the fragments punctuating Hopkins's oeuvre.

One inference appears to be unavoidable: the anxiety-producing view
that God is absent from Hopkins's early writings derives in part from the
"uncertain certitude" of Hopkins's fragmented consciousness of God. We
can plausibly imagine this emotional complex as a nondogmatic enactment, in part via the poetical fragment, of one's being poised on a Pascalian knife edge while carrying out an authentic search for God. Couched
in other terms, as Frye would have it, Hopkins's fragments, in effect epiphanic "fragments of significance," represent the poet's desire to transcend human time so as to experience and enjoy a transcendent eternity
(*Anatomy* 15). It is as if Hopkins, perceiving the disappearance of God
from history (Miller 270-359), from time to time executed a clever *imitatio Dei* by stubbornly deciding likewise to disappear. The poetic fragment would thus be one more strategy, in addition to those identified by
Robert Martin, by which Hopkins attempts to perform an antithetical van-
ishing act.

Hopkins himself, responding to Bridges's suggestion that "St. Winifred's Well" ought to be thought of as consciously contrived "fragments
of a dramatic poem," indignantly declared that "a completed fragment,
above all of a play, is the same unreality as a prepared impromptu"

(*Letters* 219). Even so, Miller views Hopkins's fragments as attempts to cope with the poet's own acute consciousness of what Norman White calls the "Victorian fragmented world" (White 401). He associates Hopkins's consciousness of world-fragment and world-unity with the poet's undergraduate essay on Parmenides (*Journals* 125-26).

> In the Parmenidean fragments Hopkins as early as 1868 finds a way to unify self, words, and world. This does not mean that he is a Victorian Presocratic, depending for the very keystone of his thought on Parmenides, although it is true that his reading of Parmenides is a turning-point in his thinking, and prepares him for the decisive encounter some years later with Scotus and St. Ignatius. (*Disappearance* 311)

In addition, another of Frye's ideas also bears upon Hopkins's poetical experiments, particularly the fragments. Is it not correct to think that Hopkins's fragments, together with his curious wordings, odd line endings, and peculiar rhymes approximate what Frye calls the "babble and doodle" that make possible a certain type of prosody (*Anatomy* 275-80)?

Precisely how essential the fragment *per se* could be for Hopkins becomes peculiarly cogent when we recall his most famous attempt at succinct self-definition: as a potsherd or shard.

> In a flash, at a trumpet crash,
> I am all at once what Christ is, ⎹ since he was what I am, and
> Thís Jack, jóke, poor pótsherd, ⎹ patch, matchwood, immortal
> diamond,
>   Is immortal diamond.

> (*Poetical* 198; #174)

The early fragments take on increasingly greater interest by their contrast with Hopkins's first poem. Hopkins would never again write a poem anything like "The Escorial." All the more striking, then, that this prize-winning poem establishes motifs central to his developing stance against history and historiography. The actual building called the Escorial is an enormous building located some fifty kilometers from Madrid. Comprising a church, a monastery, and a palace, in addition to serving as a burial place for Spanish kings, the huge Escorial was constructed by Philip II between 1563 and 1584. Because Philip's soldiers had defeated the French king's army on Saint Lawrence's feast day, the Spanish king or-

dered that the building be laid out like the gridiron on which the martyred
Saint Lawrence was reputedly roasted by Roman soldiers. Inside, it contains magnificent rooms and courts, as well as a great domed church and
a lovely cloister with an impressive central fountain. The statistics of this
gray granite structure are rather overwhelming: 37,000 square meters of
enclosed space, three-hundred rooms, eighty-eight fountains, and eighty-
six staircases. Although massive and splendid, from the outside the
Escorial appears gloomy and grim.

Both Prescott's and Hopkins's rather cliché gloom echo Thomas Carlyle's famous description of Philip II in Part 2 of *The Life of Friedrich
Schiller* (1825), where Carlyle characterizes Philip and Catholic Spain in
hyperbolic terms: "rigid cold formalities . . . [of the] cruel bigoted . . .
stony-hearted despot [whose] gloomy spirit [and] hatefulness [left him]
haggard, stern and desolate." Hopkins thus began his historiographical
career by troping a well-established early Victorian trope.[1]

The actual Escorial, a monstrous edifice, in its terrifying emotional impact something like the Kremlin, could easily come to represent for
Hopkins or for any sensitive soul the nightmare of human history and of
historiography, being mediated as it was via Prescott's account of Philip's
violent reign. For Hopkins, motifs of Hispanic religiosity, perhaps not excluding historical associations with the Jesuits and the fearsome Inquisition, could attach to any representation of the Escorial itself. Given that
Hopkins's father assisted him in the composition of the poem and even
copied it out for submission to the Highgate competition (so as to dis-
guise his son's authorship), the Escorial, in its palpable historicity, might
enter permanently into Hopkins's creative psyche. The potential for its
triggering or contributing to episodes of antithetical denial over an entire
lifetime would seem quite likely, even if disguised by the very mechanisms of denial.

What are the motifs of denial implicit in this formative episode of
Hopkins's poetical life? Any answer to this question must be complicated
in precisely the ways that Norman Holland, Harold Bloom, and other
psychoanalytical critics, not excluding Freud himself, teach us to recognize. By calling upon a historical source, Hopkins demonstrates his scholarly aptitudes and abilities; but he also to some degree thereby denies his
own powers of invention. By repeating some of Prescott's information
and opinions, he demonstrates his powers of objectivity; yet he also thereby accedes to a set of historiographical materials that from another angle
might prove problematical. He implicitly condemns the very Catholic
tradition, not excluding the austere Jesuit discipline, that he would one
day embrace in the most important decision of his public life. With "The

Escorial," he permitted himself to become a candidate for success and fame; later he would repeatedly deny any and all such ambition. He produced a finished work that not only took on a public life of its own at the Highgate school but also paved the way for him at Oxford; yet for some time thereafter, and for prolonged stretches of his life, he would not finish any work of comparable scope. Finally, and at the level of psychoanalytic theory most pertinently, he entered into a collaboration with his father. What effects the father's contributions might create, in particular his copying out the "The Escorial" and thereby symbolically expunging his son's presence in the poem, can plausibly be guessed at. Generally speaking, it seems difficult to deny the plausibility of thinking that "The Escorial" plays a part in Hopkins's developing attitude toward writing and particularly toward the writing of history.

2

"to succeed by failure":
Hopkins Against the Tradition for Lyrical Assortments

(1)   To burn always with this hard, gem-like flame, to main-
       tain this ecstasy, is success in life.

                                    Pater, *The Renaissance*

(2)   I want to write still and as a priest I very likely can do
       that too.

                                    Hopkins, *Further* 231

(3)   What of the contemporary readers whom Gerard Manley
       Hopkins almost entirely lacked, and did not seek?

                                    Wimsatt and Brooks 547

(4)   To eternize an object is to save it by withdrawing it from
       circulation; from circulation in the battering and incessant
       transaction of nature, which is life; but it is a peculiar
       method of salvation, amounting to death.

                                    Ransom 317

Concerning the necessity for an aesthetics of reception, Jauss argues: "If literary history is to be rejuvenated, the prejudices of historical objectivism must be removed and the traditional approach to literature must be replaced by an aesthetics of reception and impact" (69). But what if, in a case such as that of Hopkins, a poet removes himself from literary history so there is no reception and no impact? The consequences can be real and serious: "We accordingly lack some of the social, rhetorical, and institutional contexts that can frame a body of writing and guide our understanding of it" (Stonum 5).

Hopkins's literary fame arguably begins in 1918 with the posthumous appearance of his poems. When we say that Hopkins lived in obscurity, we refer to this circumstance, given that as an Oxonian, a Jesuit, and a scholar he was relatively well known by his Victorian contemporaries. In an age of careers and careerisms—witness Tennyson, Browning, Rossetti—Hopkins's energies went not into a *career* but into a priestly *vocation* as a member of the Society of Jesus. Almost universally, far too easily to be sure, Hopkins's critics and readers take at face value his priestly protestations against any thought of publishing his poems as a book and thereby entering the public arena.

But if we are to historicize Hopkins, we may need to reexamine, from some new perspective, this poet who adamantly refused his contemporaries' definition of *poet*. We must recall, for example, that Hopkins began writing his major poems in the 1870s. During this period, a new understanding of a career and vocation was coming into prominence. Authorial ambition as a Victorian mythos underwent change.

> [The] poetic *vocation*, in the classical sense, had come to be replaced by a poetic *career*. Whereas the former required taking certain memorial steps and imitating a ritual progress, in the latter the writer had to create not only his art but also the very course of his writings. (Said, *Beginnings* 227)

The strenuous self-fashioning Said refers to involves rivalries and cross-purposes. Hopkins would have encountered this historical paradigm shift had he aspired to a literary reputation. Only a literary vocation analogous to his priestly vocation would be a role he might aspire to for himself. As in fact, in his contradictory way, he did aspire. The relation between a career and a text is a unity between some pattern of events and the conscious transformation of such events into forms of discourse (196). With publication, a poet "begins to launch his world" (271). One of the most crucial literary events for Hopkins was his decision not to gather his poems together, edit them, and publish them in a book.

Hopkins commentators regularly miss or misinterpret signs that Hopkins with part of his mind aspired toward the career or experience of a published poet. We need only recall the ineluctable fact that he contrived for his poems to be preserved by Bridges against the possibility of posthumous publication ("if anyone shd. like, they might be published after my death" [*Letters* 65; MacKenzie, Introduction xxxiv]). Robert Martin phrases this problem both deftly and humanely: "However much poets love a dramatic gesture, they seem to have an equally sure instinct for preservation of their work" (95). Such an opinion argues for Hopkins's understandable, if sublimated, literary ambition. If nothing else, either Christian charity or common decency permits, even necessitates, our entertaining such a hypothesis. Publicly, Hopkins opted for a vocation, both poetical and priestly, rather than a career. Privately, if by quirky means, he rivalled other poets in orchestrating the course of his writings (preservation, publication) with the result we recognize today as the Hopkinsian oeuvre and status in literary history.

Two of Hopkins's poems have inordinately attracted readerly admiration and critical speculation. "The Windhover" and *The Wreck of the Deutschland* always threaten to become, each in its own way, the sort of "unwieldy excrescence of a disproportionate episode" that Thomas Warton prudently guarded against in writing the first major history of English poetry (Warton vii). Given Hopkins's oeuvre, including the twin excrescences represented by his two most written-about poems, it comes as a shock to recall that when we look at Hopkins's poetry we see something that no living person ever glimpsed during Hopkins's lifetime or in fact before 1918. Hopkins the overworked Jesuit priest never collected for publication what we possess and enjoy. Now, however, aided by the recent work of Neil Fraistat on poetical collections, we are better able to hypothesize about Hopkins's decision not to prepare a collection of his poems. Entering the realm of pure speculation, I deal in this chapter with a historical *aporia* or absence that is, paradoxically, an antithetically militant historical presence.

Hopkins chose not to follow the example of numerous other poets who gathered and ordered their poems for a published collection. The disdainful or dismayed Hopkins denies history by the public gesture of foregoing a self-fashioning act available to poets in his culture. Everywhere we look, the problem of Hopkins is a problem of beginnings or refusals of beginnings. His peculiar way of stringing words together is decidedly Viconian in its forging of novel connections "that induce origin-effects and beginning-effects" (Said, *Beginnings* 352). Yet, to begin is an intentionally productive activity which induces a painful sense of separation and loss (372). Hopkins rejected the fruitful tradition for lyrical assortments that might have enabled him to become a different, perhaps a better, poet.

We can hardly imagine the resolute but sensitive Hopkins not contemplating, with many an inward pang, various kinds of poetical collections that might work some good in the world. We need only recall that in August of 1884 he wrote to Bridges asking that his own manuscript poems be returned to him for correcting. He calls the manuscript a book: "That book could be the greatest boon to me, if you are so good as to offer it—a godsend and might lead to my doing more" (MacKenzie, "Introduction" xxxviii). This unambiguous request ought to remove any doubt about Hopkins's submerged desire or ambition. In his writing, Hopkins early on attempted to avoid many threatening forms of authority—sexual, religious, social, literary—by using vocational metaphors that blend aesthetic and religious aspirations (Smulders 161-2). Do we offer Hopkins any disrespect if we conjecture that this gifted young man, priest or not, would understandably want to follow in appropriate ways a poetical career, that he would desire to have his poems appear in a book that could find a proper audience and work its good in the world?

Hopkins's critics sometimes speak as if Hopkins had in fact given the world a personal statement in the form of a collection of poems: "He elected to enchant us and to move us, in order that he might warn us and persuade us, not only from the pulpit, as a priest should, but as a poet should—from the pages of his slim volume of poems" (Sulloway 195). Similarly, Edward Said speaks of Hopkins's "fully progressing career" (*Beginnings* 272). How inevitable, and how right, that we should hypothesize about Hopkins in relation to the book-based tradition for lyrical assortments. So we wonder: what does Hopkins deny himself and the world by excluding himself from the familiar tradition for lyrical assortments that includes among others Ovid, Dante, Sidney, Shakespeare, Milton, Pope, Wordsworth, and Browning?

How are we to historicize Hopkins's choice of a noncareer, this curious gaping absence in Victorian literary culture, in ways consistent with both tradition and individual talent? I wish to begin by stringing together, in the manner of an overture, several loosely related critical statements, together with a proposition that follows plausibly from them. Only that ought not to be which cannot be (Murray 14). The elaboration and ensembling of patterns makes it possible for society to maintain itself (Said, *World* 171). A collection of poems is an ensemble with each poem humbling itself to a pattern but finding its fullest intertextual richness as part of the pattern (Rajan 23). Historically, the book *per se* enables and represents consciousness taking a new turn (Ong 21). Thus, in justice we should conclude that not to produce a book one is capable of producing may amount to a refusal of a crucial stage in humane development and human responsibility.

The poetical career or noncareer of Gerard Manley Hopkins represents a case of self-curtailment, self-denial, or self-censorship. Despite numerous reasons urging Hopkins to assemble and publish a collection of poems, this poet of originality and distinction refused to do so. One reason for this great refusal results from a perplexity of conscience. Of his model, master, and critic Jesus Christ, he wrote:

> [H]is career was cut short and, whereas he would have wished to succeed by success—for it is insane to lay yourself out for failure, prudence is the first of the cardinal virtues, and he was the most prudent of men—nevertheless he was doomed *to succeed by failure*; his plans were baffled, his hopes dashed, and his work was done by being broken off undone. (*Correspondence* 137-38; emphasis added)

Such was the script for an *imitatio Christi* Hopkins chose to follow in his *contemptus mundi*, his antithetical decision to deny literary history by denying the reading public any experience of his poetry. This despite Jesus Christ's literary gifts, his having enacted a public career as a kind of wandering poet, and despite Hopkins's own desire for success being arguably his own most powerful drive (Bergonzi 150). Hopkins would eventually succeed, and greatly, but the route to posthumous success was to be long and circuitous. At least one critic says of Hopkins: "His was the Way of the Cross: he was to succeed by failure" (Heuser 1).

Given that Hopkins shrewdly placed his manuscripts with Robert Bridges but never himself prepared a collection of poems for publication, he places himself, ironically to be sure, both within and against the tradition for lyrical assortments. One way to achieve a focus on this puzzling episode in Victorian crisis-consciousness is to inquire into the problem of placing Hopkins's most ambitious poem, *The Wreck of the Deutschland* (1876), in relation to his other poems. MacKenzie's 1990 edition reminds us most acutely of Hopkins's great refusal and thus provokes further speculation. The arrangement in a collection being equivalent to another poem, as it were a master poem or macropoem (Ludvigson), Hopkins's refusal to arrange his poems in a collection and instead to succeed by failure represents suppression of an important macrocomposition and potentially the most crucial stage in one's artistic development.[1]

As it happens, during Hopkins's lifetime some twenty-nine poems appeared in print (Bump, "Centenary" 19). The fact that he published no collection would seem to offer at best a wornout biographical theme, unless some fresh theory should revitalize the issue. Happily, Fraistat's *Poems in Their Place* (1986), a collection of essays by diverse hands, provides a coherent assemblage of ideas, in effect a history of "lyrical assortments." A selection from these ideas undergirds my analysis in this chapter. In what follows, I identify in parentheses the author of each summarized essay, and I list each essay individually in my bibliography of works cited.

Poets carefully organize their collections, paying attention to paired poems, sequences, poems in parts, clusters of poems, and the shape of a collection as a whole. Complications arise when a poet tinkers with an arrangement; such re-ordering complicates the question whether any ordering can induce one single effect. An ordering may be narrative or argument or serial (calendrical, liturgical, numerological). A collection may be autobiographical, may imply an ideology, or may be reformed or deformed by an editor. As a narrative, it need not manifest plot in any usual sense (Fraistat, "Place").

Does a collection enact a narrative? Assuming that any sequential continuousness induces continuity, a collection may be informed by a plotless narrative resulting from a writer's use of devices such as progression, recurrence, and sequentiality. Cognitively perceived entities (certain people, places, events, ideas, and motives) may induce a strong sense of integrative narrative even where emphases shift abruptly from poem to poem. Narrative integration may be more obvious in a series of narrative poems or personal poems (Miner).

In early classical collections, *varietas* (different subjects, themes, techniques) with some loose arrangement governed the whole. Poets produced individual poems fully expecting to place them in a book, where each one would settle into a proper place according to a given decorum. Pre-Ovidian collections merely varied the forms of variety. Thus, Vergil's *Eclogues* offered ten poems varied in subject, length, choice of speaker (Theocritean or non-Theocritean voices). Horace's *Satires* offered poems grouped in three triads developing distinct subjects or personae. Horatian *Epodes* offered seventeen poems alternating between metrical sameness and difference. Horace's *Odes* employed framing poems and varying metrical ostentation. Ovid's exilic collection *Letters from the Black Sea* climaxes such classical ordering strategies. Ovid's earlier collection *Amores* had been ordered by groupings of paired poems; by contrast, the exilic letters represent a chronologically thematic account of Ovid's exile that rebukes official Roman policies. Ovid's feigned absence of order itself indicts Caesar Augustus (Anderson).

Sidney's *Astrophel and Stella* (1591) was guided by a "tradition for lyrical assortments" headed by Dante (*Vita Nuova*) and Petrarch. Sidney altered the "enabling discourse of sonneteering" by secularizing the sonneteer and the lady. He worked three major changes in the ordering of sonnet sequences: (1) he brought the lady down to earth, (2) he depicted love as humanly agonizing, and (3) he redefined the poet/lover. Sidney altered the sonnet's Augustinian aesthetic according to which the poet's creation seems to rival God's creation, symmetry and harmony generally pervade both creations, and the poet begins with a god-like plan. Initiating a major paradigm shift, *Astrophel and Stella* gives an account of Sidney's own development as a poet. Sidney moves English lyrical poetry from being mainly a metrical art toward being a narrative/ mimetic production of powerful images of human experience, thus preparing the ground for the sequences of Spenser, Shakespeare, and Donne. Such revolutionary collections secularized the sonnet, opening the way for a Milton or Wordsworth to use the fourteen-liner for broader philosophical purposes (Heninger).

In the seventeenth-century, the concept of significant order was culturally available to readers, and a collection might exhibit both chronology and deliberate arrangement. *Poems of Mr. John Milton* (1645), a retrospective arranged at the age of thirty-seven, offers a complex record of the "rising poet." In Herrick's *Hesperides* (1648), the ordering supports the English crown while distracting readers who might be unsympathetic to the crown. Jonson's *Under-wood* shows a powerful but subtle chronology, whereas Marvell's *Miscellaneous Poems* is explicitly organized by theme. Jonson's "To the Reader" asserts that he indeed fully intended to publish his poems and thus take responsibility for his literary past. Jonson uses a Pindaric ode to raise his tone a notch or two, placing it so as to disrupt an order or system: "A principle of order is thus admitted, by pointing to its disruption." Marvell's original order depends on groupings: "the point of *this* grouping is made clearer when we come to the last section of the *Miscellaneous Poems*, where a political imperative is massively reinstated" (Patterson).

Generic groupings have advantages and disadvantages in directing the reader to notice a poem's formal implications. Poetic sequences may be narrative, metaphoric, imagistic, or conceptually thematic, a sequence being construed as both part of a collection and also as one single work (Shawcross).

Between the 1645 and 1671 editions of Milton's poems, a change in the significance of *Paradise Regained* and *Samson Agonistes* results from bringing more closely together, in the latter volume, these two texts. Proximity induces "a model for dialectical opposition figured in generic strife and figuring forth different modes and extents of consciousness." Placed adjacent to each other, the two poems effectively pit an emergent prophet against a failed prophet, but the new positioning amounts to a "regressive maneuver," a generic regression. *Samson Agonistes* now expresses both revolutionary apocalyptic myth and also the cooling off of such activism into apolitical quietism. The volume as a whole becomes a poem: "*its* syntax, not that of the separate poems, governs the meaning; and the meaning itself derives from the concatenation" (Wittreich).

Alexander Pope asserted to Swift that his poems should not be "ignorantly look'd upon one by one." Pope used a collection to establish himself both inside the classical tradition and also as a commentator on current and future events: "The reader of the 1717 *Works* moves directly from the explicit prophecy in *Windsor-Forest* of Britain's political and commercial supremacy to the implicit prophecy in *An Essay on Criticism* of her literary and critical supremacy." Pope cleverly effected closure: "By placing *Eloisa to Abelard* at the end of the 1717 *Works*, Pope demonstrates that his reputation does not depend solely on his past performance" (Carretta).

Wordsworth intended to revolutionize the subject matter and language of poetry with his 1807 collection. Readers were offered an ordering "system" in the two volumes. Six sections, three in each volume, focus attention on categories such as "orchard" poems, "tour" poems, sonnets on liberty, and the like. At the end of the second volume, he placed the great Immortality Ode, a poem written almost last, as a summary statement. He offers a "continual readjustment of perspective between the simple and complex, the quotidian and cosmic," thereby producing a unique definition of Duty: "a responsible contemplation of the self, of experience, of others." Rejecting Coleridge's scornful definition of the sonnet ("a small poem, in which some lonely feeling is developed"), Wordsworth followed Petrarch's lead into psychology, engaging himself in an unparalleled involvement with the sonnet form. Two sonnet sequences adumbrate the 1807 collection. We should recall, though, that Wordsworth rearranged the whole collection for an 1815 edition, so as to intensify a Gothic-cathedral parallel for his entire oeuvre (Curran).

Browning rearranged *Dramatic Lyrics* in its various appearances (1842; 1845; 1863), emphasizing the collection itself as the appropriate unit of critical attention. In 1842, paired poems are punctuated by free-standing poems. Browning set aside chronological order of composition and arranged pairs emphasizing setting or character, hatred or love, and the like. Formal and thematic patterns link apparently dissimilar companion pieces. The 1842 volume reaches a thematic climax in "Madhouse Cells," and the final poem ("The Pied Piper") emphasizes the role-of-the-poet theme, thus focusing the assortment's major preoccupations (Bornstein).

Cultural values may be established by the very ordering of a lyrical assortment, and in a collection we may detect a personality taking on the "shadow-shape of a narrative." Walt Whitman invented the lyric-epic so as to create a new type of literary personality, based upon his own democratic sensibilities (James Miller).

Finally, Sylvia Plath's *Ariel* (1965) presents a special problem. The compiler and editor Ted Hughes imposed a different plot—his own hidden agenda—upon the collection his deceased wife had prepared. He omitted poems she included and rearranged the ordering of poems, thereby obliterating his own questionable role in Plath's sad story. Plath is made to seem a "literary dragon . . . who breathed a burning river of bale across the literary landscape." Perloff concludes: "How ironic, in any case, that the publication of Plath's poems has depended, and continues to depend, on the very man who is, in one guise or another, their subject" (Perloff).

Fraistat's *Poems in Their Place* establishes a firm context for the Hopkins who chose to occupy a special if ironical place in the tradition for lyrical assortments. We must keep in mind that the Victorian Age was a great age of "things" and collections of things. At the Crystal Palace, in 1851, the "Great Victorian Collection" provided a potent trope for English cultural history (Briggs 53-102). Widespread Victorian consciousness of the value of collections may have provided an irresistible windmill for an antithetical Hopkins not so much to tilt at as to turn his back on and pretend to ignore.[2]

Gradually we learn how to comprehend Hopkins. However, we do not yet know where to place *The Wreck of the Deutschland*. Year by year, we uncoil the mind-bending tropes embedded in every line, seemingly in every word, of that tormented modern utterance. A recent effort to elucidate the pronoun "it" in the *Wreck* typifies the close scrutiny critics apply to minute details of Hopkins's masterpiece (Cotter). Critics also endeavor to understand the *Wreck* in relation to a genre, tradition, or large influence (Bump, "Influence"). Perhaps after being unassimilable for so long, the *Wreck* is destined to remain so (Bergonzi 164). No editor or scholar has located the missing autograph of the *Wreck*, and a definitive text may be impossible to establish (MacKenzie, "Hazardous" 63-68). No one can be absolutely sure, in various senses, where to situate the poem.

Why vex oneself about the place of the *Wreck*? Did not Hopkins's first editor Robert Bridges fix it, in its opening position, "like a great dragon folded in the gate to forbid all entrance" (104)? Did not Elisabeth Schneider reinforce Bridges's characterization with the title of an influential book of criticism?[3] Even so, Fraistat's speculations about poetical collections require us to ask new questions and construct new hypotheses.

In the midst of our most confident speculations regarding the place of the *Wreck*, we recur at various levels of consciousness to Bridges's dragonish trope. A recent facsimile edition, for example, commences its second volume by offering Hopkins's mature poems beginning with the *Wreck* (Hopkins, *Later*).

Bridges, it seems likely, would have been alert to what Foucault calls the "ordering codes and reflections upon order itself" (*Order* xxi). We recall that Bridges, when sending some of Hopkins's manuscript poems to Coventry Patmore for that austere poet's vetting, cautiously placed "Pied Beauty" and other sonnets before the fearsome *Wreck* (MacKenzie, "Introduction" xxxvi). The physical place where the *Wreck* was composed has been established (Milward, "Place"), but only with difficulty can we try to place the completed poem in an ordered collection. In truth, the *Wreck*, which repels and belies stock responses invited by its title, is indeed a dragon in the gate, more literally a stumbling block or scandal. Coleridge had warned against "extravagant ravings" being placed at the opening of a collection so as to risk producing disgust throughout (Fraistat, *Book* 41). The *Wreck* focuses the problem of ordering Hopkins's poems by its tendency to overwhelm everything in its neighborhood. It functions as a transgression, in the way that the *mise en abyme* is thought to function as an embedded transgression of an embedding text. It threatened to obliterate Hopkins's other poems in the 1918 edition. In its shifting position in subsequent editions and perhaps in any imaginable edition, it only differently—no less so—disrupts and imbalances any arrangement.

Hopkins's antithetical noncareer is marked throughout by such disruptions, mainly by his self-contradictory decision both to be a poet by writing poems but not to be a poet by the simple device of not publishing a collection. Hopkins ranks among the most metaphorical of poets (Brooke-Rose 313-15), but metaphor establishes a peculiar intimacy between poet and reader (Ted Cohen 9). Hopkins refused the intimacy a published collection, with its overarching trope of sociability, could invite. Robert Martin expresses this judgment in explicit terms: "What he was forced to face directly for the first time [in 1882] was the blunt fact that his failure to write poetry was not the fault of external circumstances but of his own personality" (346). It is a touch-me-not Hopkins who proves to "forbid all entrance."[4]

No bibliomaniac, Hopkins claimed to be "altogether wanting in the spirit of a bookhunter" (*Correspondence* 107), but he was acutely aware of poetical collections. He saw and judged books by poets from the past and, surely most achingly, by his own contemporaries and friends. He kept track of Bridges's collections, on one occasion rebuking a small volume as too expensive (*Correspondence* 107). He eagerly read the 1877 sonnet sequence *The Growth of Love*. While at Oxford, he had read with keen interest R. W. Dixon's 1861 *Christ's Company*. He urged that Digby Dolben's poems be published posthumously in book form (*Letters* 17). Famous collections impinging on Hopkins's consciousness included Swinburne's 1865 *Poems and Ballads, First Series* and Walt Whitman's *Leaves of Grass*, both of which offended him by embodying an aestheticism self-consciously decadent and immoral (Mariani, *Past* 121). During 1877, when he wrote ten sonnets, he probably read George Meredith's sonnet sequence *Modern Love (Poetical* 272). Embracing the self as that which bodily interpenetrates the material world (Ong 39-40), he could scarcely fail to love the materiality of a good book.

Hopkins could always cite a precedent for his effects. What models would be available to him if he contemplated preparing a collection? Neil Fraistat, this time with *The Poem and the Book*, is again instructive on a vexing issue. One set of models would be major romantic poets, who paid careful attention to contextual and contextural effects in ordering their poems and whose books Hopkins knew. Hazarding public rejection, romantic poets used collections not only for canon-making and audience-making but also for significant self-fashioning. Pride of place frequently went to one long poem placed at the opening, or an ambitious poem placed at the end could promise even greater things to come. Centerpieces of considerable magnitude might serve the poet's intentions. Collections by Wordsworth, Coleridge, Keats, and Shelley shape a thematically complex but coherent "field," and such framings guide readerly experience (31-45). Amounting to interplay with the reader, romantic orderings were also a "means of self-fashioning and self-promotion" (31). Hopkins might have imitated Coleridge's placing a subversive poem such as the "Ancient Mariner" at the opening of *Lyrical Ballads*. He could have placed the odic *Wreck* first and exploited Coleridge's example by rationalizing the entire collection as itself an ode, thereby justifying extreme shifts in matter and manner (51-9). Or, he could follow Blake's example in *Poetical Sketches* by ignoring connective cycle and sequence, in effect producing an "anti-book" (15).

Wordsworth placed the "Immortality Ode" at the end of a collection; his admirer Hopkins could have likewise positioned the *Wreck*. The recalcitrant Hopkins knew that poetical reputations result from collections, but he chose to remain "almost a cipher during his lifetime" (MacKenzie, "Introduction" lxxv). He expended energy in casuistical explanations, such as rationalizing an overscrupulous conscience, in his efforts to justify his antithetical self-curtailment.

Given that many collections are arranged in chronological order, such an arrangement will provide a familiar cultural pattern and also give a true representation of a poet's diachronic development. However, no less an expert than Wordsworth objected to mere chronology on the grounds that it valorized the poet over the poetry (Fraistat, *Book* 33). Chronology is not one of the patterns that strongly empower poetry or critical discourse. Baudelaire championed the poet's purposive ordering that would exhibit the author's tropes and methods rather than mere accidents of chronology, as affording a truer access to the poet's soul (x-xi). Precise chronological sequence is an inorganic concept which exists only in the theoretician's mind (MacKenzie, "Introduction" lxiii). We can only hypothesize what might have been even as we speculate about putative losses attendant upon Hopkins's setting his face against the tradition for lyrical assortments.

Deracinated Victorian readers needed to feel that they were represented in the writings they would read (Mermin 145-55). In the case of Hopkins, readers in need of *propaedeutic* literature as equipment for living were cut off from one potential source of guidance. Following Fraistat, we can sketch other such putative losses. By disregarding the usual procedures for bringing forward a lyrical assortment, Hopkins deprives each poem of its richest possible intertextual framework such as the discoveries only an author can make by prolonged tinkering with pairings, sequences, clusters, poems in parts, and overall shape of a collection or a canon. He might have employed a church-calendar or liturgical positioning of some or all poems, thus supplying an ideology important for some nineteenth-century readers who were importuning one sage after another in crisis after crisis (Hollahan, *Crisis-Consciousness* 56-61).

A close relation exists between the experience of order and the experience of being (Foucault, *Order* xxi). Hopkins missed the chance to impose a continuity equivalent to a narrative, hence, the progression and recurrence that can knit together an ordered collection. By emphasizing certain characters, places, events, ideas, and motives, he could have integrated a narrative even if his emphases shifted widely from poem to poem. He could have stressed narrative poems such as "The Loss of the Eurydice" or intimately personal poems which induce an effect of narrative structure. Hopkins's admirers might give a good deal to learn, for example, how "To seem the stranger lies my lot" would fit into an arrangement by Hopkins himself.

> /To seem the stranger lies my lot, my life
>   Among strangers. Father and mother dear,
>   Brothers and sisters are in Christ not near
> \And he my peace/my parting, sword and strife,
> /England, whose honour O all my heart woos, wife   5
>   To my creating thought, would neither hear
>   Me, were I pleading, plead nor do I: Ĩ wĕar-
> \Y of idle a being but by where wars are rife.
> /I am in Ireland now; now Í am at a thîrd
>   Remove. Not but in all removes I can   10
> \Kind love both give and get. Only what word
> /Wisest my heart breeds   { baffling heaven's dark ban
>   { dark heaven's baffling ban
>   Bars or hell's spell thwarts. { This to hoard unheard,
>   { Thoughts hoarded unheard
> \Heard unhéeded,   { leaves me a lonely began.
>   { [leave]

(Poetical 181; #154)

One special feature of modern poetry being the invention of the poetic sequence—varied pieces interacting as an organic whole (Rosenthal and Gall 9)—Hopkins could have achieved a more definite place as a precursor of modern poets. His brilliant fragments of intuition could have passed from "immediate sensing" to the fullest religious insight only if he had managed an "act of *compositio*" by means of some composite structure (Weatherby 95).

As an expert classicist, Hopkins would have known how to give full rein to lyrical *varietas*. As a poet of exilic consciousness such as described by Martz (79-94), he could also have followed Ovid's example in the *Letters from the Black Sea* and given a more tightly knit account of his own exile from family, country, or God.

Hopkins is in a major sense a sonneteer (Bermann 149). Had he engaged with the sonnet-sequence subtradition of the tradition for lyrical assortments, he might have discovered an untapped ordering principle of his peculiar genius. Sonnets such as "The Windhover," "Henry Purcell," "Ribblesdale," and the terrifying poems of spiritual desolation are considered to equal Shakespeare's and Donne's in style and experiential consciousness.

Ribblesdale

Earth, sweet Earth, sweet lándscape, with leavès throng
And louchèd low grass, heaven that dost appeal
To with no tongue to plead, no heart to feel;
That canst but only be, but dost that long—

Thou canst but be, but that thou well dost; strong   5
Thy plea with him who dealt, nay does now deal,
Thy lovely dale down thus and thus bids reel
Thy river, and o'er gives all to rack or wrong.

And what is Earth's eye, tongue, or heart else, where
Else, but in dear and dogged man? Ah, thĕ heir   10
To his own selfbent so bound, so tied to his turn,

To thriftless reave both our rich round world bare
And none reck of world after, this bids wear
Earth brows of such care, care and dear concern.

(Poetical 171; #149)

Had his forty or so sonnets been ordered by the poet, following some true principle discoverable only by the poet's own heart and head, these scattered poems almost assuredly would have climaxed the sonnet-sequence tradition as forcefully as the *Wreck* culminates the odic tradition (Heath-Stubbs 108).

    As a post-Renaissance sonnet-sequencer, Hopkins would nevertheless have ready-to-hand the perfect Lady. The Virgin Mary represents one Christian model of free choice lovingly enacted (Ong 86), and Mary, of course, looms large in Hopkins's thought (Paul Barry 9-10). At the same time, he might feel some anxiety at the Renaissance sonneteer's Augus-

tinian aesthetic that equates the poet's inventiveness with God's creativity. For Hopkins to confront such a dilemma could have led to artistic
growth. The drive toward freedom of choice in Hopkins's *mentalité* functions like the freedom of play (Ong 13-14). The playful Hopkins should
have been, at least could have been, equal to the task of using a collection to induce a playful new type of sonnet-consciousness.

As early as 1877, when he was thirty-three years of age and with
twelve years yet to live, Hopkins referred to a "complete . . . set" of his
own sonnets in Bridges's possession (*Letters* 42-3). A sonnet sequence by
Hopkins could have given us a valuable literary heterocosm or Leibnizian
optional world. Hopkins played the cultural game of sonnet sequencing
but, as Wittgenstein might put it, he went only part of the way. The sonnet form, if we can accept Oppenheimer's thesis, helped to initiate modern thought, being the first lyric form of self-consciousness and self-in-
conflict (3). If Hopkins had troubled to collect, order, and print according
to his true genius even some of the forty-three sonnets included by
MacKenzie in the 1990 *Poetical Works*, he could have secured a more
important place in the history of the sonnet. He would thereby have parti-
cipated more fully in the birth of the modern mind.

Hopkins even had an excuse, in 1881, for collecting, examining, and
arranging his revolutionary sonnets. A devotee of the form, Hall Caine,
published an anthology designed to prove the impossibility of anyone's
improving upon the rhyme scheme or meter of the traditional sonnet
(Bergonzi 120). Would not Hopkins's critical reputation and English poetry in general be even more richly varied, unified, and compelling if he
had assembled a sonnet sequence in which he could have challenged
Caine's opinion? He could thereby, additionally, have confronted Petrarch's challenging assertion of the near impossibility of establishing an
ontologically stable self by means of a sonnet sequence (Bermann 20)?[5]

Complex framing techniques characterize literary modernism (Caws
263). Hopkins himself defined poetry thus: "Poetry is speech framed for
contemplation of the mind" (6). Were Hopkins open to the possibilities
of committing his unbordered soul to the confines of a book by assembling and framing a collection, he could provide both a retrospective on
his own development to any given moment and also a promise for the
future. He could arrange his poems so that they offered an even more
massive judgment on Protestant England—or Catholic England—than his
gesture at the end of the *Wreck*.

> Dáme at óur dóor
> Drówned, and among óur shóals,

Remémber us in the róads, the heaven-háven of the
    rewárd: 275
  Our kíng back, Oh, upon Énglish sóuls!
Let him éaster in us, be a dáyspring to the dímness of us,
  be a crímson-cresseted east,
More brightening her, ráre-dear Brítain, as his réign rólls,
  Príde, rose, prínce, hero of us, hígh-príest,
Oür héart's charity's héarth's fíre, oür thóughts' chivalry's
  thróng's Lórd.   280

In any event, he would be compelled to take direct editorial responsibility for his literary past. Using the *Wreck* as a *mise en abyme*, he could place it for distribution effects. To elevate and energize the prevailing tone, it could arise as a coda or a central pivot or as part of a programmatic loop as described by Dällenbach (60-71).

The overarching trope enabled by an ordering of poems might constitute a world view or root metaphor—formistic, mechanistic, organic, or contextualistic (Pepper, *Concept* 508-10). The purposive act of arranging a collection could itself have modified or even become Hopkins's root metaphor or world view. Given his Victorian cultural situation and his daring genius, what truth-effects and reality-effects he might have produced!

Dialectically, metaphors build cultures, while cultures build and sustain metaphorists (Booth 70). By tinkering with an arrangement, Hopkins could discover how to establish oppositions between poems, how to play off one sense against another. He could discover the macro-poem or phantom-poem that lurks as an informing principle of an assortment or an oeuvre. Like Pope, Hopkins could select an arrangement that expressed his own patriotic fears and hopes for Victorian England while more directly carving out a place for himself in English literary history. Had Hopkins accepted the compiler's responsibility, he might have, like Wordsworth, continually readjusted perspectives on his favorite topics such as nature, human courage, and the love of God. He could have followed Wordsworth's example—even more radically than he frequently did—of prolonged experimentation with the sonnet form. He could have followed Browning, arranging pairs of poems, building to a climax in a cluster or sequence of poems, and thereby emphasizing some chief theme or deep preoccupation. Having recognized in Walt Whitman a mind close in spirit to his own (*Letters* 155), he might have followed Whitman's example by using a book of poems to enlarge upon a new type of human personality.

The foregoing heuristic sketch of Hopkins's loss, sacrifice, or "failure," in selected terms of the tradition for lyrical assortments, leaves one main impression. Given Hopkins's familiarity with the classical and English traditions, the prospect of assembling his own collection for publication must have represented a strong temptation. Poetry collections being part of the sociology of poetry, as he would have understood, we should keep in mind that Hopkins never forgot his scattered corpus: "To escape his own powerful voice, he endured long stretches of silence, an apparently cavalier indifference to the state and condition of his parcel of songs, at the same time that one detects a nostalgia for that very same exceptional corpus of poems" (Mariani, *Past* 140). Here, the christic utterance "this is my body" becomes acutely personal and historical reality in the scattered corpus of work by a finely-tuned, perhaps too tightly strung, Jesuit priest, who happened to be one of the most remarkable prosodists in the nineteenth century.

The restless Hopkins disoriented and marginalized himself by proposing scattered, unfinished, self-contradictory projects (Bergonzi 13). Like other nineteenth-century authors, he aspired to construct a great intellectual structure, but some deconstructive or self-destructive process was at work within.[6]

> One has the distinct and disconcerting impression of a powerful, original, and well-stocked—indeed, polymathic—mind with so little equilibrium that it could not resist picking up and trying to pursue one random proposal after another. (Bergonzi 144-45)

In that Hopkins claimed to have destroyed his manuscripts as an act of self-immolation, he was one kind of book-burner. Yet, despite this histrionic "massacre of the innocents" or putative burning of his poems in 1868, his early work—sonnets, songs, ballads, narrative and dramatic fragments—survived and became part of his posthumous collected works. Do we offer this overscrupulous man the slightest insult if we choose to regard as intentional, if somewhat disingenuous, his preservation of hard-won manuscript poems? The generous work of Bridges and others in preserving these traces of a master spirit should be regarded as being consistent with Hopkins's own deepest desires. The popular notion lamenting the loss of some mute, inglorious Milton ought always to be understood, as William Faulkner somewhere says, as mere sentimentality. The true poet will guarantee that poems will see the light of day and have a chance to work their potential good in the world.

The potential materiality of a book spurs the writer on (Said, *Beginnings* 20), and everywhere in Hopkins's writings, we see a "dialectic of production" at work (Said, *World* 41). At the risk of uttering a truism, we should acknowledge that poets intend poems to be read and, to that end, to appear in books (William Anderson 47). Even an authority like Hans Walter Gabler is not unwilling to assert this seeming truism: "The composition of *Ulysses* was directed toward publication" (1891). Robert Graves would tirelessly urge that we should read poets not in anthologies but in collections. Even hemmed in by censoring forces both public and private, Hopkins might have been equal to the task of ordering his own macro-utterance for Victorian England to see and hear. The pity is that he did not try. One extreme hypothesis these speculations lead to is that Hopkins fails somewhat both as a religious poet and as a poet *per se*. The fragments of Hopkins's world for some readers "fail to cohere" (Weatherby 96).

To order a lyrical assortment may mean to designate one or more programmatic poems. By definition, a programmatic poem guides and permeates an entire assortment (William Anderson 48). The specific problem of where to place *Wreck of the Deutschland* focuses the issue of an antithetical Hopkins setting his face "against" the history of lyrical assortments. Bridges's having placed the *Wreck* first defines the problem. Other editors arranging selected editions have taken the easy way out by omitting the great ode altogether (Warner 9). James Dickey chose the honorific strategy of placing it in a separate volume by itself. As the body of Hopkins's retrieved work grows larger, each successive editor of the collected poems has dealt differently with the problem. Bridges placed it first in 1918; Charles Williams placed it fourth, following three early poems, in 1930; W. H. Gardner included more early poems and numbered it twenty-eighth in 1948; MacKenzie let it stand as number twenty-eight in 1970. In the chronologically arranged 1990 *Poetical Works*, containing 179 poems, MacKenzie includes many fragments and early poems, then designates the *Wreck* #101. What Hopkins refused to do for himself has been done by others. The assemblage of the Hopkins canon has been one of the remarkable tasks in modern literary culture.[7]

Human personality sways human behavior. Hopkins is no exception. This man of genuine intellectual gifts could not easily express his oppositional talents within institutional constraints (Bergonzi 52). How tempting but difficult it is to imagine a poetical career of which the tormented *Wreck* would be the first small step! In contemplating the increasingly more ambitious poems that *de rigueur* would normally follow, what poet would not be daunted? The example of Browning, who radically changed directions after the depressing public and critical rejection of "Pauline," offers itself for comparison. We are regularly told that Hopkins thought it best not to offer his advanced writings to an unprepared public, but he preserved poems which very likely would have reinforced the Christian faith among some Victorian readers. Reflecting upon Hopkins's refusal to become an author, we might recall Michel Foucault's famous answer to the question, "What Is an Author?": "The author is therefore the ideological figure by which one marks the manner in which we fear the proliferation of meaning." We readers share Hopkins's own apprehensions concerning the risk of being misunderstood.

One way to get a purchase on Hopkins's antithetical refusal to collect his scattered manuscript poems is to place it in the context of literary censorship, more properly, of literary self-censorship. In general, self-censorship internalizes social repression so that censorship becomes not only a manageable strategy for dissimulation controlled by the writer but also an autonomous form of writing *per se*. Censorship, on any prudent view of morality, proves fairly reasonable (Beardsley 576-83). A guarantor of social order, censorship begins with *census* or counting, so that it means keeping tabs and thus keeping control. Censorship then becomes ideological and moral control. Much of modern censorship devolves upon questions of sexual behavior and obscenity, but other departments of life come under its sway. In the area of art, according to the theological doctrine of things indifferent, an aesthetic object is neither good nor bad. Only one's use of the object determines its value. On the question of human freedom, the artist is free to enjoy not so much unbridled self-expression as the freedom to discover new modes of expression and aesthetic exploration.

> If his product is not good, it will languish and die. But if it is good, then his freedom, and even some of the peculiar and irritating uses to which it has been put, will be well rewarded; for he will have added to the whole Creation a new object, whose worth, where human beings are sufficiently aware of their own hunger to surrender themselves to it, is incalculably great. (583)

All acculturated persons practice censorship and self-censorship.

According to psychoanalytic theory, the censor is the internalized social agency by which unpleasant ideas, memories, and desires are denied or disguised from one's consciousness, as in dreams, so that the social individual can function efficiently. Censorship and self-censorship, taken together, are the double knot that binds cultural power and knowledge (Jansen 14-25).

Despite Hopkins's personal virtues and abilities, he was a conscience-stricken and disorderly archivist of his own manuscripts (MacKenzie, "Hazardous" 52). He hated to copy out his own poems (*Letters* 304). External and internal forces worked against his following through on the *Wreck* as a gesture toward public authorship. As an English ode, the *Wreck* represents a test of one's poetical calling, a "vehicle of ontological and vocational doubt," in that the English ode as a genre or form complicates the intricate negotiations between invocation and vocation (Fry 7). The *Wreck* depicts Hopkins's tormented crisis-consciousness in the violent Jansenist fashion that characterizes modern religious odes. Like every modern odist, Hopkins tries to stretch his poetical vocation into the scientific or rational sphere where vaticination itself risks being demeaned as mere superstition (275-76).

Having begun so problematically, Hopkins's career inevitably remained incomplete but not entirely *sui generis*. The unfinished poem is, in truth, an important strand in English literary heritage (Rajan 3). In a canonical sense, Hopkins's refusal to compose the macro-poem emergent only in a poet's ordering of micro-poems belongs to the historical dialectic between closure and openness. Closure stands in relation to such psychic strategies as deferral and denial, which guarantee control by saving us from relinquishment (295). Hopkins's unfinished project—his refusal to determine a place for the *Wreck* or any other single poem—is a vivid example of the literary unfinished, with its undercurrents of fragmentariness, inconclusiveness, and indeterminacy.[8]

Victorian poetry is coeval with the beginnings of psychiatry (Fass 19-57). In Hopkins's experience, the psychoanalysis of antithetical self-censorship at some point comes into play. In simple Freudian terms, the *Wreck* seems like a perverse sexual come-on, a tease, a promise of pleasures only once to be flashed but then hidden away. Hopkins's odd habit of dating all revisions of a poem only with the original date of composition, e.g., "Oxford '79," not only frustrates efforts to date the poem but also seems like anal-compulsive behavior. A Lacanian revision of Freud would have it that Hopkins wavered self-destructively between two modes of language-centered consciousness, the Imaginative and the Symbolic (Lacan 507). Harold Bloom's concept of *askesis* or self-purgation, by means of which a poet seeks to attain creative solitude, also bears upon the present case. Hopkins reacted to rivals by yielding up part of his own artistic endowment. He isolated himself from threatening precursors by forcing his own scattered corpus and thus the precursors' published books to suffer truncation.

As I will argue in chapter 3, Hopkins's struggle with any one precursor is at bottom a struggle with all of his ancestors, literary and otherwise, including his own father. What alternative was available to Hopkins? We can reasonably speculate that by enabling a tropological progress from a womblike metaphor through objectified metonymy and systematic synecdoche to a self-reflexive irony, ordering a collection might have spared him the presumed blockages that occasion such literary psychoanalysis.[9]

Numerous forces bear upon Hopkins's decision not to publish. Public and private motives for remaining out of the public eye can be found in the fact that the Victorian age, the first great age of information, threatened to expose to various forms of publicity anyone who possessed secret or private knowledge (Welsh 60-84). Moreover, Hopkins would have guessed that his diacritical and scansion marks designed to control the speech-movement and meaning of his verses would require over an entire collection so much effort and stress as to preclude any likelihood of his undertaking such a task. In still another sense, given that the city represented for Hopkins a harsh image of man's inhumanity (Forsyth 72), a poetical collection—symbolically an urban collectivity—might seem repugnant.

Hopkins's literary self-denial is also a self-obliteration, not surprising in Victorian England, known in many quarters as "*la terre classique du suicide*" (Gates 23). During Hopkins's lifetime, suicide itself was taking its place as a major trope in the history of fame (Braudy 536). The anguished, self-exiled, literally defamiliarized Hopkins attempted to avoid the central family drama that characterizes the frenzy for renown: "In the heart of aspiration is the desire for recognition by those whose approval is unconditional and therefore need never be sought, but also can never be assumed" (Braudy ix). All of these painful reasons, any one of which could be a sufficient cause, bear upon Hopkins's keeping himself out of the Victorian stream of literary history and the Victorian stream of historical consciousness.

Historical ironies continually unfold when we consider the posthumous efforts made to preserve, collect, edit, and publish this poet who refused to collect himself. Why would a poet who defines poetry as "current language heightened" (*Letters* 89) not plunge headlong into the swim of Victorian England? Why would a patriotic nationalist who considered any great work by an Englishman a "great battle won by England" (*Letters* 231) not enlist in England's effort to extend its empire? Further: if

Hopkins could accept advanced doctrines such as the theology of Christ-as-King (Milward and Schoder 49), could he not imagine Christ as a wandering, myth-bringing poet, as Bultmann and Eliade would shortly do (Perrin 19-27)?

Hopkins is a major figure in Victorian syntactical experimentation (Baker 104-05). Pursuing a poetical bravery or metrical effect, he used syntactical freedom with wild abandon (Bergonzi 170-71). Would not the task of arranging an assortment invite his type of syntactical ingenuity? Hopkins's practical intelligence in editorial matters is witnessed to in Bridges's own "Preface to Notes" ('You were right to leave out the marks'). Ironically, the problems involved in poets' preparing their collections might be well suited to Hopkins's clerical temperament, at once fussy, quirky, and domineering. As a poet, Hopkins was in the best sense a professional (Bergonzi 21). He admired God in part because, having created the world, He then became a lowly carpenter (*Further* 20). Is this charming reason not also a good rationale for Hopkins, having invented the building blocks of a poetical heterocosm, then to undertake the lowly task of compiler and editor? Given his desire to control the reader's micro-experience by odd metrical notations, we should expect that he might have assembled a collection, such an ordering being one chief means by which poets try to control, at least to influence, the reader's macro-experience.

Readers seek the momentary illusion of order that only a book-as-heterocosm can provide (Ruthven 1-15). Hopkins was a keen but unsystematic theorizer on aesthetic issues, and he undertook, only to leave unfinished, many worthy projects. To have gathered together the scattered body of his poetry would have been to reenact the Areopagitican model of truth-search. Mythically, that is, to retrieve the scattered parts of Osiris's body and assemble them into a unified whole (Rajan 11). The putative loss to Hopkins and his readers centers upon this adamant refusal.

> To place a poem in a design is not necessarily to intrude on its particularity. Indeed our awareness of the richness and specificity of a poem may be impoverished if we ignore its participation in an overall design. The poem's appropriation of that design may be a main voice of its individuality. (23)

Paradoxically, the *Wreck* and other highly individualized poems such as "That Nature is a Heraclitean Fire" or "Spelt from Sibyl's Leaves" could perhaps best find their true voices by being gathered into an organic system.

Hopkins's punctilious business habits (Bergonzi 42) could have facilitated the editorial task. He might have been his own best editor, given that he is frequently "his own best annotator" (MacKenzie, "Introduction" lxx). Hopkins was a compulsive explainer. The last word of his last poem is *explanation*, a lifeless expression yearning for a referent (Said, *World* 97) but in some deep sense typical of this querulous scholar. Had he yielded to a will to power by forcing his poems into sequencings and groupings, he could have replaced his labored "explanation" with a more vital synonym for "interpretation" (Nietzsche, "Truth" 326).

We have been informed about the death of the author, but I am representing here the death-in-life of an antithetical Victorian author who, so to speak, never lived. We might reasonably hypothesize as follows. In light of Hopkins's orthodox Christianity, his refusal to construct and fix meaning in a poetical collection can be regarded as a partial rejection of God and of all divine hypostases such as reason, science, or law (Barthes, *Sade* 145-47). By preventing public engagement with his work, he failed the poet's duty of constructing the intelligence of his age.

A poet who wishes to circumvent censorship can do so in several ways: use safe genres to hide unsafe ideas; conceal radical material in subtexts; use allusions to screen out contemporary relevance; depersonalize unsettling convictions; place dangerous opinions in dialogue; use surface unorthodoxies to hint at deep heresies; sever or disjoin contexts; or, use seemingly casual placement to establish crucial relations (Wittreich 166). Hopkins's conscience would have precluded his lightly resorting to such strategies no matter how intense the pressures of external censorship. We should look to Hopkins himself if we would understand this peculiar episode in Victorian crisis-consciousness, this denial of literary history.

Hopkins himself complained about his inability to complete tasks: "All my world is scaffolding" (*Letters* 228). He feared that Jesuit censors would thwart some of his intellectual efforts, but he also had in his own breast another, even more daunting, censor. Self-censorship is a familiar modern phenomenon. Hopkins's refusal to assemble his poems into a collection resembles an ethical choice witnessed, for example, in an obstinate Conradian hero in *Victory* (1915): "The pure life, the perfect life, is not for him an ordering of virtuous acts, but a complete negation of action" (Karl 251). Hopkins can be seen not only as a Jesuit priest enacting an Ignatian *imitatio Christi* but also as one of those sensitive spirits—Rimbaud, Wittgenstein, Valéry, Kafka, Hoffmannsthal—who, facing modern meaninglessness, enact a "legendary and august renunciation of speech" (Jameson, *Prison-House* 12).

In textual theory, the changes a writer makes in response to criticism of earlier editions of his work are designated "self-censorship." Hopkins never faced such a task, but he practiced another type of self-censorship. The pathos of Hopkins's not producing a book of poems deepens when we recall his very nearly believing, with Mallarmé, that "everything in the world exists to end in the book" (Bergonzi 177). To tell one's own story is to organize a communal symbol allowing entry into human history (Jameson, *Political* 17-102). Hopkins left the fragmented *lexias* of his story scattered across the landscape. Given that Christ's own fame-of-the-spirit depended upon the publicizing of inner worth (Braudy 151-61), not even the selective self-censorship common to traditional prayer poetry justifies Hopkins's draconian gesture.

If Christ is indeed Hopkins's only true literary critic (*Correspondence* 8), Christ might also be his only proper compiler. Hopkins would shrewdly leave the publishing of his writings to be carried out by a disciple, Bridges, so that it can be said that the poet died in 1889 but was resurrected in 1918. Yet, Hopkins could not adduce unarguable reasons for censoring himself. Invoking Christ's success-by-failure, he spoke of a "career" cut short, "hopes dashed," and "work" having been "broken off." Such Victorian commercial tropes are by no means the most obvious terms for describing the life of Christ. Hopkins was more likely adapting to his own casuistical purposes the famous definition of *success* offered by Walter Pater: "To burn with this hard, gem-like flame, to maintain this ecstasy, is success in life." But Hopkins would burn in obscurity.

Clearly, he was rationalizing his own refusal of the canon-making, self-fashioning potential of a first book, even if the Ignatian *Spiritual Exercises* practiced by Jesuits does not demand such self-censorship. Hopkins missed one part of this ascetical theology which stresses human community through person-to-person generosity (Loyola 39; Ong 77-88). The Jesuit tradition of freedom would not prohibit a poet from exercising a God-given talent. The Jesuit tradition, admittedly among the most demanding conduct-systems, warns of the risks attendant upon freedom, but it likewise witnesses abundantly to the freedom of humans to be human. Hopkins followed his order's motto *ad majoram Dei gloriam*, but this "generally despised Jesuit" (Mariani 135) missed one essential principle: "It is man who is free, and only free to be free humanly, not magically, within the full reality of the human, whose basic law has been thus defined: 'Only that ought not to be which cannot be'" (Murray 14). The

Jesuit effort to bring Hopkins's work forward since 1918 precludes any thought of monolithic, arbitrary censorship of one of its own.

Hopkins's poetry was the culmination of Tractarian devotional poetry (Tennyson 204-11). In his antithetical stance toward historiography, did he simply refuse to recognize this connection? Despite being advised by his charitable friend R. W. Dixon that "one vocation cannot destroy another" (*Correspondence* 90), Hopkins would not accept a principle that would free him to follow another line of development—Sidney, Milton, Pope, Wordsworth—all of whom humbled themselves to the tradition of lyrical assortments. It seems, then, that not the *Wreck* or any external force but only Hopkins's own oppositional temperament would "forbid all entrance" to his consciousness and his poems.

Hopkins's biography bespeaks a heroic engagement with a stressful world, even though he lived at a time when suicide was becoming increasingly available as any harried individual's destiny of choice (Gates 154). His own awareness of numerous suicides among friends from his college days prompted him to wonder if suicide were, in fact, a "dreadful feature of our days" (*Further* 254). He knew full well the "cost of silence to one's poetic reputation" (Mariani 150). What else does he lose by his antithetical refusal to engage his own literary genius directly with literary history? Obviously, he forgoes any direct role in the politics of literary reputation. By remaining out of the loop while alive, the scientific amateur Hopkins (Zaniello 1-9), who would be fascinated with computers, missed the experience of readerly feedback. As a Roman Catholic in England, he belonged to a closed, defensive, inward-looking minority. The aggressive insecurity of such an embattled group (in Hopkins's case *passive*-aggressive) intensifies in some converts, many of whom never convince themselves that they belong. Thus, they may be eager to prove their pious loyalty (Rodden 366). The "heroics of reception" (401), the making and proclaiming of any putative "St. Gerard," would accordingly be left entirely to posterity. A harrowing but maturing experience has been missed by this deconstructionist who simultaneously builds and unbuilds himself.

In the long run, Hopkins did indeed succeed by failure, becoming a major presence in the main tradition of English poetry. Yet, what if he had published a collection? Surely, as Gadamer would say, he denied himself and beleaguered Victorian readers a dialectical engagement that could have led to an advanced stage of knowledge and consciousness (64).

Only that ought not to be which cannot be. We now possess so much of Hopkins that to grouse that we do not have more might seem churlish indeed. Not to reverence the *askesis* he underwent for his beliefs would be insensitive. But not to recognize that his legacy exists despite an anti-thetical denial would be a mistake. The poet whose personal motto is arguably *"What I do is me"* ("As kingfishers catch fire, dragonflies draw flame"; *Poetical* #115) and who invents a new technologically grounded self which reconciles individual isolation with collective unity in Christ (Ong 53) might well have followed a more productive literary career. Martin puts Hopkins's conflicted desires quite succinctly: "It would be hard to find a more potent example of desire to publish struggling through conventional modesty" (315).

Hopkins had been an independent, argumentative Oxonian (Bergonzi 21), but as a Jesuit he waited year after year for some superior to suggest his assembling and ordering a collection as Rector Jones in 1875 sug-gested he compose the *Wreck of the Deutschland*. To begin to understand Hopkins's reasons, we may need to suspend any hermeneutics of suspi-cion and instead have recourse to something like Gadamer's hermeneutics of participation:

> "Participation" is a strange word. Its dialectic consists of the fact
> that participation is not taking parts, but in a way taking the whole.
> Everybody who participates in something does not take something
> away, so that the others cannot have it. The opposite is true: by
> sharing, by our participating in the things in which we are partici-
> pating, we enrich them; they do not become smaller, but larger.
> The whole life of tradition consists exactly in this enrichment so
> that life is our culture and our past: the whole inner store of our
> lives is always extending by participating. ("Suspicion" 64)

During the middle ages, the idea of the book as a significant mode of remembering, organizing, and signifying experience became well estab-lished in the culture Hopkins would inherit, but he refused to do what Chaucer did. He refused to "grant the reader the authority to complete the circle of understanding" (Gellrich 254).

Someday, when we discover a true psychology of the literary imagin-ation, we may understand the root causes of Hopkins's severe antithetical *askesis*. Meantime, Gadamer's generous belief opens a window to the winds of change, allowing us more fully to appreciate Hopkins's post-humous engagement with Victorian historiography and his contributions to our own literary consciousness.

Interchapter 2

"Past, no more be seen!" :
History and Antithesis in Poems #46-90 (1864-68)

(1)　　　　A warfare of my lips in truth,
　　　　　Battling with God, is now my prayer.

　　　　　　　　　　　　　　　　　(Poetical 83; #67)

(2)　　　　Moonless darkness stands between.
　　　　　Past, the Past, no more be seen!
　　　　　But the Bethlehem-star may lead me
　　　　　To the sight of Him Who freed me
　　　　　From the self that I have been.
　　　　　Make me pure, Lord: Thou art holy;
　　　　　Make me meek, Lord: Thou wert lowly;
　　　　　Now beginning and alway:
　　　　　Now begin, on Christmas day.

　　　　　　　　　　　　　　　　　(Poetical 86; #73)

(3)　　Behind the misleading permanence of historical terminol-
　　　ogy, we must recognize not objects, but objectifications
　　　that construct an original configuration each time.

　　　　　　　　　　　　　　　　　　　　Chartier 46

At least one-third of the poems from "The Queen's Crowning" to "To Jesus Living in Mary" are fragments, so that the same antithetical or history-denying motive discovered in poems #2-45, thanks to Goldmann and Frye, continues to bear upon Hopkins's unfinished work as a response of crisis-consciousness to time and the past. At many points of his writing life, Hopkins continues to seem like the athlete who leaves the best part of his game in the locker room, albeit for complicated reasons.

This second grouping of poems, written roughly between 1864 and 1868, are all still pre-*Deutschland* poems and thus part of the long, restrictive limbo Hopkins dwelled in until his self-fashioning genius finally kicked over the traces in 1876. In addition to more fragments and Latin exercises, several poems of substance and interest appear in this part of the 1990 edition, although nothing surfaces that would lead anyone to predict the explosive sprung rhythm of a few years later.

Not a few of these poems exhibit a Hopkins who is seriously immersed in the Victorian actualities of his own day, but only a handful of them exhibit any degree of historical density. A lively and compelling ballad, "The Queen's Crowning" (#46) glances at the past but chiefly by reason of its literary imitativeness. In "The Summer Malison" (#51), Hopkins adds a curious and interesting twist to his unfolding sense of time by wittily parodying popular almanacs with their prognostications of the coming year's weather patterns.

> Maidens shall weep at merry morn,
> And hedges break, and lose the kine,
> And field-flowers make the fields forlorn,
> And noonday have a shallow shine,
> And barley turn to weed and wild, 5
> And seven ears crown the lodgèd corn,
> And mother have no milk for child,
>   And father be overworn.
>
> And John shall lie, where winds are dead,
> And hate the ill-visaged cursing tars, 10
> And James shall hate his faded red,
> Grown wicked in the wicked wars.
> No rains shall fresh the flats of sea,
> Nor close the clayfield's sharded sores,
> And every heart think loathingly
>   Its dearest changed to bores.

(*Poetical* 69; #51)

By contrast, a deepening emotionalism unfolds in "To Oxford" (#56), where a sequence of four poems in various stages of completeness depicts a Hopkins who romantically seeks and finds in the ancient university a sweet privacy and aesthetic pleasure. The "holy ground" of Oxford embodies a version of history all compound of unspoiled naturalness, wistful beauty, and charm.

Several poems fall into that category of backward-looking perspectives of the kind frequently attempted by Victorians. A brooding monologue, "The Alchemist in the City" (#60) allows Hopkins to lament his own imagined failures to produce significant work. "The Half-way House" (#71) enables Hopkins narratively to summarize in little the history of the religious conflict between Anglicanism and Roman Catholicism. Between this last mentioned pair of poems falls one about an embattled Hopkins.

> My prayers must meet a brazen heaven
> And fail and scatter all away.
> Unclean and seeming unforgiven
> My prayers I scarcely call to pray.
> I cannot buoy my heart above;   5
> Above I cannot entrance win.
> I reckon precedents of love,
> But feel the long success of sin.
>
> My heaven is brass and iron my earth:
> Yea, iron is mingled with my clay,   10
> So harden'd is it in this dearth
> Which praying fails to do away.
> Nor tears, nor tears this clay uncouth
> Could mould, if any tears there were.
> A warfare of my lips in truth,   15
> Battling with God, is now my prayer.

(*Poetical* 83; #67)

Yet, despite, these few quasi-historical poems, and without denying the aesthetic merit of a number of the poems written between 1864-68, it seems that the explicit sort of historiographical concern established in "The Escorial" has almost been completely obliterated or submerged by other concerns in Hopkins's theologically overburdened consciousness.

The further we travel from Hopkins's youthful triumph in the historically grounded "Escorial," the more history as such tends to vanish. But if history is absent from this second grouping of poems, the antithetical spirit is not absent but abundantly present. Early in 1865, in an eight-line fragment (#48) on the classical theme of less-is-more, we find a remarkable image, "He heightens worth who guardedly diminishes; / Diamonds are better cut," which generalizes an oppositional stance toward lushness, excess, or abandonment of formal and moral restraint. Two months later, "The Summer Malison," by reason of its parodic intent, expresses a familiar sort of literary or cultural antithesis, but one perhaps a bit surprising in the pious Hopkins. Recalling the "crack'd flesh" of "The Escorial," the poem "Easter Communion" (#53) commends mortifications of the flesh, not excluding self-flagellation and the wearing of sackcloth, on the grounds of their debasing and regulating the body so as to advantage the soul:

Easter Communion

Pure fasted faces draw unto this feast:
God comes all sweetness to your Lenten lips.
You striped in secret with breath-taking whips,
Those crookèd rough-scored chequers may be pieced
To crosses meant for Jesu's; you whom the East   5
With draught of thin and pursuant cold so nips
Breathe Easter now; you sergèd fellowships,
You vigil-keepers with low flames decreased,

God shall o'er-brim the measures you have spent
With oil of gladness, for sackcloth and frieze   10
And the ever-fretting shirt of punishment
Give myrrhy-threaded golden folds of ease.
Your scarce-sheathed bones are weary of being bent:
Lo, God shall strengthen all the feeble knees.

(*Poetical* 70; #53)

Fairly regularly, Hopkins's poems and fragments of this period express religious attitudes which embody or gesture toward antithetical Christian doctrines and customs. An example would be "O Death, Death, He is come" (#54), which develops a hymnlike account of Christ's antagonism toward death itself. Likewise, the next poem, apparently an epigram from the Greek anthology, generalizes Christ's assault on death in starkly polarized love/hate terms, particularly Christ's unrelenting love of the hate-

ful sinner who would thoughtlessly choose death: "Thou canst not hate
so much as I do love thee."

Occasionally, hints of the sort of denying antithetical conflict described
by Harold Bloom betray themselves in Hopkins's lines. In the midst of
appreciating the historical and architectural delights of Oxford, he plumes
himself on being perhaps unique (literally as having no precursors):
"None besides me this bye-ways beauty try" (#56). Another outbreak of
such presumed egotism appears in "Myself unholy, from myself unholy"
(#61), an unfinished meditative sonnet expressing Hopkins's scrupulosity
that masks itself under self-loathing, the boasting of a self-proclaimed
great sinner: "tho' each have one [sin] while I have all [sins]."

Various forms of internal resistance, such as his reluctance to admit
his attraction toward the Roman Catholic church, find expression in "See
how Spring opens with disabling cold" (#62). Likewise, and even more
forcefully, in "My prayers must meet a brazen heaven" (#67), we hear
couched in antithetical language Hopkins's struggle with belief itself: "A
warfare of my lips in truth, / Battling with God, is now my prayer."
Then, "The Half-way House" (#71) states a belief in the Real Presence
of Christ in the eucharistic bread and rejects or even condemns all sects
of Christianity that forswear such a belief. All such antithetical utterances
culminate, it would seem, in a desperate outcry, "Past, the Past, no more
be seen!" (#73).

Conflicts and contradictions continue to unfold in the poems of 1866.
A furtive desire to slip away from strenuous circumstances, as if one
were an Ovidian changeling bent only upon escape from an agonizing
predicament, appears in "The earth and heaven so little known" (#74).
Hopkins here exploits a Paterian fluidity of mental impressions as a
means of gliding away from one's immediate difficulties: "O lovely ease
in change of place!" In 1866, too, one of Hopkins's best lyrics, "The
Habit of Perfection" (#77), crystallizes his deep belief in the paradox
Litzinger calls "fulfilment through denial" (Hopkins, *Poetical* 286).

The Habit of Perfection

Elected Silence, sing to me
And beat upon my whorlèd ear,
Pipe me to pastures still and be
The music that I care to hear.

Shape nothing, lips; be lovely-dumb: 5
It is the shut, the curfew sent
From there where all surrenders come
Which only makes you eloquent.

Be shellèd, eyes, with double dark
And find the uncreated light: 10
This ruck and reel which you remark
Coils, keeps, and teases simple sight.

Palate, the hutch of tasty lust,
Desire not to be rinsed with wine:
The can must be so sweet, the crust   15
So fresh that come in fasts divine!

Nostrils, your careless breath that spend
Upon the stir and keep of pride,
What relish shall the censers send
Along the sanctuary side!   20

O feel-of-primrose hands, O feet
That want the yield of plushy sward,
But you shall walk the golden street
And you unhouse and house the Lord.

And, Poverty, be thou the bride   25
And now the marriage feast begun,
And lily-coloured clothes provide
Your spouse not laboured-at nor spun.

(*Poetical* 89-90; #77)

Thus, in general, appears the overall picture of Hopkins's development, with reference to history and antithetical impulses, up to the time of his novitiate at Manresa. For about two years after this point, roughly from September, 1868, to September, 1870, there would be no poems at all.

We should pause again here to look once more at Hopkins's single most historiographical poem, "The Escorial." In 1878, eighteen years after composing his prize-winning poem, Hopkins pretended to have forgotten the date when "The Escorial" won the Highgate poetry prize (*Corres-*

pondence 5). Many of his best critics have likewise lost sight of that first step in what might have been a literary career of some recognizable Victorian type. Not a single reference to any criticism of "The Escorial" appears in Dunne's 1976 bibliography. The list of critics who completely ignore "The Escorial" reads like a partial who's who of Hopkins commentators: Bender, Cotter, Ellsberg, Harris, Lichtman, Milroy, Motto, Ong, Peters, Robinson, Sprinker, Sulloway, Thomas, Walhout, and Zaniello. Without their explicitly saying so, we can yet infer that they would agree with Gardner's opinion to the effect that important poems never issue from poetry competitions (Kitchen 25).

On the other hand, a number of critics do address "The Escorial," with varying kinds and degrees of interest and emphasis. Mariani's single comment is fairly typical:

> "The Escorial," dated Easter 1860, is a school-prize poem in Spenserian stanzas which Hopkins wrote when he was only fifteen. It bears a pale resemblance to Keats's *The Eve of St. Agnes* in its stanza form, use of narrative, luxurious descriptions, and oblique but nevertheless strong moral undertone. It demonstrates the young poet's precociousness and preciousness, but it is too sententious to manifest any personal involvement with the material. It remains what it is, a fine school exercise. (*Commentary* 4)

Fairly typical of comments on "The Escorial" is Mariani's mentioning the poem once early on but then never again referring to it in an ensuing discussion of Hopkins's oeuvre.

Despite their providing occasional comments that confer some importance on "The Escorial," critics make little of the purely historical dimensions of Hopkins's first poem. Bump notes Hopkins's attempts in the poem to combine his love of poetry with his love of painting ("Reading" 14), but he decides that this early work lacks the concentration of the mature poems (24). As if to extend Bump's remark, McChesney also contrasts the later Hopkins with the Hopkins of "The Escorial": "This soft, loose material is a strange beginning for a poet whose later utterance was to go the limits of tension and austerity" (2).

Some critics do find a complicating biographical or psychological dimension in "The Escorial." Ruggles thinks that the youthful Hopkins, in writing about the martyred St. Lawrence's sufferings, was in fact being "self-prophetic" on the score of his own future sufferings (28). By contrast, Robinson acknowledges the presence of a cloying richness in the verse but finds no masochistic hints anywhere (7-8). In sharp contrast to

Robinson, Schneider, while acknowledging the poet's metrical mastery in the Spenserian stanzas and the rich sensuousness of imagery, nevertheless insists that Hopkins betrays an inclination to dwell upon physical torture: "crack'd flesh . . . hissing on the grate." Hopkins thus exhibits a sharp inner conflict between asceticism and masochism (*Dragon* 5). Another complication arises when we take into consideration Gardner's comments. Emphasizing that Hopkins's notes to "The Escorial" announce the poet's lifelong passion for explanation, Gardner echoes and complicates Schneider's views by stressing Hopkins's interest in pain (*Idiosyncrasy* 320). However, he declares "The Escorial" to be the only poem in which Hopkins expresses a "distaste for asceticism" (54).

Some critics content themselves with an observation about some purely technical matter, as when Boyle notes that "The Escorial" foreshadows Hopkins's mature skill with verbal sound effects (xv). Likewise, Iyengar thinks the poem abundantly displays the young Hopkins's intimate knowledge of architectural details (10).

Several critics go beyond technicalities by offering comments which reinforce the likelihood that "The Escorial" involves levels of complication making it important in Hopkins's unfolding antithetical view of history. Frank detects a Hopkins who "rejects" Gothic and other forms of architecture (124). Similarly, Kitchen identifies the theme of the poem as "clashing faiths" (26). On the whole, many of the more complicated views coalesce in Loomis's remarks, where we are apprised that in his first poem Hopkins is "ideologically inconsistent" (43). Under the rubric "The Art of 'Gloom' and 'Glories': Resignation, Resplendence, or Sacral Mystery?" the critic Loomis foregrounds the problem of Hopkins's attempt to blend religious themes with sensuousness (44). Hopkins's thematic subject is "austerity," and he explores this subject until he reaches the gloomy conclusion that in the physical world death alone concludes human life (42). In the youthful poet's psyche, Loomis finds inconsistencies such as his alternating sympathy with and condemnation of Philip II (43). Thus, at the very outset of Hopkins's arduous journey toward achieved consistency between "his reverence for the life of self-sacrifice and [his] use of art as a sacramentalist activity wherein [the young Hopkins] declares his loyalty to sacrificial action," Loomis discovers a deep-seated if imperfectly expressed antithetical tension.

In my opinion, the dual strands of history and antithetical impulses in "The Escorial" establish historiography as an intricate and deep-seated element of his consciousness. This problematical complex went underground, so to speak, where it became a subterranean current that would vex and roil but also animate Hopkins's creative psyche during his entire writing life. In numerous respects, "The Escorial," one of the strongest but strangest beginnings in English literature, is the real dragon in the gate of Hopkins's poetic enterprise.

3

Hopkins Against Longfellow: Antithetical Bondings Between "The Wreck of the Hesperus" and *The Wreck of the Deutschland*

(1)   The shipwreck is always the most significant moment.

Fernand Braudel, in Kellner 187

(2)   If to imagine is to misinterpret, which makes all poems antithetical to their precursors, then to imagine after a poet is to learn his own metaphors for his acts of reading. Criticism then necessarily becomes antithetical also, a series of swerves after unique acts of creative misunderstanding.

Bloom 93

(3)   That nothing shd. be old or borrowed however cannot be.

Hopkins, *Further* 370

The next episode in Hopkins's chaotic personal drama of Victorian crisis-consciousness is more explicitly literary but no less anti-historiographical.

As in previous episodes, if we would glimpse the elusive Hopkins reacting against history we must go a roundabout way. Here, Hopkins's *modus operandi* drastically changes. The Victorian historical discourse represented by H. T. Buckle is replaced by an American literary ballad that piously reconstructed a historical event; Hopkins very nearly annihilates this earlier poem in constructing his own poem on virtually the same subject. Likewise, the literary history Hopkins evaded by refusing to publish his own poems appears in this episode embodied in one of the largest literary reputations of Hopkins's day.

A poem is one link in a chain of poems. To think of intertextual bondings is to invoke reflexive principles such as repetition, annotation, quotation, allusion, echo, parody, revision, and the like. *The Wreck of the Deutschland* functioned as a catalyst for an ambitious collection of poems by James Dickey. Elements in Dickey's *Puella* (1982) function as intertextual traces of Hopkins's matter and manner (Hollahan, "Anxiety"). Hopkins himself, possibly the most original English-language poet of the past two centuries, committed himself to a kind of historicism by believing that no poem can be so original as not to contain something "old or borrowed."

The Wreck of the Deutschland resulted from psychic pressures built up during Hopkins's self-imposed seven-year exile from poetry writing. Hopkins's pious utterance in the *Wreck* contains traces of many texts that entered into its composition. Numerous sources have been proposed for this many-layered ode. Examples include Greek myth and ritual, Ignatius Loyola's *Spiritual Exercises*, the literature of martyrdom, Revelation, "Lycidas," Baudelaire, Book of Job, and other intertextual sources (Bump, *Hopkins* 205 n. 17). One unsuspected text, Longfellow's ballad "The Wreck of the Hesperus" (1839), proves to be not so much a source as a complex precursor of Hopkins's masterpiece.

Excepting that both Longfellow and Hopkins are memorialized in Poets' Corner of Westminster Abbey, one might not be prepared to find any link between two such different men. Longfellow was the most popular American poet of his century, but he has come to be regarded, according to one critical view, as a minor figure, artificial and imitative, with no lasting influence on later poetry. According to such a dismal opinion, Longfellow appealed to the lowest intellectual common denominator and placed no burden upon his readers. The embodiment of genteel values, scholarly interests, the joys of family life, and servile responsiveness to European culture, he is mistakenly considered to have lived free of troubles or at least to have written poetry largely free of personal grief.

This all-too-familiar devaluation of a famous poet leads many readers to neglect and even ridicule Longfellow.

By contrast, Hopkins is admired—according to an equally entrenched orthodoxy—as a progenitor of advanced, difficult poetry and an influence upon many important poets (Giles). Hopkins's poetry is said to appeal to the highest reaches of intellect and imagination as well as triggering responses at the deepest levels of rhythm and image. Hopkins's life as a convert from Anglicanism to Roman Catholicism and his ordination as a Jesuit priest place him at odds with Longfellow's worldly life style. As an inventive experimentalist in his chosen art form, Hopkins makes his own personal stresses the stuff of poetry.

With this familiar if exaggerated contrast in mind, to link Longfellow and Hopkins is indeed to hypothesize an odd couple. To do so convincingly one must have recourse to an unusual theory of poetry such as Harold Bloom's hypothesis of a Freudian anxiety of influence as one genetic motive force in strong romantic poetry. My argument here posits that Hopkins saw Longfellow's poem and Longfellow's place in literary history, taken together, as an unappetizing bolus of historical fact.

Our low evaluation of Longfellow may be modified somewhat if we look at his finest effort, "The Wreck of the Hesperus." Based loosely upon an actual shipwreck in December of 1839, it is a poem of eighty-eight lines arranged in twenty-two ballad stanzas. We understand the ballad in the following terms: single exciting episode, current event, simple narrative form, impersonal material and tone, supernatural presences, strong themes such as physical courage, love, common people, domestic slant, abrupt transitions, slight characterization and description, dialogue, tragic dénouement, and incremental repetition (Holman and Harmon). The ballad stanza, four lines rhyming *abcb*, with the first and third lines carrying four accented syllables and the second and fourth carrying three, can be aptly illustrated by stanza 12 from "The Wreck of the Hesperus."

> "O father! I see a gleaming light,
>   O say, what may it be?"
> But the father answered never a word,
>   A frozen corpse was he.
>
> (Longfellow, *Poetical* 13-14)

Longfellow's narrative is simple but moving. The schooner *Hesperus* puts out to sea piloted by a doting, arrogant skipper who ignores storm warnings and subjects to a cruel death his ship, crew, himself, and his young daughter whom, for her own safety, he has bound to the mast. The

poem includes a variety of narrative and poetical elements: a vivid account of a winter sea storm; the captain's hubris ("I can weather the
roughest gale / That ever wind did blow"); the icing-over of men and
ship; the girl's momentary "thought of Christ"; the ship's collision with
deadly rocks; a shore-bound fisherman's glimpse of the frozen girl
("Lashed close to a drifting mast"); and, a closing appeal to Christ to
"save us all from a death like this / On the reef of Norman's Woe."
    A few stanzas can illustrate Longfellow's achievement:

> Colder and louder blew the wind,
>   A gale from the northeast;
> The snow fell hissing in the brine,
>   And the billows frothed like yeast.   (stanza 6)

> Then the maiden clasped her hands and prayed
>   That savèd she might be;
> And she thought of Christ, who stilled the wave,
>   On the Lake of Galilee.   (stanza 14)

> The salt sea was frozen on her breast,
>   The salt tears in her eyes;
> And he saw her hair, like the brown sea-weed,
>   On the billows fall and rise.   (stanza 21)

> Such was the wreck of the Hesperus,
>   In the midnight and the snow!
> Christ save us all from a death like this
>   On the reef of Norman's Woe.   (stanza 22)

"The Wreck of the Hesperus" was one of the poems, representing both
historiography and literary history, that Hopkins had in mind when he
responded to an actual shipwreck that shocked his antithetical poetic spirit
awake in December, 1875.
    Despite Longfellow's currently depressed reputation, "The Wreck of
the Hesperus" was famous in its day and has proved worthy of study.
Historically, Longfellow was alert to the fact that he was helping to
inaugurate an American literary type, the National Ballad. The public
welcomed his poem, with its musical lines (easy to perform on Recitation
Day), its portrayal of a national concern (shipwrecks were all too common), its tragic gloom and doom that struck a deep human chord. Even
if Longfellow did not stick literally to the facts—the *Hesperus* did not

actually wreck on Norman's Woe and the girl tied to the mast was apocryphal—the poem was widely admired and enjoyed (Hansen 52).

On the negative side, this ballad, being twice the length of its model "Sir Patrick Spens," strikes some readers as "prolix, sentimental, unconvincing" (Cecil Williams 38-9). But on the positive side, Longfellow demonstrated that he possessed the "strength and simplicity" and the "epic swiftness" of the "old balladist." In addition to the stylistic felicities displayed in *Voices of the Night* (1839), Longfellow was capable of a "hammerlike metrical faculty of striking out strong, simple lines wherein incident was everything and the personality of the author nothing" (Smeaton 47-8). Longfellow preserved an American incident that people wished to save for their posterity.

Between the extreme opinions offered by Williams and Smeaton, a more balanced view is provided by Newton Arvin. Longfellow was steeped in the ballad poetry of northern Europe. He possessed a touch of the genuine folk-poet, with his unaffected naiveté, simplicity of mind and heart, and fondness for rapid, pathetic tales, as well as a flair for improvisation. Arvin asserts:

> Hackneyed as it is, "The Wreck of the Hesperus" could hardly be surpassed as a literary imitation of the border ballad—for if the subject is native, the style is a perfect pastiche of the English or Scottish ballad, of "Sir Patrick Spens" or "The Wife of Usher's Well." It is a poem for the young, of course, without any more understanding than the subject itself carries with it, but on its youthful level, it has in it the authentic terror of the sea. (Arvin 69-70)[1]

The history of "The Wreck of the Hesperus" in Longfellow's diary and letters traces an interesting arc. Early in his writing career, Longfellow received what Andrew Hilen calls the "coin of fame" as a popular poet. Together with such poems as "A Psalm of Life" and "Excelsior," "The Wreck of the Hesperus" precipitated Longfellow's literary success of 1839-41. Mourning his wife's death, rebuffed by Frances Appleton, unhappy as a Harvard professor, the thirty-two-year-old poet found solace in literary accomplishment and fame (Longfellow, *Letters* 6:124). As different as possible from the agonized psychogenesis of Hopkins's poem thirty-seven years later, Longfellow's account of the genesis of his shipwreck poem shows the American poet exhibiting a prudent, even calculating, sense of business. He first mentions the poem in his diary (30 December 1839):

I wrote last evening a notice of Allston's poems. After which I sat till twelve o'clock by my fire, smoking, when suddenly it came into my mind to write *The Ballad of the Schooner Hesperus*; which I accordingly did. Then I went to bed, but could not sleep. New thoughts were running in my mind, and I got up to add them to the ballad. It was three by the clock. I then went to bed and fell asleep. I feel pleased with the ballad. It hardly cost me an effort. It did not come into my mind by lines, but by stanzas. (Longfellow, *Poetical* 13)

Longfellow's correspondence adds to this picture of a professional author enjoying himself while looking for his checks.

On 5 January 1840, he wrote to George Washington Greene:

I have broken ground in a new field; namely, *Ballads*; beginning with the *"Wreck of the Schooner Hesperus* on the Reef of Norman's Woe"*, in the great storm a fortnight ago. It will be printed in a few days, and I shall write more. The *National Ballad* is a virgin soil here in New England; and there are good materials. Besides I have a great notion of working upon *people's feelings*. I am going to have it printed on a sheet, and sold like *Varses*, with a coarse picture on it. I desire a new sensation, and a new set of critics. I wish you were sitting in this red arm-chair before me, that I might inflict it on you. Nat. Hawthorne is tickled to death with the idea. (*Letters* 2:203-4)

Longfellow in fact did not print his first ballad as a broadside, but he did receive the $25.00 payment he asked for, from Park Benjamin of the newspaper *New World*, where the poem appeared 11 January 1840 (2: 205-9).

A measure of Longfellow's literary prudence can be seen in his crossing out one stanza in the manuscript, four lines which preceded the present sixth stanza and which intensified the arrogance of the *Hesperus's* captain even to the point of blasphemy:

> I would not put into yonder port,
>   Nor yet into yonder bay
> Though it blew a gale, with fiery hale,
>   As on the judgment day.

(2:209 n. 5)

Longfellow and his readers remained interested in his poem until several years after the composition of *The Wreck of the Deutschland* in 1875-76. In 1845, he had objected to an illustration which Abraham Hart had chosen for the poem in a collected *Poems*: "The maiden is too much like a Roman peasant; and I do not think the fisherman looks much like a Marblehead fellow;—(Norman's Woe is on that coast)" (3:89). In 1871, Longfellow responded to Charles Lanman's praise of the poem ("always a special favorite") by copying out for Lanman his diary entry of 17 December 1839 containing his germinal thoughts:

> News of shipwrecks horrible on the coast. Forty bodies washed ashore near Gloucester. One woman lashed to a piece of wreck. There is a Reef called Norman's Woe where many of these took place. Among others the Schooner Hesperus. Also the Sea-Flower on Black Rock. I must write a Ballad on this. (5:474-5)

The perennial popularity of "The Wreck of the Hesperus" can be deduced from Longfellow's responses to readers' inquiries. In 1877, he was asked to identify the geographical location of Norman's Woe: "between Marblehead and Manchester" (6:254). The poem continued to be popular in England. Charlotte Yonge's *Monthly Packet*, a periodical for juveniles, contained an erroneous assertion that Norman's Woe was near England. In a letter to Eliza Callahan Cleveland, Longfellow authorizes her to set Miss Yonge straight on the facts. Also, he regrets that he cannot supply the origin of the name of Norman's Woe: "I doubt whether the oldest inhabitant of Manchester remembers it but I suppose it came from some ancient mariner wrecked there in the long forgotten days." He then summarizes for his correspondent the genesis of the poem and refers her to newspaper accounts of 17 December 1839 (6:281-82).

Because of Longfellow's poem, Norman's Woe became a world-famous tourist attraction. In 1878, Longfellow responded to Elizabeth Stuart Phelps, who had seen the rocks there, regretting that he himself had not stayed until the fog lifted so that he could see the rocks he had made famous (6:377). Finally, in 1880, he received the ultimate accolade for a popular poet when "a little girl nine years old" wrote to say that she had memorized his poem but failed to understand the seventh stanza. The poet explained the phrase "cable's length" as illustrating the tendency of poets, "like children," to exaggerate for effect (6:617).

Did Hopkins know "The Wreck of the Hesperus"? Madeline House records that in 1952 she and her husband Humphry found a copy of Longfellow's *Poetical Works* in the "Books Belonging to Hopkins and

His Family" (House). This may be as much historical information as we can hope for at the present state of Hopkins research. It is scarcely imaginable that he would not know the famous poem quite thoroughly.

In general, whenever Hopkins thought of versification and related poetical matters, he was likely to think of Longfellow. In his elaborate lecture notes, when he wished to illustrate his theory that the "tripping" trochaic meter when "doubled" becomes "grave and monotonous," he cites *Hiawatha* (*Journals* 274). In 1881, Hopkins critiqued a sheaf of poems by his friend Richard Watson Dixon. In a detailed letter to Dixon, he commented poem by poem, in the process judging diction, meter, accent, feeling, "instress," beauty, and the like. When he wished both to praise and blame, he invoked Longfellow:

> The Last Supper and *James and Jude* have the same freakish and almost perverse beauty as the mystery in Longfellow's *Golden Legend* and some of your own earlier *Christ's Company* pieces. Still I find less pleasure than I once used in this kind: I half think that archaic quaintness is a fallacy, that nothing was ever quaint in its time. Besides in reproducing it one is liable to fall into solecisms. (*Correspondence* 6)

Hopkins's objections to "archaic quaintness" might plausibly be extended to Longfellow's straightforward use of the ballad form in "The Wreck of the Hesperus."

In 1886, when his friend Coventry Patmore complained of being criticized for writing "goody-goody dribble" comparable to Longfellow's *Evangeline*, Hopkins responded with a letter that probes into poetical theory. Hopkins uses his defense of the rustic poet William Barnes to occasion his own complex thoughts on individual genius and literary influences, but he ends by insisting that no poet can be literally and entirely original:

> I scarcely understand you about reflected light: every true poet, I thought, must be original and originality a condition of poetic genius; so that each poet is like a species in nature (*not* an *individuum genericum* or *specificum*) and can never recur. That nothing shd. be old or borrowed however cannot be. (*Further* 370)

One of the most original Victorian poets, Hopkins nevertheless provides a generalized warrant for our believing that with the antithetical, antihistoricist part of his mind, and for intensely personal reasons which I will show, he confronted Longfellow's shipwreck ballad when he set about composing his own revolutionary poem.[2]

The Wreck of the Deutschland poses a complex set of problems. It illustrates the "sprung" rhythm which first haunted the poet's mind in his revisions of "For a Picture of St. Dorothea" (1864; 1869-72?). A two-part ode consisting of thirty-five eight-line stanzas, the *Wreck* in its first part consists of ten stanzas which recount how God touched the speaker in his own personal existence.

2

I did say yes
O at líghtning and láshed ród;   10
Thou heardst me, truer than tongue, confess
Thy terror, O Christ, O God;
Thou knówest the wálls, áltar and hóur and night:
The swoon of a heart that the sweep and the hurl of thee trod
Hárd dówn with a horror of height: 15
And the midriff astrain with leaning of, laced with fire of stress.

(*Poetical* 119; #101)

Part II commences with seven stanzas based upon a newspaper account of an actual shipwreck. Next, fourteen stanzas focus on a single passenger, the tallest of five exiled Germans nuns, who reportedly was heard to scream "Mein Gott! mach es schnell mit uns!" before she died. The last four stanzas call directly upon God to convert the English people—who may have been negligent in the affair of the actual *Deutschland*—to Catholic Christianity (Bump, *Hopkins* 94).

32

I admíre thee, máster of the tídes,
Of the Yóre-flood, of the yéar's fáll;   250
The recúrb and the recóvery of the gúlf's sídes,
The gírth of it and the whárf of it and the wáll;
Stánching, quénching ócean of a mótionable mínd;
Gróund of béing and gránite of it: pást áll
Grásp Gód, thróned behínd   255
Déath, with a sóvereignty that héeds but hídes, bódes but abídes;

33

With a mércy that oútrídes
The all of water, an ark
For the lístener; for the língerer with a lóve glídes
Lówer than déath and the dárk;   260
A véin for the vísiting of the pást-prayer, pént in príson,
The-last-breath penitent spirits—the uttermost mark
Our passion-plungèd giant risen,
The Christ of the Father compassionate, fetched in the storm
    of his strides.

34

Now burn, new born to the world,   265
Double-naturèd name,
The heaven-flúng, heart-fléshed, máiden-fúrled
Míracle-in-Máry-of-fláme,
Mid-numberèd he in three of the thunder-throne!
Not a dóomsday dázzle in his cóming nor dárk as he
    cáme;   270
Kínd, but róyally recláiming his ówn;
A released shówer, let flásh to the shíre, not a líghtning of fíre
    hard húrled.

35

Dáme, at óur dóor
Drówned, and among óur shóals,
Remémber us in the róads, the heaven-háven of the
    rewárd: 275
Our king back, Oh, upon Énglish sóuls!
Let him éaster in us, be a dáyspring to the dímness of us,
    be a crimson-cresseted east,
More bríghtening her, ráre-dear Brítain, as his réign rólls,
    Príde, rose, prínce, hero of us, hígh-príest,
Oür héart's charity's héarth's fíre, oür thóughts' chivalry's
    thróng's Lórd.   280

(*Poetical* 127-28; #101)

With its shocking subject matter and dazzling techniques, this revolutionary ode baffled its first readers and has subsequently occasioned a vast body of commentary and explication.

Numerous polymorphic generic bondings—shipwreck consciousness and sea-disaster poetry—patently link Hopkins's poem with Longfellow's national ballad. Even so, settling the question of Hopkins's antithetical reworking of Longfellow's historical ballad requires more than merely noting general resemblances. A compelling critical approach is provided by Harold Bloom's theory in *The Anxiety of Influence*, by means of which Bloom examines the psychogenetics of tradition and history. Bloom seeks to understand how romantic visionary poets manage to write original poems despite a stultifying awareness of a "demon of continuity" indwelling at the heart of tradition itself. Drawing upon a wide range of references, chiefly mystical and romantic theories, Bloom explains that the history of poetry can best be understood in terms of Freud's oedipal family romance. The son labors in the shadow of the father. Strong poets must clear imaginative space for themselves by revising earlier poets and poems. Bloom spells out his central thesis thus:

> *Poetic influence—when it involves two strong, authentic poets—always proceeds by a misreading of the prior poet, an act of creative correction that is actually and necessarily a misinterpretation. The history of fruitful poetic influence, which is to say the main tradition of Western poetry since the Renaissance, is a history of anxiety and self-saving caricature, of distortion, of perverse, wilful revisionism without which modern poetry as such could not exist.* (30; emphasis Bloom's)

For the poet who wishes not to be overwhelmed by history in the form of his predecessors, discontinuity means freedom. Bloom's most fundamental belief is that the later poet must willfully misinterpret the earlier poet; corollary to this, the meaning of any poem must always be another poem (70-1).

Bloom agrees with Kierkegaard that "he who is willing to work gives birth to his own father" (56). At this point, I must take into account the shadow of authority cast by the later poet's father, Manley Hopkins (1818-1897). As Jerome Bump notes (*Hopkins* 2), Hopkins's father influenced the poet's artistic development.

A member of an Anglican family that numbered many persons of artistic, religious, and literary sensibility, Manley Hopkins must have lodged in the memory of his loving but self-exiled son in two relevant senses: as an actuarial authority on shipwrecks and as an admirer of Longfellow. In the year of his son Gerard's birth, he founded a maritime insurance firm. Among other books, he wrote *A Manual of Marine Insurance* (1873) and *The Port of Refuge: or, Advice and Instructions to the Master-Mariner in Situations of Doubt, Difficulty, and Danger* (1887). He published collections of his own verses in 1843 and 1849, and he passed on to his son his own love of poetry.

Among various literary activities was an essay—destined never to be published—on Longfellow (56). Are we not authorized to conjecture that Gerard Manley Hopkins, before he separated himself from his Anglican family by joining the Roman Catholic Church, must have enjoyed with such a lively father numerous conversations concerning ships, shipwrecks, and the admired poet Longfellow? Would it be surprising to learn that his admired father read aloud and discussed "The Wreck of the Hesperus," an enjoyable poem they both probably had "by heart"? Where the father's interests coalesced, might not those, however conflicted, of the pious son?[3]

In searching out poetical origins, Bloom elaborates six distinct but related "ratios" (metaphorical enactments or processes). He labels these poetical strategies *clinamen, tessera, kenosis, daemonization, askesis,* and *apophrades.*

That Hopkins himself underwent a Bloomian identity-crisis is hinted at by Sprinker, who mentions a "severe *askesis*" practiced by Hopkins in composing the *Wreck* (119). Similarly, Ong comments upon Hopkins's constant practice, in effect an *imitatio Christi*, in the form of a *kenosis* or self-emptying self-sacrifice as described in Philipians 2:6-11 (112-16). Bloom himself does not discuss Hopkins at length among the strong poets (Wordsworth, Browning, Whitman, Stevens), but *en passant* he does glance twice at Hopkins. He dismisses Hopkins's "strained intensities and convolutions of diction" as being incommensurate with the burdens Hopkins seeks to alleviate in his poetic consciousness. More to the point, he complains that Hopkins allowed himself to be dominated by the Covering Cherub of historical continuity (12; 24). Even so, despite Bloom's own dismissal of Hopkins, his anxiety-of-influence theory offers, at least heuristically, a valuable explanation of the genesis of Hopkins's puzzling *Wreck*. From our own historical perspective and in terms of the currently low critical opinion of Longfellow, the American poet may seem like a decidedly "weak" poet. However, given his Victorian renown, together with Hopkins's own family background, the author of "The Wreck of the Hesperus" could loom for Hopkins as a decidedly "strong" historical and psychic presence.

Clinamen, Bloom's first type of poetic misreading or misprision, employs the Lucretian image of a falling atom which swerves and collides with other atoms so as to enable material change to occur. The later poet (ephebe) parallels the precursor for a time but then swerves in a new direction. Such a deviation from a model constitutes the central working concept of the anxiety of influence, the other five being subsumable under *clinamen*.

Tessera alludes to the ancient cultic practice of using, by joining, fragments of a broken pot so as to prove one's identity. The reactive ephebe completes his precursor by interpreting the terms of his poem in a new sense, as if the precursor had failed to go far enough. Within the framework of Freud's family romance, the ephebe claims space for himself—convinces himself of his own priority—by judging that the precursor poem falls short of full expression. The ephebe must complete the incomplete with a new poem.

In this context, Hopkins fulfilled the incomplete "Hesperus" variously in terms of content and form. The religious sentiment becomes a full-blown theology; the objective narrator becomes an intensely personalized subject; the national ballad becomes both more central to the poem and more historically significant. Formally, the clipped four-line ballad stanza becomes an explosive eight-lines of sprung rhythm and abstruse imagery.

Kenosis is a breaking device, a movement toward discontinuity with the precursor. Drawn from St. Paul, the term itself refers to the humbling or emptying-out of Jesus, his reduction from divine to human. The ephebe appears to give up his own inspiration and cease being a poet. However, this emptying-out responds to the precursor's own poem of emptying-out. Hence, the later poem still waxes relatively fuller than the earlier poem. Historical continuity equates roughly with the repetition compulsion that, according to Freud, locks people into neurotic patterns. How shall the new come into existence? One economical means is for the ephebe to engage in acts of "undoing" and "isolating" his own poetical impulses. He thus makes the father pay not only for the father's sins but also for the son's. He empties out all claim to poetical godhead. Hopkins's priestly routine, under the sway of Loyola's *Spiritual Exercises*, witnesses to his continual effort at just such a *kenosis* or self-emptying. The *Wreck* quickly establishes this note.

4

I am sóft síft   25
In an hourglass—at the wall

Fast, but mined with a motion, a drift,
And it crowds and it combs to the fall;
I stéady aş a wáter in a wéll, to a póise, to a páne,
But roped with, always, all the way down from the tall   30
Fells or flanks* of the voel, a vein
Of the góspel próffer, a préssure, a prínciple, Chríst's gift.

Part I of Hopkins's *Wreck* humbles and empties the poet, so that the
poem as a whole overwhelms the precursor, compounded of Longfellow
the celebrated poet and Hopkins's actual father who presumably admired
Longfellow's popular poem.

Like *kenosis* a form of repression, *daemonization* reacts against a precursor's sublimity. The ephebe opens his own poem to a power in the
parent-poem but a power in truth not proper to the parent-poem. His aim
is to generalize away the uniqueness of the earlier work. Bloom seems to
mean that the later poet finds that the earlier poet himself had been influenced and in his own poem betrays his own unresolved influence-anxiety.
Hopkins could allow "The Wreck of the Hesperus" into the *Wreck of the
Deutschland* because he intended to redistribute (the root meaning of
daemai) and reattribute Longfellow's daemon to other sources. The energy in the precursor poem is not Longfellow's own but various generic
entities such as sea poetry, shipwreck poetry, Protestant theology, sentimentality, or the ballad form itself. Central to Hopkins's form is the self-
diminishing shift from Hopkins's own existential predicament in Part I to
the historical framework in Part II. As a result of this violent shift,
Longfellow seems decidedly the more "human," as Hopkins looms larger
and more stylistically daemonized.

With Bloom's fifth ratio, *askesis* or self-purgation, the ephebe seeks
to attain solitude. Like some pre-Socratic shaman, he yields up part of his
own human and imaginative endowment. He separates himself from the
precursor and forces both his own poem and the precursor's poem to
suffer some degree of truncation. Certain tonalities derive from guilt over
such egotism. Essentially a sublimation of aggression, *askesis* occurs as
a self-purgation resulting in extreme solipsism. It occupies a special
position in Bloom's system in that, whereas *clinamen* and *tessera* correct
or complete the dead, and *kenosis* and *daemonization* repress the dead,
askesis in its turn directly grapples with the dead. *Askesis* centers upon
the ephebe's awareness of other selves, followed by his severe self-curtailment for the sake of solitude away from such other selves. At bottom,
the poet's struggle with any one precursor amounts to a struggle with all
of his ancestors, literary and otherwise, including, in oedipal terms, his

own father. We should be reminded of Hopkins's stated desire during his noviceship at Roehampton to undergo a *vacare Deo* (*Letters* 135).

Bloom's final ratio takes the form of *apophrades* or the return of the dead. Based upon the ancient Athenian dismal or melancholy days when the dead return to their former houses, this strategy involves the ephebe's holding his own poem open to the precursor's work (15-6). When this process is carried out by a strong poet, the effect is of a celebration of the return of his own early self-exaltation that first made poetry possible but a self-exaltation denied out of fear and only later re-appropriated (147). The central problem of *apophrades* is the burden of developing a personal style at least somewhat free of earlier models.

Was there ever a poet who answers to Bloom's description more resonantly than Hopkins? By opening his oppositional mind to the "The Wreck of the Hesperus," what a flood of ghosts he would invite. What childhood memories, family pieties and stresses, outgrown literary tastes, self-denials, and frustrated desire for fame he must then acknowledge, confront, and sublimate into his own poem. In theological terms, Longfellow's poem could be associated with the "severely displaced Protestantism," with its blocking Father-God, that Bloom blames for the failure of three-hundred years of devotional poetry after Milton (152). Hopkins the strong poet shapes his own unmistakable idiom by boldly resurrecting his dead self via a poem by a precursor who, in a real if symbolic sense, was his own father Manley Hopkins and an embodiment of literary fame. At the deepest Bloomian levels, Hopkins rebukes history by rebuking both Longfellow and his own father who had presumed to offer rationalistic advice to beleaguered master-mariners.

By contrast with the ballad form itself, Hopkins's poem presents a thorny formal problem. Hopkins himself labelled the poem an ode (*Letters* 49), and both Bender (71-96) and Heath-Stubbs place it in the odic tradition coming down from Pindar. Heath-Stubbs regards it as perhaps the last important poem in the Pindaric tradition (108). Intertextual elements besides the intensity and obscurity that derive from Pindar include Milton's meter and rhyme scheme ("On the Morning of Christ's Nativity") and the circular rhyme scheme in which an initial rhyme returns upon itself (Milton's "At a Solemn Musick"). Anderson agrees with Heath-Stubbs that nothing in the odic tradition equals Hopkins's poem for intensity and magnificence (131-38).

In examining the structure of Hopkins's stanza, we see how he could have adapted Longfellow's ballad stanza to his own unique purposes. Hopkins's eight-line stanza, rhyming *ababcbca*, represents in the first four

lines an adaptation of Longfellow's four-line stanza and in the next four
lines a wrenching amendment and elaboration.

John E. Keating's essay on stanzaic patterning in the *Wreck* reinforces
this point. Keating argues as follows. Hopkins took advantage of an opportunity to create his own stanza form. Keeping in mind that Hopkins's
line—under pressure of sprung rhythm—will not at any point scan precisely like Longfellow's but only approximately, let us set one example
before us. To Robert Bridges, Hopkins wrote that the first stanza he composed was stanza 12: "the Bremen stanza, which was, I think, the first
written after 10 years' silence and before I had fixed my principle" (*Letters* 44).[4]

12

> —On Saturday sailed from Bremen,
>   American-outward-bound,   90
>   Take settler and seamen, tell men with women,
>   Two hundred souls in the round—
>   O Father, not under thy feathers nor ever as guessing
>   The goal was a shoal, of a fourth the doom to be drowned;
>   Yet *did* the dark side of the bay of thy blessing   95
> Not vault them, the million of rounds of thy mercy not reeve
>   even them in?

Keating shows that Hopkins's stanzaic pattern is basically antiphonal:
"The latter part of each stanza typically provides some kind of response
to the opening lines" (160). In effect, Hopkins's mind thus engages in a
strenuous dialogue with itself concerning "incomprehensible mysteries"
such as God's creation being both beautiful and dangerous, the Church
though a haven being unable to protect the five German nuns, and mankind's producing both a mild St. Francis and a stern Herr Von Falk who
authored the laws that forcibly exiled the Franciscan nuns.

Keating also notes that each stanza begins with a quatrain rhymed
abab; after the fourth line, there is usually a break arising from both punc-
tuation and rhyme scheme (*abab/cbca*). Many of Hopkins's thirty- five
stanzas contain an opening quatrain that makes clear narrative sense on
its own and could be separable from the rest of the stanza. These are set
off from the following four lines in metrics and thought. Typically, in the
fifth line a new surge of prosody and consciousness arises.

14

> She drove in the dark to leeward,   105
> She struck—not a reef or a rock
> But the combs of a smother of sand: night drew her
>   Dead to the Kentish Knock;
> And she beat the bank down with her bows and the ride
>   of her keel;
> The breakers rolled on her beam with ruinous shock;   110
>   And, canvass and compass, the whorl and the wheel
> Idle for ever to waft her or wind her with, these* she endūred.

Four kinds of ideas develop from these breaks in thought: antithetical, particularizing, incremental, and reflective (155-61). Other critics note that the markedly longer last four lines provide elaboration, resolution, or prolonged tension.

To Keating's speculations, I would add my own conjecture. The first four lines represent a sprung-rhythm modification of the ballad stanza that served Longfellow's prudent aims, whereas the last four lines, more complex and far-reaching, express in an elaborate sprung rhythm the thoughts and feelings that Hopkins would be disappointed (or pleased?) to find missing in purely narrative poems such as Longfellow's. Much of Hopkins's special turns of vocabulary, syntax, and imagery occur in these stanza endings. Hopkins's bold genius shows here in his bipartite, balladic-odic stanzas as much as anywhere.[5]

En passant, an instructive contrast is provided by Hopkins's other shipwreck poem, "The Loss of the Eurydice" (1878), a poem which Hopkins considered to show "more mastery in art" (*Letters* 119). For this poem, also based upon a recent disaster, Hopkins used a form and spirit much closer to Longfellow's ballad with its abrupt story line and harsh tone. Hopkins's own response to his poem in manuscript suggests how close to the stark, objective, harsh effect of the ballad this poem seemed: "it struck me aghast with a kind of raw nakedness and unmitigated violence I was unprepared for" (79). Of course, the thirty four-line stanzas are only somewhat similar to the ballad stanza. They rhyme *aabb*; their lines measure 4,4,3,4. The approximate resemblances, relatively closer than the extreme modifications wrought in the *Wreck*, are modified by Hopkinsian oddities of meter, thought, imagery, and bizarre rhymes. One stanza may suffice to show its ballad-like qualities:

They say who saw one sea-corpse cold
He was all of lovely manly mould,
    Every inch a tar,   75
Of the best we boast our sailors are.

(*Poetical* 151; #125)

Mariani notes that a disappointed Hopkins hoped with this second ship-wreck poem to make a popular success (*Commentary* 119). To that end, he focussed on a simpler narrative account, less than half the length of *The Wreck of the Deutschland*, of the sinking of a wooden-hulled frigate in a freak storm on 24 March 1878, near St. Boniface Down. Even so, this wrenched and wrenching poem is marked by such difficult poetical braveries that it could never be popular like "The Wreck of the Hesper-us."

Sitterson notes the tendency of the modern ode to include other genres. Hopkins's ode seems perfectly to illustrate Hugh Blair's idea—applied by Sitterson to Wordsworth—that generically the ode involved "the whole burst of the human mind." Following Wordsworth, Hopkins animates his ode with a massive dose of self-consciousness, namely, the presence of Hopkins's own distressed personality and predicament in stanzas 1-10, 18, 24, 28, and 32. Hopkins, like Wordsworth, resists the odist's tradi-tional attempt to achieve "absorption into otherness." The main action in Hopkins's poem is arguably the subjective experience in the lyric frame, Hopkins's personal agony and ecstasy.

3

        The frown of his face
    Before me, the hurtle of hell
Behind, where, where was a, where was a place?—
    I whirled out wings that spell   20
And fled with a fling of the heart to the heart of the Host.—
    My heart, but you were dovewinged, I can tell,
        Cárrier-wítted, I am bóld to bóast,
To flash from the flame to the flame then, tower from the grace to
        the grace.

To characterize my own understanding of Hopkins's odic reaction to Longfellow's ballad, I borrow a critical principle from Sitterson: "indebt-edness without allusion" (31).

Given the influence of Wordsworth on Hopkins, and in light of Hopkins's praise—partly on national or English grounds—of the "Immortality Ode" (*Correspondence* 147-48), Sitterson's speculation that Hopkins's ode owes something to Wordsworth's reinforces my speculation upon Hopkins's ephebic reaction to Longfellow's ballad. Sitterson's provocative argument runs as follows. The English irregular ode was always a mixed and inclusive genre. Wordsworth was innovative in several ways: he attempted to take the form beyond the lyric to the narrative; he realized his own indebtedness to earlier ode writers (Milton, Dryden, Gray) but refused to make "overt allusion" to them; his ode converts the lyric frame itself into a mode of action or "dramatic plot"; he used the ode as an attempt to comprehend his own private self; rejecting the usual odic "sought-for moment of unself-consciousness," he preferred to explore directly the problem of "inescapable self-consciousness." Sitterson concludes: "The modernity of Wordsworth's ode is signaled by the combination of opening self-consciousness and intellectual analysis" (26-35). He might be describing Hopkins's strenuous effort to render his own antithetical crisis-consciousness.

"All the literature of the early Victorian period is infused by a peculiar distress" (Houghton and Stange xvi). We must take pains and risks in speculating about the origins of a poem as strange as the *Wreck*. We recall that Longfellow's image of a "ship in distress" (stanza 11) draws rather complacently upon the distress-image that constitutes one of the most familiar tropes in Victorian sentimentality. In the scenario I am constructing, Hopkins fixes upon Longfellow's conventional distress trope and by virtue of his own aggressive poetics twists it into something new and strange. In his career-long effort to provide an authentic Victorian definition for the metrical term *stress*, Hopkins elaborated a new meaning for the sentimental term *distress*. Together with *instress*, Hopkins's *stress* very nearly epitomizes his poetical-philosophical enterprise.

In its usual nineteenth-century meanings, *distress* stands in curious relation to Hopkins's coinages *stress* and *instress*, which date from the year 1868 (MacKenzie, *Guide* 232-35). *Instress* denotes man's process of attaining and incorporating into himself the true nature (*inscape*) of a thing. *Stress* is the meaning-kernel thereby attained (Cotter 3). Hopkins found at the crisis of Longfellow's story, in stanza 11, a melodramatic trope (*distress*) that would trigger the deepest levels of his aesthetic attitude toward certain literary conventions. Longfellow's narrative crisis or turning point occurs when his captain hears cannon fire which he interprets as indications of the dangers besetting not his own but another vessel. A minor but crucial irony here obtrudes itself. In attempting to project his own peril off onto another ship and another skipper, the captain instantly becomes a "frozen corpse." Hopkins's friend Richard Watson Dixon voiced the conventional Victorian sentiment in thinking that *The Wreck of the Deutschland* seemed "enormously powerful" by virtue of containing "elements of deep distress" (*Correspondence* 32). Even more ambitious and complex than Dixon realized, Hopkins here deviates from Longfellow in the direction of psychological veracity and intellectual intensity.

Hopkins's entire effort in poetry can be described as an effort to replace familiar terms such as *distress* with daring neologisms such as *inscape* and *instress*. His re-working of Longfellow resulted in the reinterpretation of a Victorian keyword. The word *distress* itself appears nowhere in Hopkins's great ode. In fact, only twice in Hopkins's English poems does it occur. In the early "Barnfloor and Winepress," Hopkins writes: "For us by Calvary's distress / The wine was rackèd from the press" [thematically, joy from woe] (*Poetical* 27). In the fragmentary poem "'The times are nightfall, look, their light grows less'" (*Poetical* #152), he links "man's distress" with a strong sense of despair at the onset of nightfall: "All is from wreck" [thematically, the pain of hopelessness] (*Poetical* 176). Both poems obviously approximate aspects of the *Wreck*, the latter of the two suggesting the hopelessness we infer from a plain tragic narrative like Longfellow's ballad and the former suggesting one of Hopkins's odic themes, our discovery of Christ's mercy in the midst of suffering. For Hopkins's *Wreck*, Longfellow's commonplace distress trope would not suffice.

On the other hand, Hopkins uses *stress* eight times in his English poems, always as a noun, sometimes to mean "strain" and sometimes in his specialized sense of the essence of a thing. *Stressed* appears only once, in stanza 5 of the *Wreck*. *Instressed* appears only twice, once in stanza 5 of the ode. *Instress* appears not at all in the poems themselves. Admittedly, these random statistics have their meaning only in relation to the actual poem's numerous complexities. The *Wreck* stanzas (2, 5, 6) where these key words appear are among the most crucial in Part I, at cruxes where Hopkins confronts what Longfellow omitted: the poet's historical situation, personality, and subjectivity. The relevant passages are among Hopkins's most famous:

2

I did say yes
O at lightning and láshed ród;   10

Thou heardst me, truer than tongue, confess
Thy terror, O Christ, O God;
Thou knówest the wálls, áltar and hoûr and níght:
The swoon of a heart that the sweep and the hurl of thee trod
Hárd dówn with a horror of height: 15
And the midriff astrain with leaning of, laced with fire of stress

*   *   *   *

5

I kiss my hand
To the stars, lovely-asunder
Starlight, wafting him out of it; and   35
Glow, glory in thunder;
Kiss my hand to the dappled-with-damson west:
Since, thóugh he is únder the wórld's spléndour and wónder,
His mýstery múst be instréssed, stressed;
For I greet him the days I meet him, and bless when I understand.   40

6

Not out of his bliss
Springs the stress felt
Nor first from heaven (and few know this)
Swings the stroke dealt—
Stroke and a stress that stars and storms deliver,   45
That guilt is hushed by, hearts are flushed by and melt—
But it rídes tíme like ríding a ríver,
(And here the faithful waver, the faithless fable and miss).

Given the philosophical importance of *stress* and *instress* for Hopkins's prosody, we can imagine him either recalling Longfellow's conventionally loaded but inadequate word *distress* in its crucial position in "The Wreck of the Hesperus" or, if he actually consulted a copy of that poem—as I believe he might have done—noticing it only to object to it.

He takes upon himself the heroic task of establishing the true, full, Catholic-Christian-existential meaning of *distress* as it related to a horrifying shipwreck in which the question of God's mercy was radically at issue. Both he himself personally and God Himself are affronted by the glib concept of distress as used in its limited naturalistic and sentimental senses by a merely popular poet. *The Wreck of the Deutschland* proves Hopkins's genius at re-fusing and re-forging words according to the needs of his imagination (MacKenzie, *Guide* 28). This verbal genius is force-fully illustrated by Hopkins's severe reworking of Longfellow's comfort-able *distress*-trope into his own agonized *stress-instress* trope.

Further technical alterations wrought by Hopkins on the raw material offered by Longfellow's ballad can be understood in terms of the differ-ences between simile and metaphor. Longfellow embellished his stark narrative by including eleven similes designed to vivify the rocks, the ship's crew, the sea, the ship itself, and the skipper's daughter tied to the mast. Seven of these figures form a conceptual or thematic group:

> But the cruel rocks, they gored her side
> Like the horns of an angry bull.
>
> (stanza 18)

> And a whooping billow swept the crew
> Like icicles from her deck.
>
> (stanza 17)

> And the billows frothed like yeast.
>
> (stanza 6)

> She struck where the white and fleecy waves
> Looked soft as carded wool
>
> (stanza 18)

> She shuddered and paused, like a frighted steed,
> Then leaped her cable's length.
>
> (stanza 7)

> Like a sheeted ghost, the vessel swept
> Towards the reef of Norman's woe.
>
> (stanza 15)

> Like a vessel of glass, she stove and sank,
> Ho! Ho! the breakers roared!
>
> (stanza 19)

These seven direct comparisons draw upon several areas of experience: nature (brute animal, mineral, chemical), supernature, and man-made ob-jects.

By means of four other similes, Longfellow places his most intense focus upon the suffering girl. She is made to resemble inoffensive or innocent elements in vegetative nature. One entire stanza consists of three similes devoted to the helpless maiden.

> Blue were her eyes as the fairy-flax,
>   Her cheeks like the dawn of day,
> And her bosom white as the hawthorn buds,
>   That ope in the month of May.
>
> (stanza 2)

At the end of the poem, Longfellow re-imagines the dead girl, once again vegetatively, through the eyes of the land-bound fisherman.

> And he saw her hair, like the brown sea-weed,
>   On the billows fall and rise.
>
> (stanza 21)

All of this is adequate so far as it goes, but it does not attempt to go very far. With their curious mixture of elements (ghost, bull, glass, yeast), these similes contribute to Longfellow's melodramatic effects. Hopkins might admire Longfellow's similes, but he would write otherwise.

Hopkins rejected simile for metaphor. Given his deep theoretical and practical commitment not to explicit simile but to implicit metaphor, he certainly could see "The Wreck of the Hesperus" as a challenge. Alfred Borrello's *Concordance* establishes that Hopkins did in fact use *like* (100 times) and *as* (169 times). In the *Wreck*, *like* appears only once, in stanza 6 ("But it rides time like riding a river"); *as* appears seven times in the poem, but usually as a mere conjunction, only once functioning as the overt sign of a simile, and then a very complex simile: "I steady as a water in a well, to a poise, to a pane" (stanza 4). Even Hopkins's similes vex and reward the reader like complex metaphors. In her technical study *A Grammar of Metaphor*, Christine Brooke-Rose explains that among English poets Hopkins is a highly metaphoric poet, perhaps more so than any preceding poet. Citing *The Wreck of the Deutschland* more often than any other text, Brooke-Rose notes that Hopkins's language is "more crowded with metaphor than the richest passages in Spenser, Shakespeare, or Donne." Brooke-Rose finds illustrative metaphors in twenty-seven of Hopkins's thirty-five stanzas in the *Wreck* (2-13; 15; 18-27; 29-31; 35). Unlike Longfellow's relatively mechanical similes, Hopkins's metaphoric changes, she asserts, "are not on the whole smoothly or coolly expressed in terms of logic, but either assumed as already changed and obvious . . . or breathlessly asserted." Hopkins's metaphoric language makes a strong impression: "The tension thus produced is remarkable" (313-15).

Longfellow's poem powerfully renders the authentic terror of the stormy sea, and Hopkins would have admired and, to a degree, done likewise ("Wiry and white-fiery and whirlwind-swivellèd snow"). He recognized the ballad stanza as a proven technique to induce an impersonal tone and a sharply focussed narrative. The vividly rendered "angry sea" as it tosses the *Hesperus* a hyperbolic "cable's length" was matched by newspaper accounts of the actual storm in December of 1875. Longfellow's *dramatis personae* also to some degree suited Hopkins's raw material and antithetical decorum. The skipper is an arrogant authority figure—like Bismarck and the *Deutschland's* captain—whose obtuseness precipitates the disaster. An "old sailor," whose sensible warning to put into port is ignored, prefigures the several ships' masters and pilots aboard the *Deutschland* whose collective wisdom should have prevented the wreck. The skipper's daughter, focal point of Longfellow's narrative, reinforced Hopkins's rationale for his focus on one passenger, the Tall Nun. Then, too, Hopkins's impulse to place himself, a priestly but landbound fisher of men, in his ode found reinforcement (perhaps the original impulse?) in Longfellow's fisherman who "stood aghast" but safely on shore and stared at the maiden's frozen corpse.

Only within the context of a Bloomian, antihistorical argument would many of the verbal echoes one hears in the *Wreck* be of much interest, but given my premise they urge themselves quite compellingly. Even allowing for seasonal, situational, and generic coincidence, a few examples, drawn from the relatively more narrative Part II, may suffice. In Stanza 13, Hopkins's brilliant image of the "unchilding unfathering deeps"; in Stanza 14, the expression "She struck," just as in Longfellow; *en passant*, admittedly situational terms such as "snow," "breakers," "shrouds," and "rope's end" that gain in allusive effect in relation to Hopkinsian braveries such as "black-about air" (Longfellow's "midnight dark and drear"?). Of course, all such echoes pale by comparison with Hopkins's splendid transmutation of the rope Longfellow's captain uses to tie his daughter to the mast into the "rope's end" (stanza 16) from which a "handy and brave" sailor "dandled" in his attempt to save the doomed nuns.

16

One stirred from the rigging to save
The wild woman-kind below,

With a rope's end round the man, handy and brave—
He was pitched to his death at a blow,
For all his dreadnought breast and braids of thew: 25
They could téll him for hóurs, dándled the tó and the fró
Through the cobbled foam-fleece. What could he do
With the burl of the fóuntains of aír, búck and the flóod of the
          wave?

By his agonized psychopoetics, Hopkins earned the right to replace
Longfellow's last word ("Woe") with his own final word ("Lord"). At the
crisis of the young woman's experience in stanza 14, when "she thought
of Christ, who stilled the waves, / On the Lake of Galilee," Hopkins
could find the very structural emphasis he needed. Even Longfellow's
pious but predictable ending ("Christ save us all") might give a clue for
climax and closure.

Dáme, at óur dóor
Drówned, and among óur shóals,
Remémber us in the róads, the heaven-háven of the
          rewárd: 275
Our king back, Oh, upon Énglish sóuls!
Let him éaster in us, be a dáyspring to the dímness of us,
          be a crimson-cresseted east,
More bríghtening her, ráre-dear Brítain, as his réign rólls,
Príde, rose, prínce, hero of us, hígh-príest,
Oür héart's charity's héarth's fíre, oür thóughts' chivalry's
          thróng's Lórd.   280

On the whole, Longfellow's narrative—with its contrapuntal tonalities of
scornfulness, arrogance, trusting piety, neglected wisdom, natural violence, exciting action, pathos, deathliness, terror, amazement, and desperate hope—offered fecund material to the poet-priest's exacerbated consciousness. Longfellow's simple title itself could give Hopkins his own
stark, compelling title. This was a poem that the Hopkins family would
have known and loved. What memories it might trigger![6]
    So much for what Hopkins would preserve but amend. One connota-
tion of "sprung" rhythm is that of a breaking free from long-established
metrical constraints. To speculate further about what Hopkins decided that
Longfellow left undone and then resolved himself to do is to confront in
numerous ways the disciplined outpour of intense subjectivity, experi-
mental style, daring theology, moral indignation, stanzaic enlargement,
thematic exfoliation, psychological analysis, and mental anguish that have

occasioned so much readerly astonishment and critical commentary.[7] Bloom might consider such stylistic excess both the ephebe's anxiety-provoked overcompensation for prolonged frustration and also the inevitable over-spillage from an authentic but superabundant literary genius.

Compared with Hopkins's other challenging models such as the Book of Job, "Lycidas," or John's Revelation, "The Wreck of the Hesperus" might seem decidedly minor. However, Longfellow's ballad is a real and forceful form of history, equal in provocativeness to H. T. Buckle's scientific philosophy of history. Longfellow's shipwreck poem is, as it were ironically, a life-preserving text that itself can be given a new lease on life. We should be grateful to Longfellow's excellent ballad for challenging Hopkins. We should regard it historically as itself a grounded "ship in distress" awaiting the flood-tide of Hopkins's unique combination of religious consciousness and new versification.

Longfellow rewrote historiography by writing a national ballad about an actual American disaster. Hopkins rewrote Longfellow by means of an antithetical ode ostensibly about an actual English disaster but equally about the problem of writing and rewriting history. How best to judge Hopkins's complicated responses to historiography? Perhaps I should at this point simply invoke a philosopher who valorized bodily existence and who in that sense shares an outlook with Hopkins. Somewhere in *Signs* (1960), Maurice Merleau-Ponty evaluates historiography: "to give the past not a survival, which is the hypocritical form of forgetfulness, but a new life, which is the noble form of memory."

In this central episode showing how one poem gives a new life to another poem, "Hopkins Against History" proves paradoxically to be likewise "Hopkins For History."

Interchapter 3

"being in rank-old nature":
History and Antithesis in Poems #91-135 (1870-79)

(1)   I am soft sift
                        In an hourglass . . .

                                                    (*Wreck*, st. 4)

(2)   He fathers-forth whose beauty is past change.

                                                    (*Poetical* 144; #121)

With this third of four gatherings of poems in the 1990 edition, beginning
with "*Ad Matrem Virginem*" (#91) and ending with "Who shaped these
walls has shewn" (#135), we move roughly from Christmas, 1870, when
Hopkins was writing an occasional pious exercise in Latin, up to a point
in 1879, when at age thirty-five he turned to music as another strategy for
evading inscriptions of the nightmare of history. During this period, there
occurs perhaps the most abrupt emergence of genius in English literature.
    The ten poems and fragments from "*Ad Matrem Virginem*" to "*S.
Thomae Aquinatis Rhythmus and SS. Sacramentum*" (#100) represent
Hopkins's pious submission to his priestly calling. For the most part
composed in Latin, these ten poems preceding the *Wreck* state and restate
orthodox themes and emotions associated with topics such as the mother

115

of Christ, the Jesuit order, St. Winifred, and various occasional materials. Only with the "rhythmus" in honor of Thomas Aquinas, immediately preceding the *Wreck*, does any serious antithetical strain appear: the belief, perhaps in truth a complaint, that God not only hides himself in the eucharistic host but also scatters and hides himself under physical phenomena. Without some theory of non-English poems, ideally a theory equal to the Goldmann-Frye theory of poetic fragments as antithetically expressive forms, these ten poems add little to the Hopkinsian crisis-consciousness I am representing. It is perhaps too arbitrary to borrow from Frye by suggesting that Hopkins removes himself from the mainstream of history by hiding his English light under a Latin basket.

When the *Wreck of the Deutschland* (#101) finally appears, readerly sensations are those of shock and amazement. Not even the most astute reader of poetry could have predicted such a difficult, ambitious, brilliant poem from Hopkins or from any poet similarly situated. A reviewer of the 1990 edition asked: where did such a radical prosodist come from? In one special sense, the *Wreck* is one of Hopkins's most historical poems, rendering as it does in some detail an actual shipwreck in the English channel on 7 December 1875. Yet, the *Wreck* is also the least historical in being oriented not toward the past but toward the immediate moment. Walter Ong relates Hopkins's fashioning of a new kind of modern self in part to the poet's imaginative response to the latest advances in technology: "'The Wreck of the Deutschland' is the first great telegraphically conditioned poem in English, and perhaps in any language" (*Self* 50). Hopkins, by writing literally to the moment, is writing against time and inscriptions of time.

The *Wreck* initiates or releases Hopkins's true genius by enabling the sense of immediacy that characterizes the best of his subsequent poems. Many of them sonnets, these accomplished poems establish him as an engaging and important Victorian poet. Something indeed telegraphic ("danger, electrical-horror"), something electric ("The world is charged with the grandeur of God"), something immediate and hence ahistorical or even antihistorical, from thenceforward marks his best writing by reason of his rapid-fire sprung rhythm prosody. Hopkins appears determined to keep one step ahead of the ineluctable passage of time.

Following *The Wreck of the Deutschland* (1876), the reader of MacKenzie's chronological arrangement thus encounters not only many finished poems but poems exhibiting remarkable finish. Prior to the *Wreck*, we recall, many of the one hundred items presented by MacKenzie are mere fragments. Admittedly, the entire oeuvre risks being fragmented. With any poet, even one much more prolific than Hopkins, various kinds of historical frameworks may threaten to engulf a corpus or break it up into scattered remnants:

> There is a serious risk, of course, in source studies and histories of ideas: they may construct complex patterns of historical relationships within which individual literary works have been reduced to oversimplified paraphrase or collections of fragments taken out of context. (Whitaker xv)

As I proposed in interchapter 1, the Hopkinsian fragment itself possibly represents one of the poet's most forceful, if indirect, antithetical gestures against history. At the same time, I must agree with Whitaker that any attempt to historicize an oeuvre runs the risk of fragmenting and thus obliterating the oeuvre.

It is worth noting here that Whitaker's version of Yeats's "dialectical dialogue" with history can provide an illuminating contrast with Hopkins. Yeats sought to follow a gnostic path so as to escape from a fatalistic cycle of the individual self engaged in opposition to history. He enacted a visionary dialogue with history, spinning out elaborate systems of mythic rationalization in *A Vision*. Like Hopkins, Yeats struggled with history on both microcosmic and macrocosmic levels. Unlike Hopkins, who accepted one version of the Christian faith, Yeats resorted to numerous life-support systems, including Neoplatonism, theosophy, Rosicrucianism, magic, gnosticism, stoicism, and Blakean humanism.

History is central to Hopkins's development as it was to be for Yeats's development. The difference between these two poets on this score can be illuminated by Whitaker's generalization about Yeats.

> [H]istory was for Yeats a mysterious interlocutor, sometimes a bright reflection of the poet's self, sometimes a shadowy force opposed to that self. He conversed with it as with his double and anti-self. He could endow it with his own imaginative life, seeing it "but as an image in a looking-glass"; but he could also expect it to disclose all that he sought, all that seemed contrary to his own conscious state, all that lurked in his own depths, unmeasured and undeclared. This visionary and paradoxical dialogue—both strikingly individual and highly traditional—was a central fact underlying Yeats's complex and sustained growth. It led him beyond a facile subjectivism toward an awareness of his own more comprehensive nature and toward a passionate self-judgment that was also a judgment of the dominant qualities of his time. And it enabled

him to view history as a "necessity" which, when accepted and understood, might "take fire" in the head and become a "freedom or virtue." (4)

By contrast, Hopkins's strategies to evade or rewrite history contributed to his very different poetical utterance, not a Yeatsian dialogue *with* history but a desperate monologue, as it were a sotto voce buried life today difficult to comprehend, *against* historiography.

Among English poets, Hopkins is unusual in denying history at a literal level by completely eschewing in his verse the very word *history*. For such an omission to carry much weight, we need only recall Philippa Levine's account of the flowering of English historiography between the years 1838-1886, a period almost coterminous with Hopkins's lifetime. Levine notes that *history* was becoming a Victorian keyword of wide applicability and genuine discursive power.

> Historical studies ranked alongside those of the sciences as the dominant intellectual resources which shaped Victorian culture, providing the means to justify, to deplore, to praise or abuse, to determine the means and portents of the changes affecting the structures of society so profoundly in this period. (1)

For any Victorian writer to avoid the word *history* altogether would seem to be a noteworthy omission.

In *Crisis-Consciousness and the Novel*, I examined the complex processes by which many writers worked out their representations of human life in part by means of a crisis-trope centering upon what George Eliot characterizes as the "great noun" *crisis*. Hopkins shares with some other poets a reluctance to use the word *crisis*.[1] In many respects, the word *history* seems no less important as an enabling and characterizing key word for the emergence of modern consciousness. Many poets do in fact participate in the process by which *history* becomes a trope at least the equal of *crisis*. Excepting a rare figure such as Thomas Traherne, nearly every English poet before Hopkins and nearly every contemporary Victorian poet used *history* as part of a time-trope and a consciousness-trope.

A brief canvass of the uses to which English poets have put the word *history* can vividly suggest, by way of contrast, some of the consequences of Hopkins's decision to forego the trope-inducing word that appealed so strongly to his contemporaries. To begin, we might usefully list some familiar names of English poets who did incorporate *history* in their poetry:

Skelton, Marlowe, Jonson, Sidney, Herbert, Donne, Marvell, Swift, Dryden, Pope, Johnson, Wordsworth, Coleridge, Keats, Tennyson, Browning,
and Arnold.[2]

These central figures in the main tradition of English verse employ the
loaded word *history* in memorable passages and important poems. We
might begin by looking not before but after Hopkins. We find Yeats
himself, in his prolonged conversation with the past, frequently employing *history* in utterances of some thrust and import. Most notable is the
philosophical poem "Among School Children," where *history* signifies the
burden of acculturating forms which inevitably shadow one's entering the
prison house of adulthood.

> I walk through the long schoolroom questioning:
> A kind old nun in a white hood replies;
> The children learn to cipher and to sing,
> To study reading-books and history.
>
> (lines 1-4)

The importance of this poem in Yeats's development and reputation
would be enough to suggest what Hopkins sacrificed by deciding not to
invoke the Victorian history trope.

One further glance at a poet coming after Hopkins can reinforce this
point. In "Makers of History" (1955), W. H. Auden puts a sardonic twist
upon Yeats's linking of *history* with burdensome processes of accultura-
tion into conventional maturity.

> Serious historians care for coins and weapons,
> Not those re-iterations of one self-importance
> By whom they date them,
> Knowing that clerks could soon compose a model
> As manly as any of whom schoolmasters tell
> Their yawning pupils.
>
> (lines 1-6)

We glimpse here a sort of tradition or historical pattern from which
Hopkins, presumably in full self-awareness, removed himself.

Of even greater relevance would be the numerous poets, before and
contemporaneous with Hopkins, who employed *history* in figures and pro-
nouncements. Given Hopkins's own characterization of himself as
"Time's eunuch" ("'Thou art indeed just, Lord, if I contend'"; *Poetical*
#177), Shakespeare's dramatic concern with the "hatch and brood of

time" seems peculiarly pertinent. Warwick's great speech in *2 Henry IV* exhibits one range of emotion and concept enabled by a writer's recourse to a history-trope.

> There is a history in all men's lives,
> Figuring the nature of the times deceased,
> The which observed, a man may prophesy,
> With a near aim, of the main chance of things
> As yet not come to life, which in their seeds
> And weak beginnings lie intreasurèd.
>
> (iii i 80-5)

Shakespeare's insistence on history's truth-telling powers marks one of the high points of the trope's compelling history.

In Sidney and Marvell, *history* enables discursive possibilities. In sonnet 90 of *Astrophil and Stella*, Sidney insinuates into his groundbreaking sequence a comparison of Stella with history and history with the meaning of life.

> Stella, think not that I by verse seek fame;
> Who seek, who hope, who love, who live, but thee:
> Thine eyes my pride, thy lips my history;
> If thou praise not, all other praise is shame.
>
> (lines 1-4)

An equally revolutionary analogy, equating nature with truth, appears in stanza 73 of Marvell's "Upon Appleton House, to my Lord *Fairfax*."

> Out of these scatter'd *Sybyls* leaves
> Strange *Prophecies* my Phancy weaves:
> And in one History consumes,
> Like *Mexique Paintings*, all the *Plumes*.
> What *Rome, Greece, Palestine*, ere said
> I in this light *Mosaick* read.
> Thrice happy he who, not mistook,
> Hath read in *Natures Mystick Book*.
>
> (lines 577-84)

Clearly, even taking only Shakespeare, Sidney, and Marvell as our exemplars, we should recognize the potential for rich meanings and provocative metaphors inherent in *history* as an emerging discursive figure.

In the next age, poets extend and deepen the range of possibilities, as passages from Dryden, Swift, Pope, and Johnson illustrate. In "Religio Laici," Dryden links *history* with vital issues of the day such as tradition, authority, and the relations between writing and speaking.

> Tradition written therefore more commends
> Authority, than what from voice descends;
> And this, as perfect as its kind can be,
> Rolls down to us the sacred history
> Which, from the Universal Church receiv'd,
> Is tried, and after for itself believ'd.
>
> (lines 350-55)

Swift used "The Faggot; Written in the Year 1713, when the Queen's Ministers were Quarrelling Among Themselves," to urge his modest belief in the past of the Ancients as a source of exemplary wisdom and exemplary folly.

> In history, we never found
> The consul's fasces were unbound;
> Those Romans were too wise to think on't,
> Except to lash some grand delinquent.
>
> (lines 27-30)

In *The Dunciad*, Pope places a personified History, together with such good company as the admirable powers Science, Wit, Logic, Rhetoric, Morality, and Tragedy, temporarily under the footstool of Dulness. History seethes with resentment but wisely bides her time for revenge: "But sober History restrain'd her rage, / And promis'd Vengeance on a barb'rous age" (IV, 39-40).

In his turn, Johnson provides in "The Vanity of Human Wishes" a version of history very noble and lofty. History equates with moral vision and the broad classical view of life.

> Let hist'ry tell where rival kings command,
> And dubious title shakes the madded land,
> When statutes glean the refuse of the sword,
> How much more safe the vassal than the lord;
> Low skulks the hind beneath the rage of pow'r,
> And leaves the wealthy traytor in the Tow'r,

> Untouch'd his cottage, and his slumbers sound,
> Tho' confiscation's vulturs hover round.
>
> (lines 29-36)

To cite such poets as these, from Shakespeare to Johnson, would be an adequate rationale for questioning Hopkins's deliberate avoidance of *history*.

Among the romantic poets, Wordsworth, Coleridge, Keats, and Byron bend their individualized genius to the task of defining *history* for a new epistemology and consciousness. For Wordsworth, in *The Excursion*, history is "time's slavish scribe" who must hold a monitory mirror up to human nature, as for example violent Frenchmen during the later stages of the revolution.

> Scorn and contempt forbid me to proceed!
> But History, time's slavish scribe, will tell
> How rapidly the zealots of the cause
> Disbanded—or in hostile ranks appeared.
>
> (iii 768-71)

In the case of Coleridge, a seemingly obligatory occasional poem, "Lines written in the Album at Elbingerodu, in the Hartz Forest," actually expresses some of Coleridge's most crucial beliefs regarding the dialectic operating between outer forms and inner meanings. History here equates with prophecy, but it can be read from nature only by the purest of human hearts.

> I had found
> That outward forms, the loftiest, still receive
> Their finest influence from the Life within—
> Fair cyphers else: fair, but of import vague
> Or unconcerning, where the heart not finds
> History or prophecy of friend, or child,
> Or gentle maid, our first and early love,
> Or father, or the venerable name
> Of our adoréd country.
>
> (lines 16-24)

Wordsworth and Coleridge find basically positive uses for *history*, but the romantic poets were not of one mind on the subject.

Keats's most ambitious poem, "Endymion," complains of a bleakly indifferent historical process, a "gilded cheat," that obliterates distinctions and individuals.

> Hence, pageant history! hence, gilded cheat!
> Swart planet in the universe of deeds!
> Wide sea, that one continuous murmur breeds
> Along the pebbled shore of memory!
>
> (lines 14-17)

The romantic treatment of *history* can be said to culminate or self-deflate in Byron's *Don Juan*. Here, history not only lacks powers of discrimination but is extremely clumsy.

> History can only take things in the gross;
> But could we know them in detail, perchance
> In balancing the profit and the loss,
> War's merit it by no means might enhance,
> To waste so much gold for a little dross,
> As hath been done, mere conquest to advance,
> The drying up a single tear has more
> Of honest fame, than shedding seas of gore.
>
> (lines 17-24)

Given Hopkins's familiarity with these romantic precursors, his unwillingness to resort to *history* increasingly takes on potential significance.

When we come to Hopkins's famous contemporaries like Matthew Arnold, as well as Tennyson, Meredith, and Browning in some of their more complacent moods, we are afforded a glimpse of metaphors that might explain why Hopkins would refrain from using the figure.

Admittedly, Arnold could seem to echo Byron's jaundiced historicism when he characterized history as a wide sea of indiscriminately jumbled human actions. In "To the Duke of Wellington: On Hearing Him Mispraised," Arnold wrote:

> . . . thy track, across the fretful foam
> Of vehement actions without scope or term,
> Called history, keeps a splendor due to wit,
> Which saw one clue to life, and followed it.
>
> (lines 11-14)

By no means, though, is Arnold's sardonic image of history typical of the
Victorian sages.

We have already noted how Pater, upon reading Renan, was enabled
to "relax into historicism." By contrast with the intense Hopkins, the trio
of Tennyson, Meredith, and Browning indeed relaxed into the vogue of
historicist figuration. Tennyson uses *In Memoriam* to predict that history
would play an unambiguous role in the march of progress toward an
enlightened future.

> As one would sing the death of war
> And one would chant the history
> Of that great race, which is to be,
> And one the shaping of a star.
>
> (poem 103; lines 33-36)

Likewise, Meredith used "Earth's Secret" to urge that history functions
as a source of wisdom, itself something on the order of a Victorian sage.

> They, hearing History speak, of what men were,
> And have become, are wise. The gain is great
> In vision and solidity; it lives.
>
> (lines 9-11)

Finally, under the problematical dramatic persona of one "Mr. Sludge,
'The Medium'" Browning judges *history* to be as essential to Victorians
as sacred scripture or the mother's milk of experience, knowledge, and
wisdom.

> I ask
> Next what may be the mode of intercourse
> Between us men here, and those once-men there?
> First comes the Bible's speech; then, history
> With the supernatural element,—you know—
> All that we sucked in with our mother's milk,
> Grew up with, got inside of us at last,
> Till it's found bone of bone and flesh of flesh.
>
> (lines 833-41)

As these examples testify, the finicky Hopkins might find in a contemporary poetical trope bordering at times on glibness many sufficient reasons
for despising and doing otherwise.

In the interval between Shakespeare's confident assertion ("There is a history in all men's lives") and Byron's jaundiced complaint ("History can only take things in the gross"), a great falling off had occurred. Hopkins enters history hard on Byron's heels and chooses to reject history, or at least one sort of history, outright. Taking note of the fact that Hopkins's own sermons, unlike his poems, frequently draw upon the Victorian trope induced by the loaded word *history* (Foltz and Bender), we can now begin to calculate the cost of his forgoing the word in his poems.

It bears repetition that following the *Wreck* the other poems of 1876-79 are, like the *Wreck* itself, of such rapidity and intense immediacy that they seem in effect to escape from history. One such poem explicitly defies time by replacing evolution with devolution.

The Sea and the Skylark

On ẽar and ear two noises too old to end
    Trench—rîght, the tide that rãmps against the shore;
    With a flood or a fall, low lull-off or áll róar,
Frequènting thère while moon shall wẽar and wend.
Léft hànd, òff lànd, I hẽar the lark ascend,   5
    His rash-fresh re-winded new-skeinèd score
    In crisps of curl off wild winch whirl, and pour
And pelt músic, till none's to spill nor spend.

How these two shame this shallow and frãil tówn!
    How ring right out our sordid turbid time,   10
Béing pure! We, life's pride and cared-for crown,

Have lost that chẽer and charm of earth's past prime:
Our make and making break, are breaking, down
To man's last dust, drain fast towards man's first slime.

(Poetical 143; #118)

Merely to name a few other rapid-fire poems is to advance the present argument: "The Starlight Night," "The Windhover," and "Henry Purcell."

We have here reached by still another curious route the central paradox of Hopkins's antithetical response to history. He rejected the great historiographical enterprise of the Victorian period (including Buckle's scientific history), literary history of the standard kinds, and Longfellow's

rewriting of actual events. Even so, his own antihistorical poems bequeath
to us a compelling record of a modern self enacting its own existence, or,
as we say today, self-fashioning its own history. We would do well to
recall Suzanne Langer's insight into Shakespeare's dramatic forms: "Yet
it is a poetic art, because it creates the primary illusion of all poetry—
virtual history" (306).

4

Hopkins Against Frederick II:
"The Windhover," *De Arte Venandi cum Avibus*,
and Modern Consciousness

(1)   Source study is wholly irrelevant here; we are dealing
        with primal words, but antithetical meanings, and an
        ephebe's best misinterpretations may well be of poems he
        has never read.

                                                    Bloom 70

(2)   That's why the wise won't jump beyond his station,
        To greater heights presented him by luck,
        But always keeps his tastefulness and tact.

                                    Frederick II, in Oppenheimer 65

(3) Flutters the fuckgale, standgale,
    Galefucker (yes, names for him respectable
    Dictionaries actually enshrine)—kestrel, windhover, kingdom
    Of daylight's dauphin in his a little-dappled-flattened
    Clinging to meshes of fine wire.

    Trails from his left claw a chick: more such
    Pus-yellow fluffs or powder-puffs of dead
    Chicks from a farm
    Sag under these wired-in naked branches dropped

By these half-dozen tedium's dauphins on this
Wet staleness of their ground.

A stink of fox, from curled foxes
Asleep on quarry ledges in the next cage,
Sneaks round.

Geoffrey Grigson, "Wild Life Park"

One of Hopkins's readers, asking if the Victorian Hopkins might have been the poet of the future, decided that he was not (Robert Adams 559). The next episode in Hopkins's unfolding crisis-consciousness opens up the possibility that the inventor of sprung rhythm may indeed have been—no less than Matthew Arnold or George Eliot—a proleptic or prophetic Victorian who perceived what stringent life-conditions lay in wait for their beleaguered fellow men. In this episode, relations between discursive forms and forms of cultural power become more and more important.

Hopkins's symbol for the modern poet and for modern man is a caged bird: "Hopkins's repeated attempts to free himself from the constraints of his, in part, self-created cage produced only smaller and smaller cages to contain his stylistic energies, until in the end, the bird had not sufficient room to sing" (Sprinker 120). Geoffrey Grigson's encaged "half-dozen tedium's dauphins," reenacting Hopkins's grim vision of modern life, drives home one principle of Victorian crisis-consciousness: historically, *Te deum* becomes *tedium*.[1]

We have already seen how we may have to go roundabout in historical gyres in order to deal with any Hopkinsian clue in full view. Henry Thomas Buckle's *History of Civilization in England*, the tradition for lyrical assortments that nearly defines poetry itself, and a national ballad by a conservative versifier—such episodes require strenuous explanation before we can glimpse Hopkins in his antithetical stance toward Victorian life as represented by Victorian historiography. Now, alerted by Harold Bloom's most provocative opinion—"an ephebe's best misinterpretations may well be of poems he has never read"—we confront another episode, perhaps the most abstruse, in Hopkins's antithetical role in the formation of modern crisis-consciousness. In this episode, we will see Hopkins reacting to coordinate problems of personal discipline and literary representation.

"The falcon cannot hear the falconer." Thus, in 1919, one year after Hopkins's poems first appeared, Yeats bequeathed an anachronistic image for cultural disintegration. "The Second Coming" offers a cyclical philosophy of history which has been interpreted as often and variously as the "The Windhover" itself. In Yeatsian criticism, the art of falconry comes into critical play. Of a certainty, we should not be surprised to find strong poets being more concerned with language-effects than with informational correctness. Yet, in depicting his decentered falcon, Yeats betrayed ignorance of the fact that in the British Isles falconers do not use vocal calls but rely upon visual signals to control their birds (Hohenstaufen 243). More to my purpose, though, when Yeats thought of a falcon, he correctly thought of a falconer. Yeats's own falcon was originally, in at least one manuscript version, simply a hawk (Jeffares 203).[2] We will do well to recognize that a falcon is a hawk that has been trained or broken to the discipline of falconry. Hopkins would have known this. In 1877, he wrote: "No sooner were we among the Welsh hills than I saw the hawks flying and other pleasant sights soon to be seen no more" (*Correspondence* 148).

Dictionaries and handbooks regularly define *falcon* in disciplinary and representational terms: "any hawk trained to hunt and kill small game; in falconry the female is called a *falcon*, the male a *tiercel*" (*Webster's New World Dictionary*, 1986). Hopkins referred to "The Windhover" not only as the best thing he had ever written but also as the "Falcon" poem. Let us remind ourselves once again of the physical appearance of the poem he so highly valued.

The Windhover:

to Christ our Lord

I caught this mŏrning morning's mînion, king-
    dom of daylight's dauphin, dapple-dáwn-drawn Falcon, in his
      riding
  Of the rólling level úndernéath him steady aír, and stríding

High there, how he rung upon the rein of a wimpling wing

In his ēcstasy! then off, off forth on swing,   5
    As a skate's heel sweeps smooth on a bow-bend: the hurl and
      gliding
  Rebuffed the bíg wínd. My heart in hiding
Stirred for a bird,—the achieve of, the mástery of the thing!

Brute beauty and valour and act, oh, air, pride, plūme, here
    Buckle! AND the fire that breaks from thee then, a billion   10
Tímes told lovelier, more dangerous, O my chevalier!

No wŏnder o͜f it: shéer plód makes plóugh down sillion

Shíne, and blue-bleak embers, ah my dear,
Fall, gáll themsélves, and gásh gŏld-vermílion.

(*Poetical* 144; #120)

If histrionic gestures in a ritualized sport such as wrestling resemble diacritical writing, as it were a set of comments placed above the wrestler's body (Barthes, *Mythologies* 18), then likewise can Hopkins's odd markings be regarded as a burdensome if liberating symbol for the material gear employed in falconry to control the bird. The disciplinary paradox of controller and controlled had been noted in English poetry as early as Chaucer's *Parliament of Fowls:* "The gentyl faucon, that with his feet distrayneth / The kynges hand" (lines 337-38).

A falcon is a bird trained to falconry. We should pause over this technicality. A mistake is made when a Yeats or a Hopkins writes about a falcon without closely attending to the discipline of falconry. In such cases one mars one's discourse by ignoring, for example, the sexual differentiation between *falcon* and *tiercel*. Feminist criticism has sensitized us to the consequences of such a gaffe.[3]

We can not have our Hopkins simultaneously one of the most careful of poets at the same time that we would have him careless in composing the best sonnet he would ever write. When Hopkins refers to a "Falcon" he brings into his poem both a falconer and the ancient art of falconry. It seems quite certain that he intended such a frame of reference. Perhaps he would be surprised to learn that this clue in full view, however subject to interpretation, would not be obvious to any alert reader.

We are told by commentators that *windhover* means "kestrel" (but not "peregrine" or "gerfalcon"). Why did Hopkins not write *Kestrel* ("dapple-dawn-drawn Kestrel"), given that metrically and in other respects *Kestrel* would fit his intention? The word *windhover*, like the dedication "to Christ our Lord," appears only at the head of the poem, and therefore has at best only a peripheral function and status. As Gérard Genette would say, the very word *Windhover* in the title is paratextual and hence problematical (261). If we assume that—as with "Buckle"—Hopkins is providing another historiographical clue in full view, we may be afforded compelling answers to vexing questions.

Falconry is, to borrow Claude Lévi-Strauss's terms, culture rather than nature, the cooked rather than the raw. Encyclopaedias regularly define falcons as part of a discipline. Thus: "The falcon is a hawk-like bird that is trained to hunt other birds in the sport called falconry" (*World Book*

Encyclopaedia, 1976). Oddly, Hopkins criticism has never raised questions bearing upon this one central fact: birds are not falcons until they are disciplined to falconry.

Historically, falconry is a method of hunting game with trained hawks. Persians invented it more than 4,000 years ago. In the middle ages, it was a popular sport among the noblemen of Europe, becoming less widespread only after the invention of guns and after the demise of feudalism. Training a falcon is an art that requires abundant skill, months of effort, and endless patience. The bird must first be "manned" or made comfortable in the presence of humans. Then it must be "broken" to a hood placed on its head when it is carried to and from the field. The hood is removed only when the game is spied; the falcon is then turned loose to pursue the game. The bird must be trained to "lure," so it will not fly off with the game.

What, then, might be the implications of Hopkins's not anticipating Yeats (so to speak) by including a falconer along with his famous "dapple-dawn-drawn Falcon"? Have we come upon another obvious but clever strategy for antithetical consciousness, the overlooking of which by his readers might cause the poet consternation and puzzlement.[4]

Suppose we ask again: what about written history, particularly literary history? A possibility, admittedly abstruse, then suggests itself. Historiographical relations may exist between Hopkins's nineteenth-century English sonnet about a falcon and a thirteenth-century complex consisting of the invention of the sonnet by Giacomo da Lentino which has ties to an important treatise on falconry by Giacomo's master, the sonneteering Emperor Frederick II of Hohenstaufen. Issues raised by New Historical critics—issues such as the relations between consciousness, discourse, knowledge, and power—may help to untie this intricate knot.[5]

We can begin by wondering why Hopkins's best sonnet includes a falcon? And why, by the poem's end, we are reading not about a bird but about a plough and dying embers? Assuming that "The Windhover" may be a key moment in Victorian crisis-consciousness, here is the line of inquiry I will follow.

Prompted by Paul Oppenheimer's hypothesis that the origin of modern consciousness is owing in part to Giacomo's *duecento* invention of the sonnet, we can speculate afresh about "The Windhover" as a sonnet about a falcon. According to Oppenheimer, modern consciousness arises, between the years 1225-1230, with the silently-read, inward-turning, problem-solving, logical-seeming sonnet. Frederick, arguably the first modern man, encouraged Giacomo's experimentation and himself composed sonnets. Additionally, his book *De Arte Venandi cum Avibus* (*The Art of*

Hunting with Birds, c. 1245) historicizes and promotes an ancient activity that is also thereby linked to the origin of modern consciousness.

Examining Hopkins's celebrated "dapple-dawn-drawn Falcon" alongside Frederick's encyclopaedic falcon ("bird life [expresses] attractive manifestations of the processes of nature") permits us to witness—if not fully understand—a new episode in Hopkins's antithetical crisis-consciousness of the past. Like the revolutionary Frederick II, Hopkins may have perceived, both in and via the sonnet form, a consciousness that would prove essential to forms of discipline required by the modern predicament.[6]

"The Windhover" can bear much historical weight, having already borne more commentary than any other nineteenth-century English poem of comparable length. Hopkins could have adapted from his mentor Walter Pater a dialectical view of history. Accordingly, history's purpose is to mediate between the familiar and the strange: "History animates man's urge to change the familiar and at the same time to preserve it" (Iser 68). By transcending history via a narrative grounded in a particular person, place, and time, Christianity itself enacts one version of this problem (Kemp 5). The falcon in "The Windhover" is regularly interpreted as an allusion to Christ, but it may be that the noun *Falcon* in the second line initially alludes to an acculturated bird such as Frederick described in *De Arte Venandi*. As in previous episodes of Hopkinsian crisis-consciousness, we must traverse a wide field to get a new glimpse of the antithetical poet rewriting history.

Oppenheimer's account of the invention of the sonnet grounds itself in Freud's principle that frustration is the beginning of self-consciousness (Oppenheimer 10). The classical world had valued introspection; witness Oedipus's frustration before eventually attaining to crucial self-knowledge. But the medieval mind practiced an "amazing and easy ignorance of self." Everyman looked outward, not inward, believing that any limiting self-ignorance would be more than compensated for by God's grace. In the middle ages, allegory and spiritual edification replaced internal knowledge. Not until the invention of the sonnet early in the *duecento* would European man in any great numbers once again methodically practice the art of self-consciousness (9-12).

Modern literary thought, then, begins with Giacomo's invention, the first lyric form since the classical era intended mainly for introspective, silent reading. As the first lyric of the self in conflict, of self-consciousness, the new form can be traced to Plato's *Timaeus*, with its mathematical architecture of the soul and of heaven itself. Early in the *duecento*, Giacomo's invention was understood as a new way of thinking about mankind, a way to acknowledge and solve previously intractable emotional problems (4).

Provençal courtly love poetry preceding the sonnet differed from its successor. Allegories of courtly love implied that individuals must rely strictly upon institutions, namely, the Church, rather than self-questionings or personal communication with God. Impersonal allegory ignored the self. In the courtly love triangle, with its amusing artifice, the persona is a lover or poet or performer standing at a distance from the love object. Personal torments are suppressed. A histrionic rhetoric induces Ptolemaic truth-effects by means of a comprehensive explanation of reality. Medieval man was enjoined to avoid self-consciousness by a system which posits man's separation from God the Creator. Men are mere beasts or machines; salvation comes through faith; the remote lady reminds the lover that he must look outward for help (4-9).

Such was the medieval culture that Giacomo's fourteen-line sonnet would seriously change. Intended as a meditative instrument of self-absorption and self-scrutiny, it contributed to—Oppenheimer thinks it initiated—modern consciousness (12). As the sonnet enabled a new literary intimacy, courtly poets began to value the form as an epistolary conduit for dialogue between poets (38). The sonnet became widely fashionable, but at a deep level it transformed literature so that verbal images could induce a symbolism connected to the subconscious mind. Details became symbols functioning as "gateways to internal conflicts" (27-8). By its octave-sestet structure, the sonnet allowed the poet to ask and answer personal questions, to solve intimate problems, and to discover his own inner nature (33). In this tradition, we have the personal signatures of Shakespeare, Milton, and Wordsworth. Even the peculiar intimacies of the *Divine Comedy* ("the first silent epic") were made possible by Giacomo's invention (37).[7]

Giacomo da Lentino's biography is factually incomplete but richly sublimated into two other historical phenomena, the sonnet form itself and the achievements of his master Frederick. A lawyer or courtly *notari*, thus one who wrote and disputed while acquiring legal knowledge and expertise, Giacomo was a student of philosophy whose duties included transcribing masses of documents. Schooled in the *trivium* (*grammatica*, *rhetorica*, *dialecta*), Giacomo presumably complemented Frederick's own brilliance, as witnessed by the emperor's giving Giacomo the power to appoint all other court *notari* (18-19).[8] Oppenheimer reads Giacomo's personality in part from his literary invention, arguing that Giacomo anticipated Frederick's program by inventing the poetical form which subsumes past and present in a nexus of silence, introspection, intimacy, and individual consciousness. The sonnet opens up the frontiers of modern experience and feeling.

Some time between the years 1225 and 1230, Giacomo constructed the first sonnet, using a peasant-song form (*strambotto*) for the octave and a sestet derived philosophically and mathematically from ideal ratios— 6:8:12—informing the *Timaeus* (189). Recognition of a radical congruence between Giacomo's mathematico-architectural sonnet and Hopkins's own thinking about the sonnet form has been made possible by Hardison. He cites a "curious mathematical interpretation" in a passage from Hopkins's correspondence with R. W. Dixon, where Hopkins writes:

> It seems to me that this division is the real characteristic of the sonnet, and what is not marked off and moreover has not the octave divided again into quatrains is not to be called a sonnet. For the cipher in [line] 14 is no mystery, and if one does not avail oneself of the opportunities which it affords, it is a pedantic encumbrance and not an advantage.
>
> The equation of the best sonnet is:
> $$(4 + 4) + (3 + 3) = 2x4 + 2x3 = 2 (4 + 3) = 2x7 = 14$$

Hardison thinks that even if Hopkins's unexplained "cipher" is rejected as over-ingenious, the sonnet is nevertheless an entirely unnatural form, with the Italian sonnet being perhaps the most unnatural [read *logical*] of the various types (196-97). Hopkins's cipher, I believe, would prove simply to be one's sense of emptiness, following upon logical resolution and cathartic satiation, typically experienced at the end of a sonnet.

Giacomo's sonnet manifested three main features: a strong departure from performance-based poetry, the treatment of emotions with logic, and an endless self-referentiality. Oppenheimer notes:

> In thus announcing a new individuality and self-consciousness in poetry, the sonnet form must have seemed ideally suited to an emperor, and an intellectual as well as a political community, Frederick's court and the students at his new university, passionately attracted to the frontiers of emotions and experience. (23)

Almost certainly, Giacomo would have made his literary intentions clear.

> Giacomo would have explained what he had done: reproduced the architecture of the soul, even the architecture of the meditative mind of God, in words on a sheet of paper. He might have added

that the new form was designed to bring its readers, and those who
wrote in it, closer to understanding the biblical assertion that man
has been made in the image of God, the silent mind-creator of
everything, who was to be wooed with prayer, or words, or poetry.
(23-4)

The sonneteer "addresses himself not to any outsider but to the form
itself" (184). At a stroke, Giacomo turned the mind inward and modified
consciousness from thenceforward. Problem-solving modern man would
increasingly use sonnet-like strategies to induce and reduce frustrations
caused by unanswered questions.[9]
    Assuming that "The Windhover"—like any sonnet—stands in an in-
teresting relation to Giacomo's invention, and even given Hopkins's
awareness of the form, we yet must admit that Giacomo's own sonnets
could be, as Bloom would have it, influential poems that the later poet
perhaps "has never read." What, though, of the fact that "The Windhover" is a sonnet about a falcon? Here our search makes an unsettling
swerve if we take careful note of Giacomo's patron, the first modern
ruler, Holy Roman Emperor Frederick II, author of an authoritative treatise on falcons.
    At his imperial court in Sicily Frederick initiated a secular *modus
vivendi* based on reason. Thus radically centered, he followed the skeptic's decentering path by challenging both traditional science and papal
authority (Oppenheimer 4). Under the sway of this active but meditative
ruler, human personality acquired unprecedented importance (12). A
member of the royal Hohenstaufen family, Frederick II (1194-1250) was
crowned king of the Romans at age two, king of Italy at age four, and
Holy Roman Emperor at age twenty; he became self-proclaimed king of
Jerusalem at age thirty-five. He ably governed his Sicilian kingdom, establishing the University of Naples in 1224 and making the University of
Salerno the best medical school in Europe. Throughout his life, he fought
with popes and emerging towns in Germany and Italy. Praised as *Stupor
Mundi* (The Amazement of the World), he achieved fame as an administrator, soldier, and scientist. Gifted in languages, he encouraged the development of sculpture and poetry. His book on falcons, *De Arte Venandi
cum Avibus*, is still consulted by experts. Frederick occupies a high place
in George Sarton's history of science (Wood and Fyfe xlii-xlvii), and he
is decidedly part of the history of fame (Braudy 217-18).
    In the modern world, men and women read and write silently and
alone, thus generating a new definition of the self (Oppenheimer 25).
This rich inner life begins under the reign of Frederick. He championed

reason and experimentation for the sake of new knowledge. Love of beauty and a desire to gain access to the actual world guided his every action (21). Living in a culturally diverse Sicily, Frederick followed his open-minded, anti-clerical, scientific curiosity. Resisting papal power, he was excommunicated three times. On such occasions, he further offended authority by issuing orders in the name of Christ rather than the interdicting pope.

Frederick in part initiated modern thought by accepting as truth whatever is proved by force of reason and nature. He set aside the medieval reliance upon biblical analogy; he debunked unthinking reliance upon Aristotle and other authorities. He employed political theatrics in creating the first secular state. In Jacob Burckhardt's opinion, Frederick was the first ruler to transform a political state into a work of art.

Delighting in mathematical puzzles and games, Frederick created dazzling effects when his royal entourage—including not only judges and jugglers but circus performers, dancing girls, and a menagerie of exotic animals—traveled the countryside. Oppenheimer represents the spectacle thus:

> The threat and delight were there for all to see, the declaration of independence, the announcement of the importance of the individual soul and consciousness. Frederick's procession was a heavenly and earthly caravansary, a mingling of dreams, exotic visions, and splendors. (17)

Thus Frederick as *immutator mirabilis*, the creator of the amazing. In his secular universities, a polyphony of voices could be heard as Roman law was studied alongside the classics. Aided by the poet Pier della Vigna, he drew up for Sicily rational laws based upon ancient Roman law.

"Our work is to present things that are as they are." Frederick's book on falcony expresses his scientific outlook, his grasp of the importance of cultural discipline, and his awareness of the problem of discursive representation. Extant in an illuminated copy in the Vatican library, *De Arte Venandi cum Avibus* represents one of the first modern historico-scientific texts. A serious threat to the established model of nature, it was the world's first sumptuously illustrated encyclopedia on the history, traits, requirements, and habits of many kinds of birds (storks, ducks, swallows, falcons). A major work of natural history, its frank empiricism and disavowal of traditional science threatened the church's Ptolemaic and Aristotelian system (Oppenheimer 14-15).

First assembled some twenty years after Giacomo's first sonnet, *De Arte Venandi*, like Frederick's other projects, might well have been influenced by Giacomo's logical, dialectical sonnet form. Owing much to Aristotle's general lore in *De Animalibus* and much to first-hand observation, *De Arte Venandi* itself is an imposing book of more than four-hundred pages, beginning on a sociotherapeutic note ("falconry enables nobles and rulers disturbed and worried by the cares of state to find relief in the pleasures of the chase"), touching upon economic problems (the poor may participate in falconry so as to "earn some of the necessities of life"), urging the inherent nobility of an activity highly disciplined and conscientious (4-6), and ending with an image of imperfectly disciplined falcons leaving the hunt and gravitating toward each other: "it is the habit of falcons to fly toward another of their kind whom they see in flight" (414).

Frederick's technical treatise divides into six books, providing abundant information on the anatomy and habits of birds (I), the rearing, feeding, and seeling (temporary blinding) of falcons, as well as the hoods and implements used in falconry (II), types of lures and types of hunting dogs used with falcons (III), habits of gerfalcons and methods of hunting with them (IV), the hunting of herons with falcons (V), and, the hunting of water birds with the peregrine falcon (VI).[10]

One passage from *De Arte Venandi cum Avibus* can suggest Frederick's thought-style:

> Once in the saddle with the falcon on his fist, the falconer should ride along slowly and in localities where the bird, unaccustomed to the motions of the horse and other new sensations, will have less cause than usual to take fright.
>
> The first excursions of horseman and falcon should be made to places where there are no ravines, no forests, and but little water, where they are not likely to meet vehicles, many men, or other animals, and where there are no bushes or brambles, because the falcon will be alarmed by all these objects and their accompanying noises. (195)

The falconer's gloved fist may be taken as a symbol of the discipline.

Falconry, combining the maximum of nature with the maximum of culture, the maximum of freedom with the maximum of constraint, is a site where power circulates from element to element as it is being exercised. We recall Chaucer's figure: "The gentyl faucon, that with his feet distrayneth / The kynges hand." Falconry as represented by Frederick

138 Hopkins Against History

may be another "poem" that Hopkins never read. But it almost certainly interacted dialectically with Giacomo's sonnet form and hence would bear upon any subsequent sonnet.

To get a purchase on this issue we may need to circle the way the falcon circles. *De Arte Venandi* is a book that might have developed along either of two other motivated lines: the purely spiritual or the purely physical. Certain discursive features, including Frederick's illocutionary message of discipline *per se*, invite us to examine his historico-scientific treatise from the perspective of two other famous discipline manuals. One of these books belongs to Hopkins's past; the other belongs to his future, as gloomily imagined by Geoffrey Grigson. Ignatius Loyola's *Spiritual Exercises* (1541) and Michel Foucault's *Discipline and Punish: The Birth of the Prison* (1975) may help us to achieve deeper understanding of Frederick as a historiographer against whom Hopkins would react. These two books exemplify the coordinate problems of discursive representation and discipline which concern both Frederick and Hopkins.

Hopkins the Jesuit relied upon *Spiritual Exercises* as a conduct book. Loyola's masterpiece of religious retreat, like Frederick's book, is among other things a discourse on representation, on the coding and decoding of signs in a systematic discipline. The retreat master guides souls by judging reactions and motives. Such skills depend upon the spiritual art of interpreting God's signs to the retreatant (Robert Gleason 23-4). A retreatant has a structure of discipline to shelter within and to struggle against. Accepting an Augustinian view of history based upon the combat between Christ and Satan, *Spiritual Exercises* lays down a procedure by which the retreatant can make contact with "the mind that was in Christ, Jesus." The four-week retreat is a silent time of spiritual work, moving from a humbling week-long preparation, through two weeks of meditation upon the public life of Christ, and concluding with meditations upon Christ's risen life. Motifs include service, contemplation, combat with Satan, and indifference to earthly creatures. Just as Frederick's ideal falconer would respect the letter and the spirit of *De Arte Venandi*, Loyola's retreatant ought not merely parrot biblical passages (22).

Convinced that Ignatian discipline means learning how to tolerate God's silence, Roland Barthes interprets *Spiritual Exercises* as a knowledge-discourse that leads to knowledge-power (*Sade/Fourier/Loyola*). *Spiritual Exercises* attempts to transcend history by employing four operations (self-isolation, systematic articulation, rhetorical ordering, theatricalization) that, according to Barthes, effect a change in historical understanding: "the violence that enables it to *exceed* the laws that a society, an ideology, a philosophy establish for themselves in order to agree among themselves in a fine surge of historical intelligibility" (10). To be sure, such violence works suavely on various discursive levels. Ignatius's manual is addressed to the retreat master but also by the master to the retreatant, the retreatant to God, and by God—necessarily a wordless address—to the retreatant (41-2). At the end, one has attained an Ignatian indifference remarkably like the ideal neutrality of a value-free scientific objectivity, something like Frederick's treatise on falconry. We might also appropriately imagine something like Hopkins's own "heart in hiding."

Foucault's *Discipline and Punish* reinforces the human implications of Geoffrey Grigson's image, "these half-dozen tedium's dauphins" trapped in dismal wire cages. The prison illustrates the power of normalization by means of official knowledge-power in modern society (308). Foucault's style of discourse could be adapted both to the Ignatian account of spiritual life and to Frederickian falconry under its sterner aspects.

Foucault lays down a "political technology of the body" (3-31) similar in effect to Frederick's anatomy of birds. Next, allowing for differences in noise levels, we are shown a "spectacle of the scaffold" (32-69), a public arena of punishment, reminiscent of Frederick's account of the spacious but constrained field of falconry. Foucault's "art of punishing" leads through an encyclopaedic "semio-technique of punishment" to the advent of a new politics of the body via a calculated economy of controls (73-103). In a remarkably Frederickian chapter ("The Gentle Way of Punishment"), Foucault praises the "development of a knowledge of the individual" under control by means of verbal and non-verbal discursive signs. Lamenting that in the eighteenth century a "coercive, corporal, solitary, secret model" of punishment came to prevail (104-31), Foucault propounds a major disciplinary theme: "The art of punishing, then, must rest on a whole technology of representation" (104).

Foucault's "Discipline" section (135-228) closely resembles Frederick's method. Punitive principles render bodies docile by a penitentiary art of distribution, control of activity, organization of one's time, and disposition of energies. Procedures include hierarchical observation, normalizing judgment, and regular examination. Holding sway over the entire system is a visual technology like Bentham's panopticon, allowing penal authorities to observe the prisoner at every moment. Such visualization could seem to adapt to relations between prisoner and jailer many features of Frederick's account of the visual contact essential to falconer and falcon.

Foucault describes the closed architecture of the prison itself (231-308). A new historical category—the carceral *per se*—has emerged in western culture: "The carceral texture of society assures both the real capture of the body and its perpetual observation" (304). Society must discipline and punish itself if it is to discipline and punish prison inmates. In Frederickian terms, falcon and falconer must be able to see and thus regulate each other.

Foucault's "carceral city," like Loyola's retreat, helps us to understand both Giacomo's sonnet and *De Arte Venandi*. Historically, as the task of administrating masses of people grew more essential to civilization, a process evolved for controlling the "disciplinary individual" (308). Technicians of behavior devised mechanisms which brought about a turning point: "the arrangement of power-knowledge over individuals." The prison internalized the carceral city. From inside the prison there appears to be "no outside" (301).[11]

The carceral city depends upon knowledge about persons: "Knowable man (soul, individuality, consciousness, conduct, whatever it is called) is the object-effect of this analytical investment, of this domination-observation" (305). A double function operates: "a soul to be known and a subjection to be maintained" (285). Happily, the carceral network of power-knowledge made the human sciences possible (305); unhappily, like the blood sport of falconry, it is underwritten by violence: "we must hear the distant roar of battle" (308).

How do these two disciplinary treatises bear upon Hopkins's literary reinscription of Frederick's discourse? Hopkins, I think, confronts Giacomo's sonnet and Frederick's treatise, two poems he perhaps "has not read," from a precarious position located historically somewhere between *Spiritual Exercises* and *Discipline and Punish*. Falconry involves class distinctions and predatory slaughter; it is one of the "barbaric acts that sometimes underwrite high cultural purposes" (Veeser xi). Likewise, treatises on child-rearing—witness Benjamin Spock's—incorporate Frederickian discipline. In "The Windhover," Hopkins may have perceived that modern human beings would experience stressful conflicts analogous to those embodied in the discipline of falconry, particularly as made aesthetically manageable in Giacomo's self-enclosed sonnet.

Falconry has a literary tradition of more than five-hundred books in a dozen languages covering more than a thousand years. The iconography of falconry invites an Ignatian or a Foucauldian perspective. A practitioner of this difficult sport must accept a "unique subjective relationship with a living bird" (de Chamberlat [vii]). Such a relationship requires expert skills (leathercraft, meteorology, aerodynamics). Falconry has been documented in paintings and sculptures. De Chamberlat's *Falconry and Art* presents hundreds of paintings representing the physical arena of falconry. Generally "superb" in effect, this iconography develops—via representations of places, people, and paraphernalia—a nexus of key motifs: places (landscape and airscape, spaciousness, beauty, centeredness), people (excitement, piety, sobriety, sufferance, service, interdependence), and paraphernalia or "furniture" (technology, control, materiality). An exhilarating sensation of flight colors the effect, but in falcon iconography we regularly view expressions of the sad wisdom of self-restraint.

Falconry is linked with its material furniture. Gloves, lures, perches, cadges, hoods, bags, rings, jesses, creances—these and other implements inculcate disciplined responses that guarantee the falcon's return to the falconer. Both Ignatian and Foucauldian, falconry requires the falconer to act as a substitute parent who understands the bird but never resorts to coercion. Locked into a man-bird-dog triangle, the falconer finds pleasure in the aesthetics of the discipline. The training never ends. Symbolically (and perhaps most sonnet-like), the device called a *cadge* is an enabling but confining material technology: a quadrangular wooden frame with legs and shoulder strap, carried by a man standing inside the frame. It is used to transport birds to the hawking ground, and it may serve us as a material symbol for the falconer's carceral role as an imprisoned servant to the birds he himself imprisons.

Hopkins liberated but disciplined English prosody by his invention of sprung rhythm. We might do well to reflect once again upon Geoffrey Grigson's mordant "Wild Life Park," cited at the head of this chapter, where we are shown the windhover in a cage, "a little-dappled-flattened / Clinging to meshes of fine wire." Grigson gives us a compelling figure for twentieth-century man. Was Hopkins prescient, even prophetic, in his falcon sonnet? We may plausibly inquire if the discipline represented in *De Arte Venandi*—regarded as a redeeming tragic ritual—undergoes a paradoxical reduction via Hopkins's sprung rhythms in "The Windhover" or a dozen other "sprung" poems? Barthes speaks of the "eruptive force of a coined word" (*Sade/Fourier/Loyola* 7). Hopkins's coinage *sprung*, a word that carries a genuinely seminal value (Said, *Beginnings* 266), can signify an escape or release from prison. Hopkins seems to have perceived that modern men would find their freedom only by becoming entrapped within urban constraints. More simply, in the cages of their own selfhood.[12]

Modern history arguably begins as an attempt by art and science to occupy one house (George Levine 3-32). The appeal of Giacomo's sonnet for Frederick and Hopkins might be that it promises a symbolic human habitation. Architecture was one of Frederick's chief avocations. He designed and constructed more than sixty fortresses and castles, in addition to many hunting lodges and *loca solatiorum* (Wood and Fyfe lxxxix-cx). Hopkins, with his own architectural awareness—witness the "rigorous compulsions" enforced by the "mason's levels" ("To Oxford [ii]")—matches, in little, Frederick's sensibilities. We might note too that the homeless Hopkins used houses and homes to represent moral discipline.[13]

The New Historicism reminds us that every expressive act is embedded in a network of material practices (Veeser xi). Likewise, cultures redeem individuals and construct themselves by means of the metaphors produced by materially acculturated individuals (Booth 70). Frederick's and Giacomo's double-bind representation of falcon discipline in sonnet and treatise becomes an energy-producing trope as potent as Henry Adams's Virgin and Dynamo (Lesser 378-80) and no less problematical. If Hopkins in his reading encountered references to Frederick's disciplinary theme in *De Arte Venandi cum Avibus*, he would discover a material metaphor capable of redeeming deracinated human beings via a rigorous discipline. As recently as John Cheever's novel *Falconer* (1977), with its terrifying atmosphere in Falconer's Penitentiary, we see evidence of the enduring value of Frederick's falcon-trope for writers depicting the prison-house of cultural forms (Brombert). Frederick was more interested in human beings than birds. Only a literal-minded reader would overlook how *De Arte Venandi* adapts itself to the discipline of human beings.[14]

Hopkins produced a great Victorian sonnet by drawing upon the unlikely subject of falconry, a decidedly ancient, even outmoded, practice. Each in its own way—Giacomo's sonnet form, Frederick's *De Arte Venandi*, Loyola's *Spiritual Exercises*, and the Foucauldian prison—dialectically triggered historical turning points. Dialectical imagination attempts to perceive turning points from the inside, but revolutionary turning points occur as moments of confusion, disorientation, and *aporia*. As readers, we attempt to confront not only historiographical traces but also history in process (Brown, "Turning" 9-23). For Frederick and for Hopkins, groping for metaphors which could shape a vision of the future, the falcon is a centering sign of dialectical turning or crisis-consciousness.[15]

Hopkins's falcon, erupting at an intersection of tradition and individual talent, carries an ethical charge. His falcon-centered poem, with its theme of exaltation tempered by humility, resembles a sonnet by Frederick himself. Here may be the Bloomian precursor poem that the later poet never read. Frederick anticipated Hopkins with a sonnet-theme of modest self-fulfillment through ground-hugging self-denial. As Englished by Oppenheimer, Frederick's poem reads like prudent advice but also like a proleptic gloss upon "The Windhover."

Balance, providence and true refinement
Make any man both savvy and aware,
And every sort of grace means better judgment
And every sort of wealth produces care.

No mass of money, no matter how abounding,
Can make a coward a man of bravery.
Only habits of life with solid grounding
Can offer people true nobility.

The man placed in a lordly high position,
Who swims in money, falls hardest in the muck,
Believing his rank to be a solid fact.

That's why the wise won't jump beyond his station,
To greater heights presented him by luck,
But always keeps his tastefulness and tact.

(Oppenheimer 65)[16]

In other words, sheer plod makes plow down sillion shine. In "The Wind-hover," the falconry trope is overheated by sprung-rhythm urgencies; in Frederick's poem, it is under-determined, refined to a shadow. Yet, by some cultural process not easy to understand—surely not mere coincidence—this is very likely one of the historiographical discourses against which Hopkins shadow boxes.

Frederick's sonnet and "The Windhover" develop one concept: grounded habits of life prevent one's leaping beyond one's proper place. For both king-poet and priest-poet, falconry symbolizes the disciplined consciousness we need in our encounters with nature, self, and God. Frederick's poem and "The Windhover" form a chiasmus in that one poem sublimates the discipline of falconry in a forthright ethical statement whereas the other bodies forth a disciplinary ethic in the form of an acute consciousness of falcon, plow, and embers. Such a process, simultaneous building-up and building-down, human beings regularly use to constitute themselves as fully human (Giddens 49-95). Frederick named his treatise an "art" of falconry. Could his dialectical movement between pure science and literary art soberly imply that objective science may have its limits?

In my chapter 2, we saw that poems are written with a final resting place—more properly a living space—in mind. "The Windhover," in its antithetical relation to Giacomo's sonnet and Frederick's *De Arte Ven-andi*, exhibits just such a need for legitimation. We can propose of Hop-kins's backward-looking poem what Barthes concluded about historical criticism: "[It] is not an 'homage' to the truth of the past or to the truth of 'others'—[rather] it is a construction of the intelligibility of [its] own time" ("Criticism?" 260). Hopkins's poems appeared at long last in the twentieth century, and we know that "The Windhover" has helped to constitute our century's rhythmical and moral intelligence.

By Hopkins's time, the introspection induced by Giacomo's invention became in many instances a retreat into the mind, necessitating the human science of psychiatry (Fass). The sonneteer must always be haunted by an anxiety attendant upon a fear lest no formal solution to the octave's formal problem be forthcoming in the sestet. Such anxiety likewise char-acterizes falconry: "This is a moment of intense, heart-fluttering excite-ment, even for the most experienced falconer. Will the bird come back on seeing the lure? Its safe return signifies that the battle is won" (de Chamberlat 20). Emotions common to falconry equal the love-sickness of the Renaissance sonnet as well as the sonnet's longing for completion in some logic-effect: "For [the falconer] is always haunted by the fear of losing the companion to whom he has devoted so much time and effort, and with whom he has shared so many stirring moments" (14). The crisis-inducing, crisis-resolving sonnet form probably influenced Freder-ick's appreciation of falconry, of discipline, of experience, of science, of truth. And it probably influenced Hopkins in similar ways.[17]

Historically, the lore of falconry is always in danger of being lost (Salvin and Brodrick 1). We may continue to wonder: did Hopkins directly know *De Arte Venandi*? We cannot be sure. Hopkins critics gen-erally attend to other matters, being mainly concerned either to validate the orthodoxy of Hopkins's theology or construe his inscapes and his sprung rhythm metrics. Given Hopkins's interest in nature, he could have encountered the classic *Falconry in the British Isles* by Salvin and Brodrick, published twice (1855; 1873) before he wrote "The Windhover" in 1877. This famous book makes no mention of Frederick or *De Arte Venandi*, but most books on falconry do cite the great treatise (Harting 168-69; de Chamberlat 17).[18] Of course, any Victorian reader could know Frederick from reading Dante's *Divine Comedy*.

Hopkins could understand, as Frederick himself should have under-stood, that falconry may disorient and unbalance even a seasoned veteran. The strenuous discipline can seem like a "skilful helter-skelter process" (Richard Oke, in Wood and Fyfe 593). Hopkins never tells us if his bird is broken to falconry, and interpretations (Dunne 305-13; Bump, "Reading" 129-45) regularly identify the bird with Christ or nature. But, as in previous episodes of Hopkins's crisis-consciousness, we ask again, what of history? Perhaps we may guess correctly if we keep in mind that a falcon is a bird consciously introduced into a ritualized art.

Two readings of "The Windhover" offer themselves in the historical context Oppenheimer invites us to explore. First, we might assume that Hopkins's bird is not broken to falconry. Assuming an episode of the raw rather than the cooked, a paraphrase would read as follows. This morning I glimpsed a splendid natural sight, a kestrel in flight, at once bright, assertive, sprightly, and ecstatic as a fine horse prancing on a long rein. From my privileged perspective, I was moved by the bird's actions, combining natural gusto and beauty as it pushed against its natural limits. My epiphany was almost unbearable. Yet I realized that the humblest things push themselves to their limits, in the process displaying an individuating brilliance.

Next, let us imagine that the bird is not the "gaudy and irresponsible" natural or "raw" creature of Sulloway's version (123) but has in fact been trained to hunt. The transitive verb *caught* invokes the entire discipline, with its snares, traps, and restraints. The nouns *minion*, *kingdom*, and *dauphin* induce a sense of royalty, of Frederickian power. The capitalized noun *Falcon*, more specific than would be essential to a poem celebrating bird-flight in general, invites or requires us to think of falconry. The technical image of riding, striding, ringing on a rein, swinging, and sweeping invites us to appreciate a discipline with a disciplined eye. Every treatise on falconry emphasizes mastery, so we are prepared for Hopkins's exclamation over "the mastery of the thing." Frederick himself might thus exuberantly have exclaimed. Nothing in the body of the poem enforces a Christ-chevalier equation (*Poetical* 379). However, Frederick was descended from Norman kings, so he makes a plausible candidate for the utterance "O my chevalier!"

A paraphrase would run as follows. This morning, like an observant falconer, I observed a hunting bird going through its paces, most royally as befits its lineage. I found nothing disappointing in the bird's performance as it enacted falconry exercises. I was moved to think of the long line of brilliant men (not excluding Frederick?) who preserved and advanced this dangerous sport with its fusion of energy and restraint. Yet I am not surprised by the bird's performance, since everything in culture (plow) and nature (ember) flashes forth such radiance. Anything intent upon being itself will give off signs of its self, and in human life such behavior carries an ethical charge. The discipline is all.

The truth may lie somewhere between these two readings. Perhaps we have here an artist rejecting any one answer, preferring instead to enact at once a crisis, a question, and a consciousness. "The Windhover" excites and baffles readers in part because Hopkins sets his face against Frederick's secular enterprise, a liberating but crippling program symbolized by the furniture of falconry. He gives us a lowly kestrel instead of a magnificent gerfalcon, yet he convinces us that it too can be splendid. In the final triplet, he insinuates another antithetical premise: a plough, like a trained bird, may reflect brilliance, but an ember, like any untrained creature, may even more richly "gash gold-vermilion."

Hopkins would perhaps reject Frederick's skeptical program for Christian Europe, but he does so in a self-enclosed literary form invented under Frederick's skeptical program for historical change. He never tells us whether the speaker of his poem is adept at falconry. He uses the final pair of images, plow and ember, to reduce himself to an empty character at an empty center, but an empty center or cipher on which the preoccupied falcon can count, a point where counting and moral existence can begin. Hopkins thus ironically realizes Frederick's ambitious modern program. He employs sprung rhythms to release, but odd diacritics to control, Frederick's bird within Giacomo's tight sonnet form. Thereby, he locks the bird, his reader, and himself into discursive constraints and a new form of consciousness appropriate to the constraints of modern life.

In the history of the sonnet, poem after poem expresses the longing of a pent-up soul to fly away to some perfect world (Oppenheimer 122-23). Yet the form also functions as "a tiny emblem of human power and involvement in life's perplexing rhythm" (Bermann 49). A curious forward-into-the-past motif emerges when we consider "The Windhover" as analogous, if abstrusely so, to Hopkins's gestures against Henry Thomas Buckle's ideological historiography, or to his refusal to enter literary history, or to his rewriting of Longfellow's reinscription of American history. At the heart of this paradox are to be found the dialectics between science (Frederick's treatise) and art (Giacomo's sonnet). Given science's ameliorations of human suffering, it threatens to obliterate all competing paradigms. As Gadamer says: "The shift of the ontological definition of the aesthetic to the sphere of [mere] aesthetic appearance has its theoretical basis in the fact that the domination of the scientific epistemological model leads to the discrediting of all the possibilities of knowing that lie outside this new method" (75). Hopkins certainly perceived and resisted the early stages of this historical shift.

Science is first, and the rest are nowhere. From inside, there appears to be no outside. Hopkins's reliance upon poetry becomes historically interesting when he bases a famous sonnet upon the falconry trope that Giacomo and Frederick used to initiate modern consciousness. This description of two falcons calling to each other, over a time-fissure of seven-hundred years, ends in a reflexive irony. Only once did Hopkins write about falconry. Yet in humbling himself to this outmoded discipline, he bequeathed a new understanding of the modern condition. "The Windhover" can be viewed as an erotic poem—buckling, plowing, gashing—about a bird known vulgarly as the windfucker (John Gleason). Geoffrey Grigson uses "Wild Life Park" to emphasize this linguistic oddity and to depict Hopkins's windhover in its most degraded condition, on public display in a filthy wire cage.

Hopkins apparently saw that the diminutive but intense sonnet form represents the predicament of modern man, living in a world where living space will shrink and where internal self-restraint will become more necessary and more difficult to maintain. Grigson's updating but downgrading of "The Windhover" fulfills the grim prophecy represented by Hopkins both in his great falcon sonnet and in a political poem like "Tom's Garland."

Tom's Garland:

on the Unemployed

Tom—gárlanded with squat and surly stéel
Tom; then Tom's fallowbootfellow piles píck

By him and rips out rockfire homeforth—sturdy Dick;
Tom Heart-at-ease, Tòm Navvy; he is all for his méal

Sure, 's bed now. Low be it: lustily he his lòw lót (féel   5
That ne'er need hunger, Tom; Tom seldom sick,

Seldomer heartsóre; that treads through, prickproof, thick
Thousands of thorns, thoughts) swíngs though. Commonweal
Little Í reck ho! lacklevel in, if all had bread:

What! cóuntry is honoúr enough in all us—lordly head,   10
With heaven's lights high hung round, or, mother-gróund
That mammocks, mighty foot. But nó way sped,
Nor mind nor mainstrength; góld go garlanded
With, perilous, O nó; nor yet plod safe shod sound;

                    Ûndenizened, beyond bound   15
Of earth's glory, èarth's ease, all; noone, nowhere,

In wide the world's weal; rắre gŏld, bŏld stèel, bắre
                    In both; cằre, but shằre cắre—
This, by Despắir, bred Hangdog dull; by Rage,
Manwolf, worse; and their packs infest the age.   20

(*Poetical* 195; #171)

By reconstructing the disciplinary falcon trope earlier constructed by
Frederick II and Giacomo da Lentino, in a literary form they invented,
"The Windhover" takes us back to the moment in history when an emperor and his lawyer sat down to invent the dialogue of the mind with
itself and foreshadowed the encaging consciousness Hopkins (and we ourselves) came to inherit.

Interchapter 4

"world without event":
History and Antithesis in Poems #136-79 (1879-89)

(1)   Now Time's Andromeda on this rock rude.
                                         (*Poetical* 163; #138)

(2)   The supersessive shifting of descriptions of the world—
        the scientific history that describes the principles and
        shapes of constant supersession—leaves no possibility for
        a resting place for the mind.
                                         Kemp 161

(3)   Yet God (that hews mountain and continent,
        Earth, all, out; who, with trickling increment,
        Veins violets and tall trees makes more and more)
        Could crowd career with conquest while there went
        Those years and years by of world without event
        That in Majorca Alfonso watched the door.

                                         (*Poetical* 201; #176)

Throughout his life, Hopkins warred within himself over many issues.
When he faced up to his own antithetical spirit, he would very likely

produce a lasting piece of literature. Robert Martin characterizes Hopkins thus:

> As a man he was torn apart when he was in doubt, but it was pre-
> cisely when he was impelled, perhaps neurotically, to examine all
> aspects of a problem, including its unattractive side, that his poetry
> came most fully alive. (263)

The final grouping of poems in the 1990 edition includes poems which have established his place in literary history as a major minor poet.

A world of constant agitation may be, paradoxically, a "world without event." As Karsten Harries thinks, modern art aspires toward instantane-ousness and, hence, toward an obliteration of time and history (82). One impression induced by a reading of Hopkins's late poems—including such energized performances as "Felix Randal," "The Leaden Echo and the Golden Echo," "Spelt from Sibyl's Leaves," "Tom's Garland," and "That Nature is a Heraclitean Fire and of the comfort of the Resurrec-tion"—is of an immediacy, at times amounting to an urgency and even a frenzy, resulting from his poetic forms' barely containing his over-loaded emotional content. A familiar phrase from the Heraclitean poem—"In a flash, at a trumpet crash"—aptly characterizes this rapid-fire pace.

To understand such urgent prosodic effects we might have to turn to poems like those of Emily Dickinson, where condensed form iconically expresses an indeterminacy, an immediacy, a sense of reality as NOW! and hence as being true to a modern sense of instability in nature and culture (Hagenbüchle). The overall effect in Hopkins is that of a "world without event" constituted predominantly of rapid-fire events that leave no resting place for the mind. Recalling the Viconian principle that his-tory itself is engendered only by the removal of immediacy (Said, *Begin-nings* 373), we can see, as with Hopkins's committing his consciousness to fragments, the poet struggling to remain one step ahead of time and thereby to deny history.

In the poems from "The Cheery Beggar" to "To R. B." Hopkins has come a long way from the direct historiography of "The Escorial." He provides a gallery of characters (bugler boy, farm laborer, schoolboy, soldier, unemployed navvy). He depicts religious and social events (first communion, wedding, school play). He develops strong themes (sin, sacrifice, pollution of nature, worship, time's passage, beauty). Even in time-burdened poems like "Andromeda" and "St. Alphonsus Rodriguez," some timeless force such as myth or piety effectively overrides or obviates mere history. These poems depict some of the most intense personal experiences ever recorded, but history has almost entirely vanished.

On the other hand, if history has vanished under the combined pressures of Hopkins's desperate piety, exacerbated sprung rhythms, escape into nature or immediacy of sense experience, nevertheless certain antithetical sentiments are present in abundance. In order to observe antithetical ideas and emotions at work, we need only re-read the Terrible Sonnets (the Sonnets of Desolation, as MacKenzie labels them [*Poetical* 443-45]). Here we witness the dismaying spectacle of a devout priest undergoing moments of melancholy, terror, darkness, confusion, agonizing temptation, and isolation—emotions as painful to contemplate as any ever rendered in verse.

Justus quidem tu es, Domine, si disputem tecum; verumtamen justa
loquar ad te: quare via impiorum prosperatur? etc. (Jerem. xii: I)

Thou art indeed just, Lord, if I contend
With thee; but, sir, so what I plead is just.
Whý do sínners' ways prosper? and why must
Dísappóintment all I endeavour end?
Wert thou my enemy, O thou my friend,   5
How wouldst thou worse, I wonder, than thou dost
Defeat, thwart me? Oh, the sots and thralls of lust
Do in spare hours more thrive than I that spend,
Sir, life upon thy cause. See, banks and brakes
Now, leavèd how thick! lacèd they are again   10
With fretty chervil, look, and fresh wind shakes
Them; birds build—but not I build; no, but strain,
Time's eunuch, and not breed one work that wakes.
Mine, O thou lord of life, send my roots rain.

(*Poetical* 201; #177)

Experiencing these private terrors, these "events in the mind," we might reasonably feel that, just as consoling nature has disappeared from Hopkins's purview, so too has human history been denied. Hopkins makes us feel that he is very nearly the first human ever to suffer such agonized consciousness.

Many questions present themselves when one inquires into a poet's conversation with history. Issues of metaphysics, origins, governing images and tropes, contingencies and facticities of human life, problems of separateness and community, memory and eschatology, consciousness and personality—all these and many more urge themselves upon us in our inquiry. We feel compelled to wonder: is Hopkins a millennialist, an apocalyptic, an evolutionist? Does he view history as necessarily cyclical or linear? Is there a simple or a complex relation obtaining between Hopkins's aesthetic principles and his view of history?

In the modern world, everything, including God, nature, time, place, and man, seems to come under the sway of history, with history being regarded variously as bleakly purposeless or grimly teleological (Simpson 240-41). To arrive at some formulation of a writer's vision of history is no easy undertaking. How difficult such an effort can be, and the tortuous rhetoric one may resort to in the effort, can be seen in the following statement concerning another Catholic writer, Flannery O'Connor.

> O'Connor's metaphysical sense, which derives from her Catholic belief, is the intrinsic foundation for both her vision of history and her artistic technique. Moreover, I assume her metaphysics, historical vision, and artistic technique all derive specifically from her belief in Christ's Incarnation and Redemption of human history—a belief which, ideally, made her historical sense and her artistic sense inseparable within the creative act. (Desmond 3)

As Desmond thinks, first comes a theology or theological predisposition, then a metaphysics, and then, somehow in tandem, an artistic technique and a vision of history.

Since I commenced my own study under the skeptical shadow of David Hume, I can sympathize with any such effort to establish priority and cause-effect relations between motives buried deep within a human psyche. If Hopkins is a Christian, how can he entertain any view of history other than Augustine's view, by reason of which the only history that matters is Christ's war with Satan? And yet, even an Augustinian view may undergo changes in the actual life of a human being as gifted and conflicted as Gerard Manley Hopkins.

It would be too glib to say of Hopkins that in his end was his beginning, but as I examine his responses to historiography, I must repeatedly look back at his first gesture at authorship. "The Escorial" won a prize and showed a certain kind of historical promise, but at least one critic speaks of "The Escorial" as "soft, loose material" which is a "strange beginning for a poet whose later utterance was to go the limits of tension and austerity" (McChesney 2). Perhaps, though, material soft and loose might in fact be the perfect material for a poet aiming ultimately at tension and austerity. More to the point, we are reminded that beginnings are inherently interesting and problematical, as Edward Said has demonstrated in *Beginnings: Intention and Method*.

Said pursues a single purpose: to locate and identify a type of literary production characteristic of the deracinated modern world. He focuses on the last quarter of the nineteenth century, Hopkins's own mature period. At that time, major writers began to produce literary works that repeatedly begin themselves anew amidst numerous cultural perplexities and ruptures. Said rejects the notion of any "origin" stemming from some preexistent mode of being such as God, Nature, or History. He prefers to believe in the writer's ability to initiate some self-fashioning "beginning." He writes that a beginning is impossible without a willed intention to continue writing, an intention that itself creates value and meaning.

Said discovers a relation between beginning and being. In the modern world, where traditional discourses have been undermined, we should always inquire where a poem, or a poetical oeuvre, or a poetical career, begins. With the first word, the idea, the literary mode one adopts, the historical period one lives in and through? Does one's beginning come from an Other or from one's own lonely but inventive self? Said's account of the complexities inherent in modern literary beginnings draws upon many literary artists. His major exemplar is Gerard Manley Hopkins.

Said's speculations upon Hopkins's numerous beginnings touch upon several important concepts: the modern struggle to become a writer, tensions between repetition and innovation, construction of a literary persona and career, biological analogies with writing, parallels between God's fecundity and a writer's sexuality, and the writer's self-sacrifice of his literary gifts. Said's final comment on Hopkins's paradoxical habit of beginning but not beginning, of being a poet who would be no poet, focuses on Hopkins's final word *explanation*, "the poorest substitute for a poetic text" (274).

> In a very poignant way, Hopkins recognizes that his "creative" text is now behind him; he has passed it because he can no longer add to it. In common with most modern writers, Hopkins regards the text and his career as entities that stand apart from the rest of his life; what the text preserves is a potent authority that seems to taunt its beginning source in the author himself. (275)

Assuming, then, that beginnings, no less than closures, reward our closest scrutiny, any amount of critical attention paid to "The Escorial" seems justified. Truly, in Hopkins's beginning ("lonely began") is his end.

To seem the stranger lies my lot, my life
Among strangers. Father and mother dear,
Brothers and sisters are in Christ not near
And he my peace/my parting, sword and strife,
England, whose honour O all my heart woos, wife   5
To my creating thought, would neither hear
Me, were I pleading, plead nor do I: Ĩ wẽar-
Y of idle a being but by where wars are rife.
I am in Ireland now; now Í am at a thîrd
Remove. Not but in all removes I can   10
Kind love both give and get. Only what word
Wisest my heart breeds   { baffling heaven's dark ban
                              { dark heaven's baffling ban
Bars or hell's spell thwarts. { This to hoard unheard,
                              { Thoughts hoarded unheard
Heard unhéeded,   { leaves me a lonely began.
                  { [leave]

(Poetical 181; #154)

At this point, I need to reprise the main antithetical points I have already established in interchapters 1-3. Hopkins began his poetical career
as a prizewinning historical poet whose set piece "The Escorial," written
with aid from his father, contained twenty-four explanatory footnotes
referring to details from one of his primary sources, Prescott's *History of
the Reign of Philip II*. He would never again write a poem anything like
"The Escorial," but to a striking degree the poem establishes denial and
related motives central to his reactions against historiography. By relying
heavily upon a written source, Hopkins demonstrated his scholarly abilities, but he likewise thereby qualified or diminished some dimensions of
his own powers of invention. By repeating some of Prescott's information
and opinions, he demonstrated powers of objectivity but also subordinated
his youthful genius to historiographical materials that in other perspectives might prove self-contradictory. He implicitly condemned the very
Catholic tradition, including the Jesuit order, that would one day provide
him with a spiritual home. With "The Escorial," he became a likely candidate for success and fame; later he would repeatedly deny such ambition. He produced a finished work that took on a limited public life of its
own, but for some time thereafter, and for prolonged stretches of his life,
he would not finish any work of such scope. He collaborated with his
father, who symbolically expunged his son's very presence in the poem.
On the whole, it seems reasonable to conjecture that "The Escorial" might

play a crucial role in Hopkins's developing attitude toward writing and particularly toward the writing of history.

Some critics detect knotty implications in "The Escorial." The youthful Hopkins, in writing about the martyred St. Lawrence's sufferings, seems "self-prophetic" on the score of his own future sufferings. By contrast, a cloying richness in the verse almost borders on masochism, as Hopkins betrays an inclination to dwell upon physical torture ("crack'd flesh . . . hissing on the grate"). Hopkins thus wavers between asceticism and masochism. In addition, Hopkins's notes to "The Escorial" announce the poet's lifelong "passion for explanation."

Many levels of complication testify to Hopkins's unfolding antithetical view of history. An antithetical Hopkins "rejects" Gothic and other forms of architecture; the theme of the poem may be "clashing faiths"; Hopkins is "ideologically inconsistent"; he struggles to blend religious themes with sensuousness; his subject is "austerity," which he explores until he reaches the grim conclusion that only death can relieve human suffering; he alternately sympathizes with and condemns Philip II. Thus, at the beginning of Hopkins's journey toward achieved consistency between self-sacrifice and art as a sacramentalist activity, we can glimpse a deep-seated if imperfectly expressed antithetical conflict.

The dual strands of history and antithetical impulses in "The Escorial" establish historiography itself as an intricate and deep-seated challenge to consciousness. This challenging complex subsequently submerges and becomes a subterranean current that will sporadically vex but animate Hopkins's creative psyche. In numerous respects, "The Escorial" is the real dragon in the gate, Hopkins's self-fashioned dragon, of his poetic achievement. The more we reexamine "The Escorial," the more we see not so much what might have been—had Hopkins for example followed the Browning model by basing poems on specific readings in history—but what actual results proceed from his rejecting a mode of writing in which he had succeeded early in life. Hopkins appears in this light to be, as the Irish say, someone who cannot stand prosperity.

The most recent study of the Escorial, Kubler's illustrated *Building the Escorial* (1982), reminds us, as we leave Hopkins's first poem, how rich the Escorial can be for the aesthetic imagination. Hopkins, we remember, became to no small degree a mannerist poet (Storey). As Kubler thinks, the mannerist style in architecture and other arts provides rich materials for psychohistorical analysis (124-26). The aesthetic principle underlying the Escorial is essentially Augustinian (131-34), one that in various ways roots itself in the mind of the Jesuit priest Gerard Manley Hopkins. The challenge to Hopkins's hyperactive mind that could presumably arise from the historical research he carried out in composing "The Escorial" might have produced a different Hopkins from the unique Hopkins we actually inherit. Perhaps we should leave "The Escorial" on a parting note from Kubler: "Old buildings still require the historian to discover the values that were intended by their makers" (126).

It seems pointless to ignore that Hopkins's various strategies for denying history relate in intricate and subtle ways back to his first and most historiographical poem.

Chapter 5

"most secret catgut of the mind": Hopkins, Music, and the Erasure of History

(1)   *All art constantly aspires toward the condition of music.*
                          Walter Pater, "The School of Giorgione"

(2)   I am teaching myself the piano so as to be independent of
       others.   Hopkins, *Journal* 241

During Hopkins's lifetime, when symbolism was becoming a chief mode of literary representation, music became an important symbol for emotions of the ineffable kind (Hertz 21). It thereby became a means by which beleaguered Victorians—including Hopkins—found temporary refuge from their troubles. In its evanescence and its escapist possibilities, music might seem to be the least historical of human experiences. Suppose, though, that we ask yet again: what about history? What if we recall the Nietzschean belief, echoed by Frye and Kramer, that music can annihilate history by erasing verbal inscriptions of the human past?

In an earlier episode of "Hopkins Against History," I seemed to take the poet to task for electing a silence peculiar to the non-publishing poet, the poet who would be no poet. In this next, and final, episode, I may seem to be taking to task the overworked genius who wrote "Henry Purcell" and "Spelt from Sibyl's Leaves" for pretending to possess a cultural competence, in music, where he had little or none. Music occasioned some of Hopkins's strangest behavior, but verbal musicality contributed to some of his finest poems. Witness the following.

Binsey Poplars

felled 1879

My aspens dear, whose airy cages quelled,
Quélled or quenched in leaves the leaping sun,

Áll félled, félled, are áll félled;
   Of a fresh and following folded rank
      Not spared, not one   5
      That dandled a sandalled
    Shádow that swam or sank
On meadow and river and wínd-wándering

   weed-winding bank.

  Ó if we but knéw whát we do
      Whén we delve or hew—   10
   Háck and rack the growing green!
     Since Country is so tender
    To tóuch, her béing só slénder,
    That, like this sleek and seeing ball
    But a prick will make no eye at all,   15
    Whére we, even where we mean
      To mend her we end her,
       Whén we hew or delve:
 Áfter-comers cannot guess the beauty been
   Tén or twélve, ónly ten or twelve   20
    Strókes of havoc únsélve
     The sweet especial scene,
   Rúral scene, a rural scene,
   Swéet especial rural scene.

(Poetical 156-57; #130)

    My purpose is not to rebuke the poet who bequeathed such beautiful language but rather once again heuristically to hypothesize where this ontological prosodist came from, this poet whose antihistoricist aesthetic could produce poems of such flawless musicality.

    Perhaps, though, I have already hypothesized enough. Perhaps it is enough to have delineated an adversive Hopkins working at cross-purposes with Henry Thomas Buckle but in the process immortalizing that forgotten historian in one of the greatest English sonnets? Perhaps it is enough to have represented a recalcitrant poet as he refuses to risk censure by ordering his poems in a lyrical assortment? Perhaps it is enough to have demonstrated how a rivalrous Hopkins rewrote but raised to a higher level of art an American national ballad? Or, perhaps, it is enough to have shown how a Victorian sonneteer intuited a historical connection between the discipline of the sonnet form and the discipline of falconry, in the process refining Victorian consciousness of modern man's reduced spiritual circumstances?

Enough is usually enough, but in this case, enough may not be quite enough. One further episode remains to be examined. Hopkins spoke confidently of music in connection with his poetry and also in and of itself. Music, as the most evanescent form of human expression, is potentially an antithetical mode. This final episode in Hopkins's crisis-consciousness begins with a new question: what is the musical dimension, if any, of Hopkins's antithetical response to history? My procedures, after establishing a Victorian framework, will be to examine a handful of poems in which Hopkins turns to music. These include five poems with undeniably "musical" titles: "The Loss of the Eurydice," "At the Wedding March," "The Bugler's First Communion," "Henry Purcell," and a piece once labelled "On a Piece of Music."

Cultivated people of Hopkins's generation valued music as a social act with implications for gentility, social cohesion, love of beauty, morality, progress, historical amelioration, cosmopolitanism, and culture in its old-fashioned sense. In this final episode, Hopkins almost comes off badly as pretending to have mastered a Victorian art that he was unwilling or unable to study in any approved way. More to the point, he comes off as a typical Victorian resorting to music as an alternative to the harshness of modern existence. Once again, we recognize an antithetical spirit acting out a protest against inscriptions of history, at times against the "little history" inscribed in his own poems. History, particularly literary history, would be associated in Hopkins's mind with the orthodox running rhythm—e.g., iambic pentameter—that largely dominated English poetry in the Victorian era. Hopkins rebelled. We can console ourselves that by making a musicalized sprung rhythm the linchpin of his literary enterprise, Hopkins bodied forth not music proper but verbal acoustics, a mode in which human consciousness takes on rhythms of work and play (Bücher 331).

Writing history may be, as Novick thinks, like nailing jelly to the wall, but the historian usually has hammer, nail, jelly, and wall. In dealing with music, we have the hammer, the nail, and the wall, but the object to be nailed seems, under one's very gaze, to vanish. Treitler's query—"How is historical thought about music possible?" (1)—may be understood to motivate my inquiry. The antithetical Hopkins takes on a new appearance as we witness him—in a series of gestures alternately arbitrary, arrogant, pathetic, and heroic—rejecting history by aspiring toward a Paterian condition of music but finally opting for the kinds of truth possible only to authentic poetic language.[1]

During Hopkins's lifetime, music was becoming part of a "large cultural act of human self-definition" (Kramer vii). Occasionally, Hopkins decided that like many of his fellow men he would, so to speak, refine himself out of historical existence by redefining himself aesthetically through music. Before we condemn such gestures as escapism, we should recall that English writers from Collins to Coleridge had felt compelled to acknowledge a growing uncertainty about language's expressive and representational powers. Their replacement for language was frequently some misty and even mystical type of music (Kevin Barry 178). We are called upon to distinguish between Hopkins's musical escapism in his tormented personal life and the actual poems that resulted from his musically conditioned linguistic consciousness.

A peripheral but interesting problem is Hopkins's occasional pretensions to musical genius. An instructive framing device is provided by Samuel Johnson and Carl Jung. For Jung at his most mystical, music emerges as a primal psychic force that precludes or predates musical training: "The mysterious interconnectedness of word and music, then, reaches beyond the known into the unknown—endowing the participant with a gift of great magnitude" (Knapp 211). By contrast, wise old Samuel Johnson recognized that music, more so than any other form of expression, requires training: "There is nothing, I think, in which the power of art is shown so much as in playing the fiddle" (Ehrlich 1). Hopkins himself never advanced beyond the stage of a cultivated Englishman's musical sensibility, but his poetical engagement with music proved fruitful.

Hopkins's most evanescent reaction to the nightmare of Victorian history should be understood within guidelines provided by a literary musicologist. Steven Scher thematizes his essay "Literature and Music" by means of an epigraph hinting at the difficulty, even the impossibility, of any poet's escaping from words to music. Thus: the motive power which drives a poet to music may be a "longing for the lost Paradise, for that original unity which can never be regained." Hopkins, I believe, yearns with an intense desire for a lost paradise as represented in the myth of Orpheus, for a fusion of word and tone. He hints at some inward private knowledge—"most secret catgut of the mind" (*Correspondence* 110)— some hidden access to unheard melodies, that both places him at the center of Victorian crisis-consciousness and also motivates his own poetic consciousness.[2] In the long run, though, the inner music he heard was less like formal music and more like some melancholy music of humanity.

Scher cautions anyone who would negotiate the tricky waters between poetry and music. Despite the familiar assumption that music is the art most closely allied with literature, many correlations prove to be illusory. Parallels are proposed by persons lacking any specialized knowledge of the two disciplines. Practitioners of musico-literary criticism begin their explanations at too high a level of generalization. Too often we find affinities and analogies even before we acquire any knowledge of the basic principles, critical possibilities, and interpretive strategies of the two arts (225-26). Scher might be describing Hopkins's own solipsistic reliance upon the "secret catgut of the mind" and his plans for studying music on his own so as to become "independent of others."[3]

Relations between literature and music should be divided into three categories. First, music and literature: vocal music, where text and composition are inextricably bound; oratorios, cantatas, madrigals, operas, and ballads. In such symbiotic works, both components must be simultaneously present. Musicologists have largely dominated this area of study, which asks where and how word interacts with tone. Literary critics have also studied musical settings of poetic texts, questions of priority, and questions of appropriateness of text to musical score. Second, literature in music: impact of literature on music, as in program music; literarization of music as distinct from pure or abstract music; tone poems and similar expressive pieces. A long-standing theoretical debate considers the question whether music, being made up of sounds, can in truth carry any conceptual meaning whatsoever. Third, music in literature: this category embraces exclusively literary productions. Here we see how poets attempt to musicalize literature or to verbalize music. As if anticipating the problem with Hopkins, Scher thinks that literary texts cannot transcend the confines of literary texture and become musical texts. The most rewarding study of literature will be to look for manifestations of music in literature (226-29).[4]

Scher's cautionary account of the pitfalls endangering all efforts to fuse word and tone should make us skeptical of any Victorian escapes— including Hopkins's—into the lotus land of pure music. Biographies of Hopkins make it evident that his sporadic gestures toward musicianship were quite conventionally Victorian even when they bordered on the absurd. Granting that, we should still remind ourselves that at some deep psychic or psycho-physical level, some somatic level where rhythm in general fuses with music and prosody to form a consciousness of life's basic processes, Hopkins was on the right track. Witness his intensive debate with Darwin's anthropocentric view of sound and language, a debate in which Hopkins defends a logocentric view (Nixon 132-42). Witness, too, his remarkable invention of sprung rhythm, surely one of the nineteenth century's most musicalizing efforts to liberate and redefine human energies.[5]

Joseph Brodsky defines prosody as "a repository of time within language" (357). In phenomenological terms, cathectic rhythm represents our effort to "flood the channels of passing time with a sense of the relationships that constitute us, so that they can there acquire a sense of tangible presence." The sprung rhythm that is Hopkins's chief contribution to our civilization can be understood as a "convergence" of the music of poetry and the poetry of music: "the shaped flow of time produced by the unfolding of a structural rhythm, especially where that rhythm has a cathectic basis" (Kramer 241). We are dealing here with something like a Freudian electric charge, but we might be describing Hopkins's antihistorical consciousness that the world is "charged with" God's presence.

God's Grandeur

The world is charged with the grándeur of God.
    It will flame out, like shining from shook foil;

    It gathers to a greatness, like the ooze of oil
Crushed. Why do men then now not reck his rod?
Génerátions have trod, have trod, have trod;   5
    And all is seared with trade; bleared, smeared, with toil;
    And wears man's smudge and shares man's smell: the soil
Is bare now, nor can foot feel, being shod.

Ánd, for all this, náture is never spent;
    There lives the dearest freshness deep down things;   10
And though the last lights off the black West went
    Oh, morning, at the brown brink eastward, springs—
Because the Holy Ghost óver the bent
    World broods with warm breast and with ah! bright wings.

                                    (Poetical 139; #111)

Hopkins's intense consciousness of self interacts dialectically with his excitable sprung rhythms. Kramer does not cite Hopkins—few historians of music do—but he provides one viable context for construing as antithetical gestures against history the poet's gestures toward music as a substitute for poetry. One impression induced by Hopkins's musical expectations is that they resemble the wish for simultaneous self-excitation and self-oblivion as described by Nietzsche in "On Music and Words" (Dalhaus, *Between* 116).[6]

Before we look at Hopkins's consciousness of music as a means to expunge himself from history, we might take a clue from Wilhelm Dilthey on the subject of music: "The point of departure is the actual world of sound itself" (373). From childhood onward, Hopkins took an interest in many kinds of sounds. He responded to raw sounds such as a bird song or the human voice. Precociously talented in word-play, he speculated upon various pronunciations of Latin words by his fellow Jesuits; he discussed foreign languages; he speculated that differences in auditory habits might account for differences in speech sounds; he noted dialectal variations; he was aware of the influence of Welsh poetry upon the consonantal-chiming in his own verses; he lamented the auditory degeneration of modern English; he noted the existence of "alto cuckoos and soprano cuckoos"; he winced at the crash of a felled tree. Even though the prosodic treatises he planned to write on Miltonic rhythms, Dorian measures, and the philosophy of rhythm itself were never written, he maintained his interest in the sounds of nature and the nature of sounds until his death (*Journals* 11-12). In general, sounds were one means by which Hopkins attached himself to the real world.

A sonnet dated 1882 illustrates one antithetical meaning that sound carried for Hopkins. "Ribblesdale" has for its general theme the now-familiar but then-new environmentalist's complaint that man does not take sufficient care of the earth. The effectiveness of this complaint depends upon Hopkins's characterization of earth, which he accomplishes in terms of the lovely but tongueless plight of "sweet Earth, sweet lándscape."

Ribblesdale

Earth, sweet Earth, sweet lándscape, with leavès throng
And louchèd low grass, heaven that dost appeal
To with no tongue to plead, no heart to feel;
That canst but only be, but dost that long—

Thou canst but be, but that thou well dost; strong   5
Thy plea with him who dealt, nay does now deal,
Thy lovely dale down thus and thus bids reel
Thy river, and o'er gives all to rack or wrong.

And what is Earth's eye, tongue, or heart else, where

Else, but in dear and dogged man? Ah, the heir   10
To his own selfbent so bound, so tied to his turn,

To thriftless reave both our rich round world bare
And none reck of world after, this bids wear
Earth brows of such care, care and dear concern.

                                        (*Poetical* 171; #149)

Earth has "no tongue." It can only exist in a patient but mute vulnera-
bility. But Earth can find a tongue in humankind, in "dear and dogged
man." This naturalistic proposition represents a philosophical attitude
toward sounds of all kinds. To represent sounds would become a moral
imperative for a poet who believed man ordained to syllable earth's own
mute consciousness.

   Birdsong mediates between natural sounds and cultural sounds such as
music. A mild winter scene in "Winter with the Gulf Stream" (#7; 1863,
1871) in the 1871 version associates sound with physical vigor: "A
simple passage of weak notes / Is all the winter bird dare try." More am-
bitiously, "The Nightingale" (#76; 1866) exploits one type of birdsong for
its power to terrify an anxious woman as she awaits her husband's return
from a sea-voyage. Hopkins here develops an emotional fluctuation between silence and sound. He thus prepares us for antithetical dialectics
between silence and sound to be elaborated in poems such as "The Habit
of Perfection" (#77; 1866) and "*Nondum*" (#78; 1866). Hopkins yearns
for silence but in "*Nondum*" complains of God's silence, as four of the
nine stanzas show.

            We guess; we clothe Thee, unseen King,
            With attributes we deem are meet;
            Each in his own imagining   15
            Sets up a shadow in Thy seat;
            Yet know not how our gifts to bring,
            Where seek Thee with unsandalled feet.

            And still th'unbroken silence broods
            While ages and while aeons run,   20
            As erst upon chaotic floods
            The Spirit hovered ere the sun

Had called the seasons' changeful moods
And life's first germs from death had won.

And still th'abysses infinite   25
Surround the peak from which we gaze.
Deep calls to deep, and blackest night
Giddies the soul with blinding daze
That dares to cast its searching sight
On being's dread and vacant maze.   30

And Thou art silent, whilst Thy world
Contends about its many creeds
And Hosts confront with flags unfurled
And zeal is flushed and pity bleeds
And truth is heard, with tears impearled,   35
A moaning voice among the reeds.
                                      (*Poetical* 92; #78)

As in Browning's "Porphyria's Lover," a remote God does not say a
word.

Other birds stimulate other forms of consciousness. In "Spring" (#117;
1877), Hopkins's ecstatic description of a vernal scene includes a thrush
whose "echoing timber does so rinse and wring / The ear, it strikes like
lightnings to hear him sing." In another sonnet of 1877, "The Sea and the
Skylark," Hopkins incorporates birdsong more structurally. He expresses
dissatisfaction with his fellow men ("our sordid turbid time") by contrasting them with "two voices too old to end," the sea's somber roar and
the lark's thrilling song.

On ear and ear two noises too old to end
    Trench—right, the tide that ramps against the shore;
    With a flood or a fall, low lull-off or áll róar,

Frequénting thère while moon shall wear and wend.

Left hand, off land, I hear the lark ascend,   5
    His rash-fresh re-winded new-skeinèd score
    In crisps of curl off wild winch whirl, and pour
And pelt músic, till none's to spill nor spend.

How these two shame this shallow and frail tówn!
    How ring right out our sordid turbid time,   10

Béing pure! We, life's pride and cared-for crown,

Have lost that chêer and charm of earth's past prime:
Our make and making break, are breaking, down
To man's last dust, drain fast towards man's first slime.

(*Poetical* 143 ; #118)

Expressive sounds represent a high point of evolutionary consciousness
from which backsliding humankind seems to be devolving towards
"man's first slime."
    "The Caged Skylark" makes explicit the encagement implied in "The
Windhover." It develops an analogy between the bird "scanted in a dull
cage" and the soul in its "bone-house." Bird and soul sing "sweetest
spells," yet both fall into depressions and dull rages.

As a dare-gale skylark scanted in a dúll cáge,
    Man's mounting spirit in his bone-house, mean house,
    dwells—
That bird beyond the remembering hís free fells,
This in drudgery, day-labouring-out life's age.

Though aloft on turf or perch or poor low stage   5
    Both sing sometímes the sweetest, sweetest spells,
    Yet both droop deadly sómetimes in their cells
Or wring their barriers in bursts of fear or rage.

Not that the sweet-fowl, song-fowl, needs no rest—
Why, hear him, hear him babble and drop down to his nest,   10

But his ówn nést, wíld nést, no prison.

Man's spirit will be flesh-bound when found at best,
But úncúmberèd: meadow-dówn is nót distréssed

For a ráinbow fóoting it nor hé for his bónes rísen.

(*Poetical* 148; #122)

Hopkins tries to find consolation in the belief that bird and soul will find
rest within their respective cages ("no prison") or in some post-resurrec-
tion body (MacKenzie, *Guide* 92).

A final image of birdsong as a complex state between brute nature and music appears in "The May Magnificat" (#126; 1878). Intended to praise Christ's mother as a source of fecundity, this poem reaches its climax, in stanza 11, in a birdsong:

> And azuring-over greybell makes
> Wood banks and brakes wash wet like lakes
> And magic cuckoocall
> Caps, clears, and clinches all—

> *(Poetical* 154; #126)

Generally, then, in a Hopkinsian hierarchy of sounds, birdsongs of the lark, nightingale, thrush, and cuckoo mark a paradoxical stage between other natural sounds and properly musical sounds.

Hopkins's enthusiastic but discriminating responses to sound yield specific insights. Two poems from 1866 depict an antithetical attitude toward sound's shadowy companion, silence. We confront here the sort of painful consciousness that, as Freud might say, breeds antithetical poets. Written during Lent of 1866, "*Nondum*" is a 54-line poem which develops implications of Isaiah xlv.15: "Verily Thou art a God that hidest Thyself." Not sound but silence oppresses Hopkins's consciousness in this outcry to an obdurate God (Mariani, *Commentary* 36-8). Human language dies in a "vast silence" of "being's dread and vacant maze." We move here close to the center of Hopkins's experience of nightmarish modern history. Like many of his Victorian contemporaries, he expresses dismay at a post-Darwinian world of "unbroken silence." What awaits may be only a final silence of the sort that terrified Pascal. Admittedly a piece of Victorian rhetoric (MacKenzie, *Guide* 27), "*Nondum*" expresses an individual's encounter with the terror of silence as vividly as Pascal's famous outcry, "*Le silence eternel de ces espaces infinis m'effraie*" (*Pensees* #206).

Hopkins regularly polarizes his thoughts on silence. Only a month or two before writing "*Nondum*," he had composed "The Habit of Perfection" (#77). This 28-line poem centers his priestly vow of poverty in terms of a rejection of sensuous delights. At the outset of this elegant expression of denial, he begins by rejecting ear-delighting sounds and inviting silence to share his bed.

> Elected Silence, sing to me
> And beat upon my whorlèd ear,

> Pipe me to pastures still and be
> The music that I care to hear.
>
> Shape nothing, lips; be lovely-dumb: 5
> It is the shut, the curfew sent
> From there where all surrenders come
> Which only makes you eloquent.

                                        (*Poetical* 89-90; #77)

This desire for "unheard spiritual music" (MacKenzie 25) seems designed as a compensatory contrast with the anguished complaint against God's silence in "*Nondum.*" In that "The Habit of Perfection" is regarded as the verbally most complex and enduring of Hopkins's early poems, his dismissal of sound—along with the other senses—together with his antithetical acceptance of silence, complicates any future resort to music, including "unheard melodies" on a presumed "secret catgut."

Some musical terms occurring in the poetry would suggest some acquaintance with rudiments: (1) NOUNS: chords, strain, close, note, music, strings, cadence, singing, chime, score, rehearsal, march, tune, pitch, carol, song, dominant (2) VERBS: sing, chaunt, pipe (3) ADJECTIVES or ADVERBS: Gregorian, melodiously, musical, dominant (4) INSTRUMENTS: trumpet, timbrels, harp, horn, bugle, string, bell, bass, viol.

In the 1990 edition of 179 fragments and poems, fewer than twenty seem, by their titles alone, to bear upon sound or music. Judging by titles, eight poems seem, by various stretches of the imagination, to promise peculiar sounds: "The Cheery Beggar," "Hurrahing in Harvest," "The Leaden Echo and the Golden Echo," "The Nightingale," "The Sea and the Skylark," "The Caged Skylark," "To His Watch," and "A Voice from the World." Only five titles promise music: "The Loss of the Eurydice," "At the Wedding March," "The Bugler's First Communion," "Henry Purcell," and "On a Piece of Music."

The heart of the matter resides generally in some twenty or so poems that contain musical allusions or analogies. They stretch across the oeuvre, with the most important pieces congregating toward the end. In the preceding four episodes of "Hopkins Against History," where we have seen Hopkins evading but heroically rewriting Victorian historiography, we have been moved to admire the poet's wayward but resourceful genius. His music poems body forth compelling evidence for a musical erasure of history which, in the last analysis, occasions yet another heroic refusal to knuckle under to the nightmare.

Some ten or so early poems offer glimpses of Hopkins's procedures for working music into his poems. Hopkins sometimes relies upon familiar, even cliché, musical associations. Thus, mermaids express their loneliness with a piteous "antique chaunt" ("A Vision of the Mermaids"); thus, too, in a scriptural setting, pleasant-sounding timbrels are contrasted with "the waking trumpet, the long law" ([A soliloquy of one of the spies left in the wilderness]); souls who enjoy God's bounty shall "laugh and sing" ("Spring and Death"); the "towers musical" of Oxford make one in a list of details expressing Hopkins's loyalty to that place hallowed by the memory of Duns Scotus ("To Oxford"); Easter celebration includes dance to the accompaniment of harp and horn ("Easter"); and, devotees of the Virgin Mary sing her praises (*Ad Mariam*).

Such predictable associations by no means exhaust Hopkins's poetic interest in music. As early as "A Vision of the Mermaids" (#6; 1862), he constructed from music a strong emotional climax to a poem that ends on a Prufrockian note of historical escapism:

Then they, thus ranged, 'gan make full plaintively
A piteous Siren sweetness on the sea,
Withouten instrument, or conch, or bell,
Or stretch'd chords tuneable on turtle's shell;
Only with utterance of sweet breath they sung   130
An antique chaunt and in an unknown tongue.
Now melting upward thro' the sloping scale
Swell'd the sweet strain to a melodious wail;
Now ringing clarion-clear to whence it rose
Slumber'd at last in one sweet, deep, heart-broken close.   135
  But when the sun had lapsed to ocean, lo
A stealthy wind crept round seeking to blow,
Linger'd, then raised the washing waves and drench'd
The floating blooms and with tide flowing quench'd
The rosy isles: so that I stole away   140
And gain'd thro' growing dusk the stirless bay;
White loom'd my rock, the water gurgling o'er,
Whence oft I watch but see those Mermaids now no more.

(*Poetical* 14; #6)

In its musical references and its musicality or euphony, this passage displays genuine if rudimentary musical knowledge hand and hand with competence in versification.

More revealing is Hopkins's use of a musical term (*treble*) in an intellectually complex sense in "The beginning of the end" (#59; 1865). In the first sonnet of a three-sonnet sequence concerning the death of a love, he speaks of his "lessened" love as being greater than that of other men. He specifies his remaining passion as being "treble fervent":

> But ah! if you could understand how then
> That *less* is heavens higher even yet
> Than treble-fervent *more* of other men,
> Even your unpassion'd eyelids might be wet.

Hopkins here complicates his theme by using *treble* so that its several meanings (high pitched, tripartite, shrill) reverberate hints of complex emotional ideas that range beyond music into general human experience.

Music, in the form of songs of social comment, can witness to human contingencies and even help to solve human problems; thus, music can function as the sound of history (Palmer x). But music can also encourage pure escapism from history's perplexities. The romantics whose thoughts, feelings, and forms were to influence several generations of nineteenth-century poets went to great lengths to assert aesthetic control over the contents of life and literature. In an effort to master the contingencies, they did not hesitate to attempt the emancipation of absolute or pure music from sullied and contingent language. Concerning music, though, some technical preparation is required, even if no guarantees assure that even the best prepared composer can dominate or determine any audience's response: "Technical know-how is a prime requisite for composition, but the use and interpretation of any created object are, for better or worse, usually beyond the control of the creator" (Neubauer 210). Hopkins surely turned to music during certain crises of his life in part because he desired to impose control upon the human realities—the human histories—that threatened to overwhelm him. His self-identification with Sidney Lanier in some respects epitomizes his complex expectations of music (Martin 379).

Two other poems of 1865-66 show Hopkins's increasing confidence in the practice of incorporating associational effects of music into his poetry. "The Nightingale" is a ballad-like narrative in which Frances expresses her fears that her husband Luke will not return safely from a sea voyage. At the end, Luke is reported to have drowned at the very moment she herself had wearily lain down to rest. The heart of the poem (st. 4-7) describes the terrifying effect on Frances of the song of a nightingale when Frances would have preferred to hear only Luke's footfall:

'I thought the air must cut and strain
The windpipe when he sucked his breath
And when he turned it back again
  The music must be death.
With not a thing to make me fear,   40
A singing bird in morning clear
To me was terrible to hear.

'Yet as he changed his mighty stops
Betweens I heard the water still
All down the stair-way of the copse   45
  And churning in the mill.
But that sweet sound which I preferred,
Your passing steps, I never heard
For warbling of the warbling bird.'

(Poetical 89; #76)

Hopkins gradually works toward a consciousness of the emotional implications of natural sounds that can override or obliterate human sounds.
  A more technically ambitious poem and one more central to Hopkins's
development is an untitled sonnet "'Let me be to Thee as the circling
bird'" (*Poetical* #70) in which he announces that he has discovered his
own *raison d'être* in an unquestioning love of God. This expression of
a joyous new spiritual condition is accomplished almost entirely in technical musical terms (note, strings, cadence, strain, dominant), somewhat
on the order of a metaphysical conceit:

Let me be to Thee as the circling bird,
Or bat with tender and air-crisping wings
That shapes in half-light his departing rings,
From both of whom a changeless note is heard.
I have found my music in a common word,   5
Trying each pleasurable throat that sings
And every praisèd sequence of sweet strings,
And know infallibly which I preferred.

The authentic cadence was discovered late
Which ends those only strains that I approve,   10
And other science all gone out of date
And minor sweetness scarce made mention of:

I have found the dominant of my range and state—
Love, O my God, to call Thee Love and Love.

(*Poetical* 84; #70)

This low-keyed sonnet establishes that for Hopkins music would henceforth be available both as antithetical metaphor and as therapeutic escape from human time.

We might expect that Hopkins would henceforth employ more musical references, but only a few poems make even cursory reference. The historically occasioned *The Wreck of the Deutschland* (#101), despite its strong acoustic effects, makes only one unambiguous reference, to a "madrigal start" (st. 18), as metaphor for an emotional rush experienced by the narrator's own heart as he contemplates the watery death of the exiled nuns. In "The Silver Jubilee" (#102; 1876) we learn that bells and bugles are forbidden by English law from signalling the jubilee of a Roman Catholic bishop. The only music that Hopkins can invoke in this occasional poem will be the "chime of a rhyme." More directly related to one of Hopkins's central beliefs bearing upon the individualizing selfhood of each of God's creatures, "As kingfishers catch fire, dragonflies draw flame" (#115) lists bells and "tucked strings" as musical objects that by their actions fling out their names so as to identify or express their inner natures: "Selves—goes its self; *myself* it speaks and spells, / Crying *What I do is me: for that I came*" (emphases Hopkins's).

Other brief allusions to musical elements hint at consciousness-effects. In "To what serves Mortal Beauty?" (#158; 1885), dangerous beauty stimulates desire or vanity more forcefully even than the dance inspired by the music of Henry Purcell. The agony of nocturnal despair occasions pangs that can be represented only by a musical figure: "Pitched past pitch of grief" (one of the few musical references in the Sonnets of Desolation). Hopkins's epiphanic realization that he shares in Christ's paradoxical lowliness-cum-grandeur manifests itself in "a flash at a trumpet crash" in the poem "That Nature is a Heraclitean Fire" (#174; 1888). In an untitled sonnet—"The shepherd's brow" (#178; 1889)—Hopkins laments man's misery by contrasting it with the angelic high tragedy. It mournfully asks: "What bass is *our* viol for tragic tones?"

Surprisingly, perhaps, no major utterance on the relations of music and poetry occurs explicitly again until the final poem ("To R. B."), where Hopkins rather conventionally equates poetry with "immortal song," with "the roll, the rise, the carol, the creation" of genuine art. We can now turn to five poems where Hopkins most fully recuperates for poetry what might have been lost to music.

Conventionally, music can induce a "delirium of self-confidence" in the listener (Mellers 159). Hopkins ultimately critiques such convenient euphoria. A poem that by its title alone could indicate an antithetical attitude toward music, a sort of companion piece to *The Wreck of the Deutschland*, is another shipwreck poem, "The Loss of the Eurydice" (1878). Given that in Greek mythology Eurydice is the beloved mate of Orpheus, progenitor of music and poetry, a certain line of inquiry seems to be suggested. Even allowing for the fact that Hopkins's *Eurydice* is a wooden-hulled, nine-hundred-ton frigate, we might expect some allusion to the myth of Orpheus the great musician. Yet myth itself can take on overtones of myth-as-history, and Hopkins surprises his reader by avoiding any such overt intertextuality.

"The Loss of the Eurydice" is a poem of thirty four-line stanzas, rhyming *aabb*, with lines either four beat or three beat. The poem contains some of Hopkins's most daring experiments in run-over rhythms and strange rhymes. Stanzas 4-7 can adequately suggest the ballad-like method and some of the technical oddities:

> She had cóme from a crúise, tráining séamen—
> Men, boldboys soon to be men:
>   Must it, worst weather,   15
> Blast bole and bloom together?
>
> No Atlantic squall overwrought her
> Or rearing billow of the Biscay water:
>   Home was hard at hand
> And the blow bore from land.   20
>
> And you were a liar, O blue March day.
> Bright sun lanced fire in the heavenly bay;
>   But what black Boreas wrecked her? he
> Came equipped, deadly-electric,
>
> A beetling badbright cloud thorough England   25
> Riding: there did storms not mingle? and
>   Hailropes hustle and grind their
> Heavengravel? wolfsnow, worlds of it, wind there?

(*Poetical* 149-150; #125)

The poem recounts, responds to, and judges the implications of the historical foundering, on 24 March 1878, of the British naval training ship *Eurydice*, off the Isle of Wight, with the loss of some three-hundred crew. Given the ship's name, we encounter here another Hopkinsian clue in full view. The loss of the *Eurydice* perhaps ineluctably reenacts the loss of Eurydice, Orpheus's own greatest failure.

A summary of the poem might read as follows. The *Eurydice*, in which Christ the Lord had an interest, went down at a clap, bearing a precious cargo of "training seamen." Nearly home from a Bermudan cruise, she sank before a sudden storm coming off the land (st. 1-5). A clear March day lulled the captain and crew; a storm cloud hurled off Boniface Downs, and she was "gone with the gale" (st. 7-11). The captain went down with his ship; two sailors only were rescued by a schooner; one "sea-corpse cold" impressed itself upon spectators' memory (st. 12-21). The loss of these Englishmen provokes a leap of imagination in Hopkins, so that he laments the loss of Catholic England to Protestantism. He wonders why Christ would permit an entire nation, once devoted to Mary and her Son, to be lost (st. 22-26). Appropriate tears are wept by mothers, wives, and sweethearts; but such mourners should cease mourning and instead kneel to Christ (st. 22-28). Hopkins himself asks Christ to "have heard" his prayers for grace toward the drowned sailors (st. 29), since, even though hell brooks no "redeeming," yet newly-dead persons may find forgiveness if timely prayers intercede for them (st. 30).

Among numerous poems that use individual musical compositions as subjects, Calvin Brown found many poems on Orpheus (*Tones Into Words* 11). Few poets encountering the name "Eurydice" in any context would be able to resist at least a conventional nod toward Orpheus, in whose myth Eurydice is an important figure. Hopkins makes no mention of Orpheus or Eurydice themselves, but it is to their rich story that we should look.

Eight years after composing "The Loss of the Eurydice," in a letter of 23 October 1886, Hopkins explained to Dixon his own general view of Greek mythology. Such pagan mythology, he wrote, is more than mere fairy tale, partaking to some degree of the "historical part of religion." When he considered "the great fact of heathenism," he was appalled at the spectacle of men setting up works produced by their own minds and imaginations in place of God's works. Additionally, the Greek gods, he complained, are "unnatural rakes." Even so, he concluded on a positive note that could have implications for his own aesthetic consciousness:

But I grant that the Greek mythology is very susceptible of fine treatment, allegorical treatment for instance, and so treated gives rise to the most beautiful results. No wonder: the moral evil is got rid of and the pure art, morally neutral and artistically so rich, remains and can be even turned to moral uses. (*Letters* 146-47)

Given such an opinion, Hopkins ought to have been able to use the beautiful myth of Orpheus, as other poets have done, to develop ideas and values. If the myth of Orpheus were at all present in "The Loss of the Eurydice," it would very likely be in just such an "allegorical treatment" as Hopkins approves of in his letter to Dixon. But Hopkins, so Jude Nixon thinks, in fact repudiated the entire classical system (202-5).

The myth of Orpheus would attract Hopkins's attention. Orpheus, great Thracian hero, distinguished himself not by warlike exploits but by an amazing musical talent, of both lyre and voice. This son of Apollo calmed wild beasts and moved trees and rocks by his music. He performed miraculous rescues for the Argonauts. His powerful voice and harmonious lyre won over even the implacable deities of Hades. When his beloved bride Eurydice was taken in death to the underworld, he boldly descended into Hades to rescue her. By charming Hades and Persephone with his song, he won permission to take her back to the light of day. Tragically, however, in leading her out of Hell, Orpheus experienced a failure of nerve and looked over his shoulder, against Hades's injunction, to assure himself that his cherished wife was indeed following him. By his momentary weakness, he lost her forever to the somber abode of the dead. Subsequently, some versions have it, inconsolable Orpheus killed himself. More generally, though, it is believed that by refusing to love other women, the grieving widower Orpheus provoked Thracian women to kill him. They tore his head from his body, flinging it with his lyre into the river Hebrus. The head goes on singing and delivering oracles (*Larousse* 211).

Even though "The Loss of the Eurydice" contains numerous sound effects of wind, water, and ship's tackle, almost nothing musical forces itself upon our attention. Only one delicate touch, in the second stanza, makes us even faintly remember Orpheus: when the *Eurydice* sinks, a sort of musical accompaniment comes from sheep bells worn by grazing flocks on Boniface Downs ("flockbells off the aeriel / Downs' forefalls beat to the burial"). Such sheep bells, serving as they do to calm and regulate the flock, function as equivalents for Orpheus's beast-taming song. They also remind us that Orpheus's song was able only, as it were, to accompany Eurydice's sinking beneath the ground but not to prevent her loss to Hades.

This single musical image carries us toward the heart of Hopkins's complex attitude toward Orpheus and toward music itself. He leaves Orpheus out of a poem where normally the god of music and poetry would be given a central place. Hopkins must have recognized that Orpheus, as musician, faithful husband, and would-be rescuer, should be adaptable to his poetical intentions. However, if he knew the entire myth, as doubtless he did, he would recall—what many commentators and poets choose to ignore—that Orpheus *failed* in his attempt to rescue Eurydice. Of the three parts of the myth—great musical exploits, loss of Eurydice, posthumously immortal but tragic song—the central part enacts Orpheus's nervous *failure* to rescue his beloved wife (Hollahan, "Orpheus"). Intelligent and honest about such matters, and under the sway of Christian doctrine positing Christ as the only redeemer, Hopkins perhaps could not but choose to leave Orpheus out.

We should note that despite scattered references to music in the New Testament, Christ's main form of expression was non-musical. If Orpheus the great musician appears in Hopkins's conclusion, it is only negatively, ironically, and tragically:

> But to Christ lord of thunder
> Crouch; lay knee by earth low under: 110
>   'Holiest, loveliest, bravest,
> Save my hero, O Hero savest.
>
> And the prayer thou hearst me making
> Have, at the awful overtaking,
>   Heard; have heard and granted   115
> Grace that day grace was wanted.'
>
> Not that hell knows redeeming,
> But for souls sunk in seeming
>   Fresh, till doomfire burn all,
> Prayer shall fetch pity eternal.   120

Here, in one of Hopkins's most ambitious musical poems, music has been judged and found wanting. We recognize oppositions and cross-purposes such as we have glimpsed in previous episodes of Hopkins's antithetical crisis-consciousness.

During Hopkins's mature years, music "kept the flag of romanticism flying in a generally positivist age" (Dalhaus, *Realism* 120). Even Hopkins's admirers should recognize that the poet sometimes gushed over music much as other Victorian nonmusicians gushed. We might understandably wish that Hopkins could have merely relaxed into an untrained impressionism and learned, in Peter Kivy's words, how to emote over music without losing his self-respect (132-49). But he would not or could not. In 1879, Hopkins's most sustained interest in music seriously began (Mariani, *Commentary* xiii). This is the year during which he was stationed in Oxford until October and then in Bedford Leigh near Manchester. It is the period when he wrote four important poems which, by their titles alone, would seem to develop musical subjects. These four poems are "Henry Purcell" (#131; April), "On a Piece of Music" (#135; May), "The Bugler's First Communion" (#137; July), and "At the Wedding March" (#141; October). Taken together, they suggest what Hopkins may have thought, in forms of poetical discourse, about music as an escape from or erasure of historical or real-world difficulties. In these four poems, Hopkins employs a good deal of variety; the subjects of the four poems are a composer, a piece of music, a musician, and a socio-religious ritual incorporating music.

Hopkins never humbled himself to the systematic commitment and application needed, as Ruth Finnegan defines it, to acquire and practice musical skills (133-42). Yet he could respond with some degree of cultivated sensibility to certain styles of music. Although he mentions numerous composers in his non-poetical writings, he mentions only Henry Purcell (1659-1695) in his poems. In addition to a passing reference to Purcell in "To what serves Mortal Beauty?" (#158; 1885), we find one of his most ambitious and richly obscure sonnets devoted entirely to this English composer who was organist at Westminster Abbey from 1679 to 1695.

Henry Purcell, England's greatest composer, enjoyed acclaim and admiration from his contemporaries. His career was brief but brilliant: court composer to Charles II; organist in Chapel Royal and keeper of the king's instruments; laborer upon commissions beneath his talents; composer of the first major English opera, *Dido and Aeneas*; immense range of invention within a constricting formula, the "composition on a ground"; numerous instrumental compositions of great accomplishment; unique and poignant sense of harmony; incidental music for more than forty plays, including Dryden's; oeuvre of more than five hundred works; prodigious variety of inspiration; unrivalled psychological insight; powerful expressions of sorrow and joy; and, genius for the theater. The last great English composer before a decline of two centuries, Purcell was probably the most complete musician of the second half of the seventeenth century. His only deficiency was that he was not himself a creator of new musical forms. A feverish personality, he adhered to the English masters of the past while remaining open to new currents from France and Italy (*Larousse* 195-96).

Hopkins was deeply impressed by Purcell's music. He examined Robert Bridges's copies of Purcell's music; he read W. H. Cummings' book on Purcell and visited Cummings so as to see Purcell relics and discuss the composer. A Purcell Society founded in 1876, when Hopkins was to begin his own mature career, would have helped to call his attention to this brilliant historical figure (Mackenzie, *Guide* 115).

When we turn to "Henry Purcell" itself so as to discover what it shows or says about music, we encounter an unforgettable poetic utterance but a serious problem in understanding. Hopkins's notorious difficulty of presentation appears at its worst and best in this poem. As if to acknowledge the difficulty, Hopkins provides his own prose gloss at the head of the poem:

> The poet wishes well to the divine genius of Purcell and praises him that, whereas other musicians have given utterance to the moods of man's mind, he has, beyond that, uttered in notes the very make and species of man as created both in him and in all men generally[.]

Hopkins's gloss over-simplifies the perplexed language of his splendid sonnet.

> Have fáir fállen, O fáir, fáir have fállen, so déar
> To me, so arch-especial a spirit as heaves in Henry Purcell,
>
> An age is now since passed, since parted; with the reversal
> Of the outward sentence low lays him, listed to a heresy, here.
>
> Not mood in him nor meaning, proud fire or sacred fear,   5
>
> Or love, or pity, or all that sweet notes not his might nursle:
>
> It is the forgèd feature finds me; it is the rehearsal
> Of own, of abrúpt sélf there so thrusts on, so thróngs the ear.
>
> Let him oh! with his air of angels then lift me, lay me! only I'll

Have an eye to the sakes of him, quaint moonmarks, to his
   pelted plumage under   10
Wíngs: so some great stormfowl, whenever he has walked his
   while

The thunder-purple seabeach, plumèd purple-of-thunder,

If a wuthering of his palmy snow-pinions scatter a colossal
   smile
Óff him, but meaning motion fans fresh our wits with wonder.

                                     (*Poetical* 157; #131)

A paraphrase of the poem might read thus. Among many "fair" persons
who have "fallen" (death? damnation?), Purcell is an "arch-especial"
spirit, despite his being a Protestant (ll. 1-4); I revere Purcell not merely
for the kind of musical accomplishment lesser composers might only
"nursle" but because his "forgèd feature" (style?) expresses his unique
individuality ("abrúpt sélf") and, hence, the principle of individuality
itself (ll. 5-8); I welcome his music which carries me away as a huge bird
might carry me, so that I can lie back in complete security and contemplate the "quaint moonmarks" of his under-plumage (features of style?)
(ll. 9-11); listening to Purcell, I feel as if I observed another sort of bird
("some great stormfowl") stretching its wings and thus inadvertently
expressing some essential trait (inscape); the bird illustrates the principle
that by focusing on any creaturely activity one stimulates one's own
imagination ("wits"). This theme introduces a belief to be reformulated
in "St. Alphonsus Rodriguez," where music reverts to sound and sound
reverts to the humblest human experience.

     Honour is flashed off exploit, so we say;
     And those strokes once that gashed flesh or galled shield
     Should tongue that time now, trumpet now that field,
     And, on the fighter, forge his glorious day.
     On Christ they do and on the martyr may;   5
     But be the war within, the brand we wield
     Unseen, the heroic breast not outward-steeled,
     Earth hears no hurtle then from fiercest fray
     Yet God (that hews mountain and continent,
     Earth, all, out; who, with trickling increment,   10
     Veins violets and tall trees makes more and more)

Could crowd career with conquest while there went

Those years and years by͡ of world without event

That in Majorca͡ Alfonso watched the door.

(Poetical 200-201; #176[c])

Consciousness of Purcell's musical exploits thus eventually yields to a consciousness of ordinariness as essence or inscape.

But what does "Henry Purcell" say or imply about music in itself or in its historical relations? Two metaphors in the sestet are rendered primarily as visual rather than as auditory. Purcell's music is rather conventionally an "air of angels" (l. 9), and Hopkins rather flatly asserts that Purcell's music "thróngs the ear" (l. 8). Admittedly, he contrasts Purcell's sounds with the "sweet notes" (sugary Romantic subjectivity?) of other composers, but elucidation of "Henry Purcell," so far as we can tease it out, seems not to depend upon music. The most we can say is that the poem expresses in an excitable sprung rhythm an interesting reverence for Henry Purcell the composer, a reverence expressed in some of the most intricate rhythms in English poetry.

An unshakable impression left by Hopkins's tormented sonnet on England's first operatic composer resembles the tortuous impression induced by the interfacing of operatic and literary forms. We have a battle on our hands.

> *Words and music are enemies*, perpetually jealous of one another, because each longs for the privileges of the other while *resenting intrusions on its own territory*. The aim of *music is the dissolution of sense into sound*, the aim of words . . . is to retrieve meaning and to communicate it, despite the blandishments of sound. . . . Words and music are united by *antagonism*. Opera is the continuation of their *warfare* by other means. (Conrad 178; ellipses mine; emphases added)

Given such warfare of word and tone, is it any wonder that Hopkins found as much pain as pleasure in his poetical encounters with music?

At every moment when he yearned to emancipate himself from the torments of Victorian history by emancipating music from language, Hopkins mired himself more deeply into one of history's crucial mysteries: "The paradox is that instantly upon its emancipation from poetry, music should have been held up as the ideal of poetry" (Treitler 184).

Fortunately for poetry, at the most crucial moments Hopkins opted for human language, albeit a strangely acoustical human language.

"'Who shaped these wall has shewn'" (*Poetical* #135) curiously illustrates not only how Hopkins's escape to music terminated in nonmusical consciousness-effects but also just how seductive music could be. "On a Piece of Music" is now identified as "Who shaped these walls has shewn," a poem developing an architectural analogy for the ineffable mysteries of human individuality. MacKenzie notes (*Guide* 223) that the poem deals directly with architecture but obliquely with music as an analogy for individualizing inventiveness. Thus it belongs with the other three important musically grounded poems of 1879. Following "Henry Purcell" by one month, "Who shaped these walls has shewn" may in fact contain a reference to Purcell as the composer who shows the "music of his mind" by his musical score (115). The closeness in time of composition (April; May) suggests that they may be companion poems, as do several musical terms (tune, instrument, voice, song, Re, Mi). In this case, music quickly glides toward a metaphor according to which architecture bodies forth the "man within that makes" beauty. In its turn, beauty is said to escape the black-white, right-wrong structure of simplified ethical choice.

Here we see into the heart of music's aesthetic appeal as a mode of historical escapism. The poem provides a basis for Hopkins's conflicted attempt to erase history by resorting to music. Music is a form of consciousness that allows one directly to express the mind's "secret catgut" but a form which threatens to overvault (supersede) the human voice. The poem prepares the ground for Hopkins's subordination of music to inscaped human histories such as "Felix Randal" and "Harry Ploughman." He will ultimately rediscover common human experience as the mode of his peculiar genius. We see here the conflicted Hopkins negotiating between what Jerome Bump designates as visual and auditory paradigms ("Reading Hopkins").

> Who shaped these walls has shewn
> The music of his mind,
> Made known, though thick through stone,
> What beauty beat behind.
>
> How all's to one thing wrought!   5
> The members, how they sit!
> O what a tune the thought
> Must be that fancied it.

Though down his being's bent
Like air he changed in choice,   10
That was an instrument
Which overvaulted voice.

Not free in this because
His powers seemed free to play:
He swept what scope he was   15
To sweep and must obey.

Nor angel insight can
Learn how the heart is hence:
Since all the make of man
Is law's indifference.   20

Therefóre this masterhood,
This piece of perfect song,
This fault-not-found-with good
Is neither right nor wrong,

No more than red and blue,   25
No more than Re and Mi,
Or sweet the golden glue
That's built for by the bee.

For good grows wild and wide,
has shades, is nowhere none;   30
But right must seek a side
And choose for chieftain one.

What makes the man and what
The man within that makes:
Ask whom he serves or not
Serves and what side he takes.   35

Who built these walls made known
The music of his mind,
Yet here he has but shewn
His ruder-rounded rind.   40

His brightest blooms lie there unblown
His sweetest nectar hides behind.

(*Poetical* 159-160; #135)

Hopkins here works toward an acute relation between aesthetics and morality, but Mariani (*Commentary* 159) mistakenly concludes that Hopkins favors moral judgment over aesthetic values.

I would read the poem as a rejection of music—and all such arts—as potential erasure of both human contingencies and dynamics of inner selfhood. The speaker, observing and listening to an orchestra playing a composition, is impressed by the disciplined congruence of music and performance. His mind leaps to the composer whose "thought" originally "fancied it" (st. 1). He realizes that not even angelic wisdom can predict the effect of such music on any given person, for the simple reason that *sui generis* human persons resist such constraints as pure or abstract music requires (st. 2). The composer himself may have felt free to express his powers as he pleased, but in fact he too must, at bottom, be governed by law (st. 3). In a most difficult figure (st. 4), Hopkins then states that the "air" which the composer used to constitute his music—the literal air a horn-player forces through his instrument in playing the notes or, so to speak, forces into a horn as into a vault—such air is itself an instrument which exists prior to and is necessary to the composer's supposedly "free" compositional activity. The composer, like any existentially contingent human being, poises between internal and external pressures. To understand the consequences of such consciousness, one must ask in which direction a person's intentions tend: "Ask . . . which side he takes" (st. 5). Aesthetic pleasure ("good") is to be found everywhere in nature, as it were, promiscuously; but morality appears more narrowly because a moral person must choose one position against another (st. 6). The music itself ("perfect song") neither asserts a moral judgment nor itself comes under moral judgment (st. 7). Where is the evidence for such a theory of aesthetic amorality? Not in some tome or system but in colors and sounds in their natural state, as if it were the honey produced by a honey-bee. These things provide materials for artistic appropriation but pass no moral judgment themselves.

"The Bugler's First Communion" is Hopkins only poem about a solo performer, yet this moving poem seems to say nothing about music. Hopkins the priest describes how a young soldier accepted an invitation to receive his First Communion. The priest places the consecrated host on the youth's tongue. Then, he hopes that the youth will remain worthy of

Christ. He prays that the bugler's guardian angel and fellow soldiers will help the lad to remain chaste. Hopkins feels personal satisfaction in this "freshyouth" in whom Christ momentarily reigns. But he also prays never to see the boy again, lest the boy disappoint by backsliding ("rankle and roam / in backwheels") into sinfulness. In a syntactically difficult concluding passage, an anxious Hopkins declares that he himself has vexed heaven with "pleas" on the boy's behalf; perhaps heaven will hear, respond, and protect the bugler boy. Given the poem's Hopkinsian braveries, it deserves to be viewed in its entirety.

A bugler boy from barrack (it is over the hill
There)—bóy búgler, born, he tells me, of Irish

Mother to an English sire (he
Shares their best gifts surely, fall how things will),

This very very day came down to us after a boon he on   5
My late being there begged of mé, overflowing
　　　Boon in my bestowing,
Came, I say, this day to it—to a First Communion.

Hére he knelt then ín regimental red.
Forth Christ from cupboard fetched, how fain I of feet   10
　　　To his youngster take his treat!
Low-latched in leaf-light housel his too huge godhead.

There! and your sweetest sendings, ah divine,
By it, heavens, befall him! as a heart Christ's darling, dauntless;
　　　Tongue true, vaunt- and tauntless;   15
Breathing bloom of a chastity in mansex fine.

Frówning and forefending angel-warder
Squander the hell-rook ránks sálly to molest him;
　　　March, kind comrade, abreast him;
Dress his days to a dexterous and starlight order.   20

How it dóes my heart good, visiting at that bleak hill,

When limber liquid youth, that to all I teach
　　　Yields ténder as a púshed péach,
Hies headstrong to its wellbeing of a self-wise self-will!

Then though I should tréad túfts of consolation   25
Dáys áfter, só I in a sort deserve to

And do serve God to serve to
Just such slips of soldiery Christ's royal ration.

Nothing élse is like it, no, not all so strains
Us—freshyouth fretted in a bloomfall all portending   30
      That sweet's sweeter ending;
Realm both Christ is heir to and théré réigns.

O now well work that sealing sacred ointment!
O for now charms, arms, what bans off bad
      And locks love ever in a lad!   35
Let mé though sée no more of him, and not disappointment

Those sweet hopes quell whose least me quickenings lift,
In scarlet or somewhere of some day seeing
      That brow and bead of being,
An our day's God's own Galahad. Though this child's drift   40

Séems bý a divíne doom chánneled, nor do I cry

Disaster there; but may he not rankle and roam
      In backwheels, though bound home?—
That left to the Lord of the Eucharist, I here lie by;

Recorded only, I have put my lips on pleas   45
Would brandle adamantine heaven with ride and jar, did
      Prayer go disregarded:
Forward-like, but however, and like favourable heaven heard
    these.

                            (*Poetical* 161-162; #137)

Music may be a vacation from reality such as Hopkins regularly sought by resorting to metaphor, but except for the title, Hopkins offers little in the way of music or even sound. The boy had "begged" for the priestly favor, but now the "Tongue true" is silent as the priest places the "too huge godhead" of the eucharist upon it. Hopkins's own tongue busied itself teaching Christian principles at the barrack (st. 6), but here he remains silent. The only reference approximating a sound would be the loud "pleas" (not heard but alluded to) that Hopkins had, "with ride and jar," aimed at heaven's gates. This meditative poem, uttered as the priest turns from the altar rail to replace the remaining wafers inside the tabernacle, renders a quiet moment of motivated or purposive consciousness.

Does this poem about a musician then say nothing about music? Will the antithetical strategy be simply to erase, by ignoring, the music that itself could erase both experience and the language of experience? The answer is, once again, both yes and no. One word—*fretted*—directs our attention to a musical antithesis. In the eighth stanza, arguably the "joyful" heart of the poem as distinct from the "doubtful" part, Hopkins's polarized emotions are compressed into one image: "freshyouth fretted in a bloomfall." Admittedly this is a lovely stroke of vernal imagery, yet the complex word *fretted* complicates understanding. Why, in this happiest of contexts, does Hopkins say of the beautiful boy that he is "fretted"? MacKenzie notes that in an earlier draft ("boyboughs fretted in a flowerfall all portending / Fruit"), *fretted* "refers to the ruffled blossoms as their petals are shed" (*Guide* 126). Accordingly, in this usage, *fretted* traces back to *fret*, from the Middle English *frette*, meaning "interlaced work." At one level, this allusion to a type of ornamental design still functions in Hopkins's final version. Assuming an unalloyed joy in stanza 8, then, the sense of *fretted* would be visual, ornamental (fretwork), and uncomplicated.

But *fretted* carries other meanings. Tracing back to the Old English *fretan* (*for* + *itan*, to eat), as a transitive verb it can mean to gnaw; wear away; corrode; to make or form by wearing away; to make rough or disturb; to irritate, vex, or annoy. As a transitive verb, *fret* can mean to become rough or disturbed; to be irritated, annoyed, or querulous; to worry. As a noun, *fret* can mean a wearing away; a worn place; an irritation, annoyance, or worry. *Fretted*, then, proves to be both Hopkins's device for establishing the beauty of the bugler boy and also for acknowledging Satan's worm in the apple of virtuous youth. As other parts of the poem assert, the boy, lapsing from chastity, may, and by implication certainly would, prove a vexation to himself, to Hopkins, and to God.

The bugler boy is a "fretwork" who will prove fretful, but still we wonder: what has this to do with music? Another meaning of *fret* (tracing back to Old French *frette*, a band or ferrule) refers to any of several narrow, lateral ridges fixed across the finger board of a banjo, guitar, or mandolin. In this usage, *fretted* means furnished with frets. Hopkins thus links the bugler boy to a musical instrument. Frets on a guitar not only enable but also regulate the fingering. Hopkins's antithetical intention becomes clearer and more compelling. *Fretted* can mean, simultaneously, beautiful (ornamental), vexed and vexing, and also problematically disciplining. Music is invoked as self-regulation which both sublimates and reinforces military discipline. Such discipline points toward the spiritual discipline that "favourable heaven" (st. 12) might find worthy.

The bugle usually lacks keys or valves; hence, no fingering or manual discipline is required. The bugle is an oral discipline, and it is into the bugler's open, upturned mouth that Hopkins has just placed Christ's body ("Low-latched in leaf-light housel his too huge godhead"). Since the bugler plays an unfretted instrument, an oral instrument, the bugler himself, Hopkins seems to insist, must discipline not so much his fingers as his mouth, regularly to receive the communion wafer. "The Bugler's First Communion," by means of a single complex word, adds another element to Hopkins's stern but inventive judgment of the historical status and erasive potential of music.

The last of the four music poems of 1879 condenses themes from "Henry Purcell," "Who shaped these walls has shewn," and "The Bugler's First Communion." It reveals Hopkins making his most vulnerable but most heroic refusal of any musical annihilation of his own historical being. In October of 1879, Hopkins composed a short poem that personalizes his judgment of music. "At the Wedding March" raises expectations concerning musical dimensions of a ritual ceremony, but this twelve-line poem instead offers us one of the rare glimpses of Hopkins the man within Hopkins the priest. The utterance, cited by Paul Fussell as representing sprung rhythm at its best, seems tender but conventional:

At the Wedding March

Gód with honour hang your head,
Gróom, and grace you, bride, your bed
With lissome scions, swéet scíons,
Out of hallowed bodies bred.

Eách be other's comfort kind: 5
Déep, déeper than divined,
Divíne chárity, déar chárity,
Fast you ever, fást bínd.

Then let the Márch tréad our ears:
Í to hím túrn with tears   10
Whó to wedlock, hís wónder wedlock,
Déals tríumph and immortal years.

(*Poetical* 164; #141)

The celibate priest wishes the married couple a holy life of mutuality, of "dear charity," towards each other. Then, at the march, he turns with tearful eyes to God's altar. This touching glimpse of the joys and sorrows of the priestly life, acutely moving in its own way, seems to offer little or nothing about music. Presumably, music merely accompanies a joyous occasion, a sacrament, a socioreligious ritual, but in a familiar and unexceptional way.

Upon closer scrutiny, "At the Wedding March" suggests something complex about music and human nature. In the marriage rite, music marks the couple's turn from the priest and the priest's turn from the couple. A chiasmic rupture or mutual erasure occurs. The wedding march is the couple's signal to step bravely out upon their chosen sacramental path, leaving the lonely priest to a chaste silence. We view the priest in a moment of self-pity. From his own point of view, the celibate priest is compensated by a consciousness that *his* spouse, Christ, promises "triumph and immortal years" not only to the loving couple but also to the lonely priest.

We have several good reasons to appreciate this sad, lovely little poem, but we still must wonder how it judges music. An answer is forthcoming if we note what music is asked to do in the poem: "Then let the March *tread* our ears" [italics mine]. Why does Hopkins write *tread*? No less antithetical than *fretted* in "The Bugler's First Communion," *tread* is a surprising word in this context. The word *tread*, in its various meanings, proves another clue to Hopkins's intricate but firmly antithetical attitude toward erasive music.

As a noun, *tread* refers to a mark made by treading; the act of treading; manner of stepping; and that part of the sole that touches the ground. It refers to the "sound" of treading. Such a sound, accompanied by music, the tearful priest would presumably hear receding up the aisle as the wedding party departs. As a verb, *tread* induces even more complications. It means to step but also to walk over; to beat or press with feet (trample); to subdue as if by trampling (crush); and, to form a path by treading. Most pertinently, *tread* serves three other diverse usages that complicate Hopkins's judgment of this music and perhaps of music *per se*. To tread water can be to save one's own life. In addition, *tread* can mean both to execute a dance step and, in the case of a male bird, to copulate.

We know from Gardner how attentive Hopkins was to the "inner connexions between the sounds and the meanings of words" (Hopkins, *Poems* xix). He would be attentive to the multiple meanings of a word like *tread* in the context of "At the Wedding March." Rather than escaping into music, Hopkins uses the terminology of music to examine his own privileged but constrained existence as a celibate priest. This may be the poem where Hopkins not only acknowledges but also probes into his own sexuality, even into the potential violence of his sexuality. We enjoy a privileged if brief look at the priesthood and poethood of this poet-priest who cleaves not to disembodied sounds but to embodied human souls and selves.[7]

We end on a note of deep irony. Hopkins is one of those earnest Victorians whose historical consciousness compelled him to hold the entire past of humanity within himself. At stressful moments, he resorted to music for its presumed ability to erase such painful consciousness, but in the sort of heroic desperation and leaps of antithetical wit we have seen him displaying, as for example against Henry Thomas Buckle's ideological writings, conventional literary history, Longfellow's popular verses, or Frederick II's rational program for mankind, he rises above his own griefs and fears. In some of his best poems, he converts the unheard melodies strumming the secret catgut of his mind into sprung-rhythm representations of contingent human experience and human history, if only forms of "little history." On the catgut of his innermost consciousness, he must have heard not some abstract music but a Wordsworthian still, sad music of humanity or an Arnoldian note of eternal sadness. Hopkins's final crisis-consciousness rejects the very music he might forgivably resort to as an erasure of consciousness and of history. His settled view would resemble T. S. Eliot's settled view: "The music of poetry, then, must be a music latent in the common speech of its time" (24).

We can now attempt to answer our initial question: where did this ontological prosodist come from? Surely Hopkins invented sprung rhythm at least in part as a means of denying and rewriting the prosaic rationalisms and distortions of Victorian historiography? When we say that poetry experiences a recurrent envy of what it is not, we usually think of painting or sculpture or music. Having examined five Hopkinsian episodes of a unique Victorian crisis-consciousness responding to Victorian perplexities, we can now see that poetry can also envy and seek to replace Clio's rational art.

In the preface to this book, I cited Charles James Fox's precept that the writer of a preface never thinks of the truth but only of insinuating an antithesis. As I prepare to conclude, I wish to adapt Fox's witticism to my own speculations. Whenever Hopkins's true poetical genius uttered itself, such an utterance would never embody a truth but rather an antithesis. More correctly, perhaps, an acutely antithetical truth. In the end, Hopkins's musical denial of history, intended to erase what he could not endure, produced poems that reinforce his other antithetical strategies against ideologically distorted inscriptions of history. He bequeaths to us a deep, powerful, and truthful realization, truly a permanent inscription, of one very special human history.

NOTES

PREFACE

1. Miller (*Theory* 2) stipulates for the following litany of critical antitheses: nominalization of literature versus its periodization; reification versus totalization; the notion that an authentic image in poetry is unique versus investigation of literature in terms of *topoi*, archetypes, or other fixed forms transcending the particular; novelty versus tradition; relativity or historicism versus some form of absolutism; the end of history or history transformed into an "eternal Platonic state" versus endless history; temporal form versus spatial form; hermeneutic, polyrhymthic, dialectical, or discontinuous time versus linear, organic, "natural," or continuous time; structure versus form; the notion that literature is autonomous versus the notion that it should be studied in terms of some context, biographical, social, metaphysical, or religious; microscopism versus the panoramic view; poetry as an end versus poetry as a means; yielding to the work as an experience or meaning which is its own justification versus the attempt to do something for oneself with the work, to assimilate it into the critic's own patterns of meaning; subjectivity versus reality; metaphysics versus science; poetry versus the novel; angelism versus original sin; alienation versus authenticity; disengagement, objectivity, or detachment versus engagement, commitment, or involvement; ontology versus intersubjectivity; dualism versus monism (a conviction that observer and observed are two or a conviction that they are one); criticism as interpretation versus criticism as the means of developing a theory of literature; criticism as a form of literature versus criticism as the science of interpretation or as the practice of a certain methodology. I hasten to add that, unlike Norman White, who speaks of Hopkins's "cynicism" (449), I see the poet's complicated existential and discursive strategies as being forgivable ploys by an acute crisis-consciousness struggling within stressful Victorian circumstances. I never see them as mere cynicism.

191

2. Hopkins's role in nineteenth-century consciousness has been characterized in terms of a century-long diminishment from *large* to *small* (John Holloway 98-100). Thus, one of the Sonnets of Desolation—"No worst, there is none"—is said to show Victorian consciousness at its largest and deepest, with its range and scope making it a terrifying experience. Yet, the scale and scope that threaten to make it a source only of unmitigated, unparalleled despair is blessedly brief. Holloway writes: "The larger consciousness is unquestionably there for a while, but it soon dissolves." My intention is, in part, to extend the range of Holloway's acute observation concerning Hopkins's role in the formation of Victorian crisis-consciousness.

INTRODUCTION

1. Hopkins was fully aware of his own passion for explanation, as well as of the paradoxical value-cum-redundancy of explanation as a mode of thought. In 1888, to Bridges:

> We should explain things, plainly state them, clear them up, explain them; explanation—except personal—is always pure good; without explanation people go on misunderstanding; being once explained they thenceforward understand things; therefore always explain: but I have the passion for explanation and you have not. (*Letters* 275)

Said's apt point is simply that explanation is not inherently poetical.

Hermeneutical implications of Hopkins's parting shot *explanation* can be vividly foregrounded by our recalling Dilthey's adaptation of Schleiermacher's general hermeneutic. According to Dilthey, the aim of the natural sciences is "explanation" by means of static, reductive categories; on the other hand, the aim of hermeneutics is to establish a general theory of "understanding," i.e., interpretation in which the presumed inner life of a work achieves full expression (Abrams, *Glossary* 91).

2. A comprehensive examination of metaphor from many points of view is provided by Ortony.

3. In general, I prefer Martin's biography to White's. Martin, I judge, is simply the better critic and the better writer. Even so, White also testifies abundantly to Hopkins's strangely unbalanced and exotic personality that finds expression in difficult, intense antithetical poetry.

4. Developing a historicist's consciousness is no easy matter. Pater, as characterized by Carolyn Williams, can serve as a Victorian paradigm case. Both aestheticism and historicism employ skeptical inquiry in a dialectical examination of the grounds of knowledge. Any act of perception is to be understood as an

aesthetic act. Pater's exemplary turn to history guarantees objects for contemplation, even if history itself is a priori an aesthetic reconstruction (4).

A fusion of aestheticism and historicism gradually defined Pater's techniques and themes. Beginning with attention to the particularity of each object and the unrepeatability of events, he used aestheticism and historicism to discover general form within the unique datum. He transforms the poetry of earlier times, a world already transfigured by poetry, but he transfigures it again at a higher level. By doubling the distance between representation and first-order facts, he intensifies our grasp of facts. Aesthetic value now resides in the second-order transfiguration. Historical imagination as finessed by Pater is a poetical imagination that consoles us for our inability to return to prior experiences (4-5).

Pater focuses on a few historical personages, central and emblematic, and thereby projects a sense of unity in history. But his figures are both factual and figural. Forms are at bottom "habits of organization." As in *Marius the Epicurean*, he uses a form of typology, sometimes Christian typology, so that types enable mediations between generality and particularity, identity and difference, continuity and change, repetition and novelty (7).

Typically, Pater presents a historical human figure; then he generalizes all the pertinent details as being representative of an age; then he relates both individual and period type to some cultural and historical development, some enactment of abstract forces of history. Consequently, Pater's "correlative construction of progressively more inclusive wholes makes possible the construction of an overarching developmental narrative" (8).

Once Pater becomes an aesthetic historian, he represents historical objects but also reflects upon the difficulty of such representation. His famous "imaginative sense of fact" precludes mere subjectivism or solipsism as he constantly experiments with "poised positions and slippages along a double spectrum of possible identifications and disengagements in relation to an object."

Can we in fact know the past? Historicism, which covers a wide range of epistemological opinions between a naive positivism and a naive nihilism, has always been a "struggle-concept" (56). Pater's own historicism may be regarded as a systematic, mobile, skeptical, and essentially reconstructive epistemology (57). He is Hegelian in stressing the spirit of an age. He affords a useful paradigm case for my antithetical Gerard Manley Hopkins.

5. As my speculation concerning Hopkins's reconstruction of Longfellow is the most purely psychoanalytical part of my argument, I should note here a further dimension to this problem. Norman White alludes to Hopkins's "childish petulance" (142). Almost every commentator on Hopkins remarks upon the evidence that Hopkins seems, in many respects, more like a boy-man than a grownup man. He is a person who in some ways never quite matured (Martin 101-2). No one who has objectively read Martin's biography or White's will miss the cogency of this observation. I will take the point one step further. Hopkins's girlish way of walking was admittedly in conscious imitation of

Newman's famous gliding walk, but it also had roots in psychosocial principles. It is instructive to examine the poet's mannerisms and behavior in terms spelled out in *Female Adolescence* by Katherine Dalsimer. The dynamic resemblances between Dalsimer's literary subjects and Martin's (or anyone's) representation of Hopkins are quite uncanny: intense mother-relationship, first love a homosexual crush, manic-depressive fluctuations, problems coping with the freedom to make one's own choices, reluctance to face simple facts of life, wild fluctuations between self-disparagement and delusions of grandeur, sporadic artistic efforts (poetry writing, journal keeping, musical aspirations), and the like. Dalsimer's commentary might be describing the adolescent Hopkins well into his thirties and forties. A parallel Victorian literary example of this fascinating type of human personality, appearing in the year of *The Wreck of the Deutschland*, is George Eliot's heroine Gwendolen Harleth in *Daniel Deronda* (1776). See Hollahan, *Crisis-Consciousness* 84-95.

6. In a review, Jerome Bump complains that MacKenzie's continuation of the practice of numbering the poems will have the unhappy result of perpetuating critics' habit of referring to the poems by number rather than by title ("Hopkins" 283). I agree with Bump as to the awkwardness of using the numbers. I try to avoid the worst confusions that may result from using the numbering system exclusively. The radical question as to the aesthetic validity of any chronological ordering of poems in a collection is one that, following Fraistat, I take up in chapter 2.

CHAPTER ONE

1. Robertson's editorial apparatus includes 212 asterisked and bracketed footnotes placed on the page beneath Buckle's own notes. On many of Buckle's pages, his own notes and Robertson's notes take up more space than Buckle's primary text. Generally an admirer of Buckle, Robertson could both praise and blame. He finds strengths and weaknesses in Buckle's representation of facts and principles. On the whole, Robertson's notes add up to an impressive critique that holds good to this day. A sampling, with internal brackets in (c) and (d) being mine:

(a) [*Buckle's discussion of "chance" does not proceed upon an analysis of the conception, and assumes that it is a conceptual negation of causation. In reality it has never been so. The "perfectly ignorant peoples," so far from having such an idea, have at all times ascribed phenomena which transcended their knowledge and control to unseen powers or wills vaguely resembling their own. The "doctrine of Chance" of the ancient atomists, which is disparaged below, was really an attempt to supersede the latter conception by positing sequences in nature independent of *volition*. Thus, though they did not clear their own conception, and left a free field for meaningless contrary rhetoric against an idea of "blind" chance, they in a measure prepared the way for the conception of "natural law" as distinct from "particular providence." In any critical use of the term, "chance" means simply untraced or untraceable sequence or coincidence— in other words, *unknown* law.—ED.] (4)

(b) [*The historical fact is that the doctrine of Free Will, equally with that of Predestination, arose on the ground of theology, not that of non-theistic atomism. Compare *Luthardt, History of Christian Ethics*, # 43; *Milman, History of Latin Christianity*, Bk. ii. ch. ii.—ED.] (5)

(c) [*This illustration of the idea {that consciousness is} "*merely* a state or condition of the mind," goes to show that Buckle had not realized the full force of the criticisms he cites. Briefly put, they amount to saying that consciousness *is* mind, or a name for the mind, not a "condition" into which it "may be casually thrown."—ED.] (8)

(d) [*As "disturbance" here means the whole of correlations {of men and nature}, the last clause creates a confusion. "Without such disturbance" men would not exist.—ED.] (11)

(e) [*The conception of "law" here set forth is incorrect: and the idea that one law "obeys" another must be put aside. "Law in nature" is merely a name for an observed constancy of relation between phenomena, e.g. that water boils at a certain temperature and barometrical pressure. In this sense, the alleged "general law" is merely the sum total of the so-called "special laws," the whole causation occurring in terms of specific relations: e.g. a certain organism, under certain moral or physiological conditions, and at a certain temperature, will aim at suicide, and will under conditions succeed. But the law is solely in terms of specific series, which are part of the "given state of society"—and of the environment; not of any "general" predestination to death of a given number of victims. Mr. Venn (*Logic of Chance*, 2nd ed. p. 236) records that a "sort of panic" was set up "in many quarters" by Buckle's exposition. The truth involved, however, is really on all fours with that embodied in any other set of "vital statistics." In note 32, below, Buckle points to a truer conception of law; but there also the phrasing is lax, and in the text at that point it is still more so. The phrase "prodigious energy of those vast social laws" must have been penned before the note in question.—ED.] (15). On the whole, a wry tone tempers Robertson's critical admiration of Buckle: "assertions are made that do not quadrate with the present generalization" (438).

On the whole, too, Robertson's critique of Buckle squares with my reading of Hopkins's critique in "The Windhover" and indeed in the rest of his oeuvre.

2. The world-view enacted in Buckle has become rooted in modern life. Robertson and the German historian Droysen harangue each other on the value of Buckle's work. Robertson writes: "The result is that after we have appreciatively read him, hardly any history satisfies us, so poorly does the average narrative feed the curiosity he aroused" ("Introduction" xiii). His part in the evolution of culture was to prepare minds for a science of human history based upon economics and statistics. After Buckle, regulative and determining natural

law rather than mere mystery or vague providence could be seen at work in human affairs.

For Robertson, Buckle at his best cannot be surpassed in the historian's essential talents: "fullness of knowledge, breadth of grasp, and vivacity and lucidity of presentment" (viii). In tracing theories of social causation, he displayed more color than Montesquieu, more abundance and exactitude of information than Voltaire. Buckle possessed a peculiar gift for representing large movements and causal sequences. He was thus able to contribute to the advancement of historical consciousness (ix).

A different, if ambivalent, view was offered by Droysen. Buckle is said not to define *science*, *history*, *law*, and other terms crucial to his argument. Buckle wrongly assumes science to be an activity that enlarges its domain only by transferring vital (organic) materials to inorganic categories. The very assertion that only scientific method yields knowledge is patently false. In *On Liberty*, Mill bracketed and set aside the philosophical problem of free will. By contrast, complains Droysen, Buckle dismissed the issue of free will versus determinism, arguably the most interesting problem in human affairs. Buckle's claim that history results exclusively from a dialectic between outer phenomena and human inwardness seems too simplistic to merit consideration.

Droysen would prefer that Buckle had taken account of how the human spirit, that "wonderful abridger," historically comprehends both nature and man. History emerges out of men's activities, converging upon a precise moment when human learning, insight, and wit must cope with numerous contingencies: "History gives the consciousness of what we are and what we have" (74). Buckle's vaunted historical purview with its scientific method is only one among many outlooks, others being the practical, technical, legal, social, and the like. More broadly, the moral world that Buckle rules on may in fact be ontologically unique, not at all like nature, and a complex phenomenon to be *understood* rather than *explained*. The laws Buckle advances are at bottom mere generalizations from arbitrary groupings of data. Buckle confuses an effect with a cause (77).

Droysen dismisses Buckle's four "generic" premises, namely that progress depends upon scientific method, scientific method begins and ends with the spirit of skepticism, the march of intellect will replace moral laws with scientific laws, and the only enemy of progress is suppression by church or state. The real work of culture is performed by artistic genius, reconstructive understanding, or soul's intuition, all of which elude analysis. Buckle's idea of liberty crudely isolates the individual; he entirely ignores culture, preferring his arbitrary term *civilization*; he forgets that men historically live and die for the sake of intangible values and ideas; he denies the existence of consciousness (thus seriously undermining his own position); because he can not see a thing, he denies metaphysics entirely; he is interested only in the species rather than the individual. Buckle's belief in progress does not sort well with scientific method itself, given that value-free science precludes any notion of progress (86).

[In fairness, we must note here that Buckle would find himself in a fairly large, if embattled, company on this last point. Progress is one of the root problems in historiography, along with factuality, probability, plausibility, certainty, continuity, change, law, causation, motivation, contingency, and national character. During the nineteenth century, many thinkers postulated, as a law of history, humanity's majestic progress toward moral perfection, when crime and poverty would no longer mar human happiness or the rule of orderly justice. Progress was a novel idea, quite opposite from the Graeco-Roman idea of a golden age situated exclusively and irretrievably in the past. Likewise, in positing steady improvement it differed from cyclical theories such as Vico's. Then, too, the medieval theory posited perfection only in the next world. Only with the Renaissance did earthly progress become imaginable. In Buckle's time, scientific and technological innovations indeed ameliorated living conditions; humanitarians abolished slavery; more individuals enjoyed freedom and franchise. In the twentieth century, of course, a deep pessimism has seriously questioned Comtean optimisms. Such gloom sorts better with many facts of life. Any long view of history reminds us that irrationality and destructiveness are behavioral constants. Progress seems possible but by no means certain or irreversible (Shafer 56-8). Hopkins, of course, operates within such a gloom, but as it were a fine Catholic gloom repeatedly witnessing to the "*sordidness* of things" (*Correspondence* 226-27). Equally to the point, Hopkins witnesses to the human need described by Geertz, the need to attribute significance to existence rather than merely to maintain a functioning social system (169).]

Droysen concluded that Buckle's reconciling of science with other disciplines was quite valuable: "This problem appears destined to become the middle point of the great discussion which will mark the next important turn in the entire life of the sciences."

No one can consider the growing estrangement between the exact and the speculative disciplines, the dissidence between the materialistic and the supernatural view of the world which gapes wider day by day, to be normal and true. These opposing contentions demand reconciliation, and *this must be worked out in connection with Buckle's task*. For the ethical world, the world of History, which is the problem of that task, takes part in both spheres, and it shows by every phase of human existence and action that contrast is no absolute one. It is the peculiar grace of human nature, so happily incomplete, that its ethical doings must be at once spiritual and corporeal. Nothing human but has place in this dissension, but lives this double life. The opposition is reconciled each moment in order to its renewal, renewed in order to its reconciliation. To wish to understand the ethical or historical world is to recognize first of all that it is not an apparition and does not consist of a mere mutation in matter. Scientifically to transcend the false alternative between moral and material, to reconcile the dualism of those methods and those views of the world, each of which insists upon ruling or denying the other, to reconcile them in that method which applies to the ethical and historical world, to develop them into the view of the world which has its basis in the truth of human existence and in the cosmos of the moral forces—that, it seems to me, is the kernel of the problem with whose solution we are concerned.

(89; emphasis added)

Buckle, then, had situated himself at the heart of an important historical project.

The best recent discussion of Droysen is "Droysen's *Historik*: Historical Writing as a Bourgeois Science" (Hayden White, *Content* 83-103). Droysen will surface again in my Chapter 5, where his great work *Historik* is cited as having provided the model for Dalhaus's *Grundlagen der Musikgeschichte* (1977). The relationship rises again in Treitler's *Music and the Historical Imagination* (1989), which lays the groundwork for a consideration of music and history. Treitler asserts: "Droysen wrote that no one before the mid-nineteenth century thought to speak of a history of music" (172). The sequence Droysen-Dalhaus-Treitler leads me to think that Hopkins, in his untrained way, was in fact onto something in his turning from language to music.

Given Hopkins's numerous fragments and refusal to publish his poems, both Buckle and Hopkins belong to that peculiar English category, the unfinished literary project, as described by Rajan.

3. Robertson here casts a jaundiced eye on Buckle: "[*It would be more accurate to say that many Jesuits cultivated the sciences. They were none the less the persecutors of Galileo, and they sought to have the *Discours* of Descartes condemned.—ED.]" (479).

4. At least superficially, Buckle and Hopkins have interesting things in common. Both, of course, were sensitive young men who would die young. Both were somewhat eccentric, querulous scholars who left unfinished scholarly works. Ironically, both belonged to families engaged in the shipping business. Buckle's father's shipping firm was "Buckle, Bagster, and Buckle," whereas Hopkins's father founded a firm, "Manley Hopkins and Sons and Cookes," specializing in the statistical, actuarial side of maritime insurance.

At somewhat deeper levels, too, they resemble each other. Both men faced an ordeal identified by Machiavelli: nothing is more difficult than to take the lead in introducing a new order of things. Buckle's belief in regularity would seem to be opposite from Hopkins's Scotian championing of individual selves, but in fact both men looked at raw data, perhaps necessarily, through the lenses of general assumptions. Buckle himself understood that the historian's mind is "full of conceptions of order and uniformity" (*Civilization* 6). Buckle and Hopkins believed that life is a property of all matter (*Civilization* 861); both relied upon metaphor to express essential ideas about life (*Civilization* 17 n. 32).

They worked out sharply contrasted ideas on the subject of royalty: Buckle denigrated the "protective [repressive] spirit" by which European royalty secured its power, whereas Hopkins championed the somewhat advanced theology of Christ the King (Sprinker). Yet, as a Jesuit, Hopkins could accept Buckle's principle that regularity must undergird any meaningful human activity, even if he would bridle at Buckle's belief in compulsive natural law. Buckle's 3,395 footnotes and Hopkins's numerous diacritical marks suggest a similar overscrupulousness, an adolescent showiness, and a desire to control the reader's mind. For Hopkins on this point, see Patricia Ball.

Finally, just as Buckle aspired "to rescue history from the annalists, chroniclers, and antiquarians," as well as to redeem human life from enslavement to a narrowly rigid superstition, Hopkins aspired to rescue poetry from enslavement to a fixed metrical schema, as well as more broadly to redeem his fellow Englishmen from enslavement to humdrum sameness.

5. No small part of the readerly interest in "Buckle" derives from its homely but compelling sound effects, its audible shape. We recall in this connection that Hopkins is a crucial figure in the history of sound symbolism in poetry. The whole matter of the expressive value of sound symbolism, at once mimetic and systematic, has been reexamined recently by Marie Boroff.

6. Robertson's effort to vindicate Buckle culminated in *Buckle and His Critics: A Study in Sociology* (1895). In a reasoning style itself intended to rebuke Buckle's more intemperate detractors, Robertson explains Buckle's relations to the thought of his time and to truth in general, the measure of acceptance he had received, the justice of certain hostile responses, and the benefits to be derived from a study of Buckle. After listing basic general disparagements and specific criticisms of Buckle's materials and methods, Robertson devotes a long chapter to "The Development of Sociology," where he clearly spells out Buckle's cultural role and value. He ends with an appeal for a broad, humane, historically grounded evaluation of Buckle's admittedly quirky genius.

Among Buckle's critics, Robertson lists the names of Grant Allen, Hill Burton, Charles Darwin, Matthew Arnold, John Morley, Leslie Stephen, Theodore Parker, Mark Pattison, Oscar Peschel, Franz Vorländer, Henry Maine, and Hutchison Stirling. Should we not add Hopkins's name to the list?

INTERCHAPTER 1

1. Hopkins's use of Prescott's work on Philip II establishes one link in an interesting chain of coincidence. I have already noted Henry Thomas Buckle's place in the development of the human sciences, as the human sciences are described, for example, by Michel Foucault (*Order*). One of the primary documents of the human sciences is Fernand Braudel's *The Mediterranean and the Mediterranean World in the Age of Philip II* (1949). Hopkins, in this roundabout

but curiously relevant way, can be understood as having an oblique but authentic relation to historiography as one of the human sciences.

CHAPTER 2

1. Together with Fraistat, I will assume that readers read collections straight through as totalities. But do we really read collections straight through, or do we read like the Irish poet Patrick Kavanagh?

> I found out later on that the single poem read by itself possessed far more power than when included in a volume. I seldom read a book through; when I had found and read the significant word or phrase, I would close the book, feeling that to read further would only do harm. I had been baptised again by fire and Holy Spirit. (323-24)

Reading a collection of poems in whatever order can be a more demanding task than reading a plotted narrative or expository argument.

A study of poetic careers might begin with Millgate and Lipking. Millgate describes how aging Victorian writers like Browning, Tennyson, James, and Hardy orchestrated "career closure" (1) so as to shape their posthumous reputations. Processes and consequences of "self-conscious career termination" (3) occupied these and other contemporaries of Hopkins. At the other end, Lipking describes how numerous poets began their careers. Like Milton and Arnold, young Hopkins wrote a poem on Shakespeare—"In the lodges of the perishable souls / He has his portion"—in order to capture the great precursor's spirit (224). Books of poetry about "new life" initiated the careers of Dante, Goethe, Keats, Blake, Whitman, Yeats, Pound, and Eliot. Hopkins is closer to these careerists, these new poets taking possession of poetry, than we usually recognize.

2. One historian of consciousness assigns Hopkins a special place in the relations between the art of making collections and consciousness itself. In *Consciousness Regained*, Nicholas Humphrey invokes (125) Hopkins's famous assertion that "beauty may by a metaphor be called rhyme" [agreement of sound—with a slight disagreement]. Humphrey posits Hopkinsian repetition-cum-variation as the dual principle of collecting in general. Inquiring into the reasons for our making collections, he discovers a natural human tendency to look for order. He writes that the "pleasure [collectors] get from it is linked to the satisfaction human beings take in classifying incoming information: making comparisons, uncovering relationships, and imposing order on the world" (145). Furthermore, thinks Humphrey:

> a collection is distinguished from a mere accumulation by its structure. It must have unity, it must have variety. And the relationships between the

elements become as important as the elements themselves: they must have what Gerard Manley Hopkins called rhyme. (144)

Hopkins's remarks occur in the undergraduate essay "On the origin of beauty: A Platonic dialogue." In refusing to collect his poems, he chose, it would appear, not to follow out his own exquisite understanding that a lyrical assortment would be a sign-system based on and fulfilling rhyming or ordering observations.

3. In 1968, Schneider, having modestly offered journal readers a "New Reading," then exploited the dragon image by using the journal essay as the title-providing lead essay, "Dragon in the Gate," a catchy title for a competent book of criticism. Ignoring Bridges's own suggestion "to circumvent [the dragon] and attack him later in the rear," Schneider had in fact nothing to say about the implications of such a scandal blocking the doorway to a poetical collection.

4. My sense of the violence wrought by the *Wreck* upon Hopkins's *oeuvre* owes much to Dällenbach's study of the *mise en abyme*. Essentially a transgression of a narrative (53), each *mise en abyme* roots itself in reflexivity, being a reflexion of an embedded utterance related to an embedding utterance, enunciation, or whole code of a narrative. As a parasitic means of inducing metasignification, the device places a burden upon any decoder's ability to shift registers. An embedded *mise en abyme* may work its effects via semantic compression or expression; may occur early or late in a story (though usually near the middle as a pivot); may appear *en bloc* or scattered. Always, though, it is an internalized reflexion of a work of art by a work of art. Of the seventy-five ways Dällenbach uses *mise en abyme*, some prove peculiarly relevant to the *Wreck* in context of some imagined ordering: disturbance, authorial acrobatics, decentering, energy center, bigeneric structure, and altered consciousness. Radically antithetical, so to speak. See my review of Dällenbach.

5. Hopkins's forty-three sonnets in their year-by-year chronology: 1865 (10), 1877 (10), 1879 (5), 1880 (1), 1883 (1), 1885 (6), 1886 (3), 1887 (2), 1888 (2), and 1889 (3). His last poem—"To R. B."—is a sonnet.

6. By deconstruction, I mean what Jacques Derrida originally meant: a process by which a discourse of whatever kind *simultaneously* builds something up and, to the degree possible, builds it down. Throughout Hopkins's oeuvre, in particular his antithetical stance toward history, I find signs and traces of a deconstructive personality. For a practical definition, see Hollahan, *Crisis-Consciousness* (23).

7. History silently modifies the relations between poem and poem, but the *Wreck* remains a disruptive transgressor in every edition and even in every interpretation of Hopkins. To "place" a poem can mean many different things.

A literary work may occupy various places in the imagination. Randall Jarrell arranged the reading list for his poetry course by placing the *Wreck* last, as a stylistic *ne plus ultra* (Giles 89). The *Wreck* finds various places in the thought-styles of poets as diverse as Bridges, Eliot, Ivor Gurney, Hugh MacDiarmid, David Jones, C. Day Lewis, Dylan Thomas, Robert Lowell, Elizabeth Jennings, and Seamus Heaney (iv-viii). Hopkins, in another sense, finds a place as a living presence among ordinary folk: "He lives on and flourishes in word and image, in poem and drawing, in letter and photograph, and stands brilliant and foil-like even now [1989], one hundred years after his death" (Feeney, "Archive" 28). Enthusiasm such as Feeney's has its place, but we really do not know how the *Wreck* actually relates to actual life. A brilliant if scabrous hypothesis is offered by Anthony Burgess, who situates the poem by imagining a raucous Hollywood film, *The Wreck of the Deutschland*, set amidst malevolent urban decay. A definitive positioning of the *Wreck*, like a definitive ordering of Hopkins's poems, may never be attained. We are left to wonder where Hopkins would have placed it in a seriously ordered lyrical assortment.

Critics, by their interpretive structures, place the *Wreck* in various positionings. It may be last, as a "gigantic echo-chamber" reverberating to the cacophony of Hopkins's sound effects (Griffiths 347-48). It may be fragmented and dissolved among themes of encagement, naturation, and grace (Walhout). It may be used to illustrate Hopkins's knowledge of science (Zaniello), or an episode in Hopkins's Jesuitical career (Thomas), or Victorian/Apocalyptic calamitarianism (Sulloway), or Hopkins's techno-consciousness (Ong). Perhaps it should be situated first, not as a dragon in the gate but as the birth of a poet in the mode of the elegiac sublime (Sprinker)? Better, perhaps, as the "center and circumference" of the poet's oeuvre (Motto)? Where would Hopkins himself have placed it?

8. As early as 1868, Hopkins understood how important consciousness of "organization" is to the achievement of deep form. The "two axes on which rhetoric turns," he writes, "are a "disengaged and unconditioned prepossession" dialectically modified by a "very sharp and pure dialectic or, in another matter, hard and telling art-forms" (*Note-Books* 96-97).

9. In using tropological analysis, I am indebted to Hayden White (*Tropics* 1-25). Tropes fall into an archetypal pattern informing systems elaborated by Vico, Nietzsche, Hegel, Marx, Freud, Piaget, Foucault, and E. P. Thompson. White's privileged form of this four-stage pattern derives from four post-Renaissance master tropes: metaphor, metonymy, synecdoche, and irony. These four types embody experiential processes of identification, separation, classification, and self-awareness. Piaget identifies four stages of genetic epistemology in the child: sensorimotor, representational, operational, and logical. Vico earlier described four historical ages: gods, heroes, men, and decline (*ricorso*). Freud describes four stages of dream work: condensation, displacement, representation, and

secondary revision. Thompson traces working-class consciousness in four stages: relative obliviousness, self-willed apartheid, new sense of society as a whole, and final division into workers and intellectuals. In these examples, the dialectical movement is from naïve consciousness (metaphor) to sophisticated self-consciousness (irony). For White, tropology offers a valuable model both of discourse and of consciousness itself. He wavers between believing that the four-stage process is merely analogous to or is in fact ontologically the same as the figures of speech.

Kenneth Burke, Paul de Man, Harold Bloom, and others have also identified master tropes. In rhetoric, a trope is any figure of speech that effects a twist or turn in sense and meaning, a shift from a literal to a figurative sense. Tropology identifies and interprets tropes in literary discourse. Unquestioned master tropes include metaphor, metonymy, synecdoche, and irony. Other candidates put forward include aporia, hyperbole, litotes, and metalepsis. For an author or a fictive character, a trope is intended to achieve self-expression and self-definition. By means of a trope, a rhetorician also achieves a formal critique of his content and form.

Hopkins never commits his metaphorizing genius to the distancing metonymy and ordering synecdoche of a public career. Hence, he could never achieve the ironical perspective on his own poetical self that only a collection, more so a published collection, could provide.

CHAPTER 3

1. Both Longfellow and Hopkins depict Gothic/Romantic emotional extremes. Hopkins's yoking of terror ("Thy terror, O Christ") and horror ("a horror of height") in stanza 2 of *The Wreck of the Deutschland* has connections not only with the odic poet's aspirations to sublimity but also with emotional extremes appropriate to the Gothic mode. A succinct discussion of Gothic/Romantic emotionalism is provided by Robert Hume. In addition, Jerome Bump places Hopkins's emotional *tour de force* in the tradition of the Sublime, more specifically the "dynamic sublime" and, finally, the "sacrificial sublime" ("'Wreck'" 111).

2. That Hopkins kept up with American poets and poetry is clear from his references to Sidney Lanier, Whitman, and Poe (*Letters* 192). When Fr. Henry Coleridge, editor of the Jesuit periodical *The Month*, invited Hopkins to submit his shipwreck poem, he said (in Hopkins's words): "there was in America a new sort of poetry which did not rhyme or scan or construe; if mine rhymed and scanned and construed, and did not make nonsense or bad morality he did not see why it shd. not do" (*Further* 138). Fr. Coleridge, of course, rejected Hopkins's strange poem, which seems to many readers closer to Whitman than Longfellow.

3. Anecdotal evidence: when I presented my hypothesis to a Hopkins Centenary Symposium at Rockhurst College in Kansas City (October 19, 1989), the eminent Hopkins scholar Peter Milward, S.J., commended my speculations, saying that his own father had "The Wreck of the Hesperus" *by heart* and recited it repeatedly to his family. Thousands must have done.

4. Intertextuality—Bloomian or otherwise—is entwined with intention. Robert Alter tried to dismiss intertextuality on the grounds of its lacking the "writer's active, purposeful use of antecedent texts" (112). A more satisfactory understanding of Bloomian intertextuality vis-à-vis allusive poetry in general ("influence on an artist [is] always mediated in some degree by the artist's contemporaries") appears in Bump ("Influence"). Among critics, Sprinker most fully embraces Bloom's theory as an explanation of Hopkins's creative genius: "Hopkins is trapped in what Harold Bloom has called the anxiety of influence, the paradoxical situation of the modern poet in which he is compelled to honor and to imitate his precursors and to differ from them at the same time" (Sprinker 140). Sprinker makes no mention of Longfellow. For a competent if somewhat tentative application of Bloom to a body of texts, see Daniel Mark Fogel's *Covert Relations* (esp. 165-67).

5. What is the relation between sprung rhythm and ballad rhythm? Thanks to Edward Stephenson (*What Sprung Rhythm Really Is*), we can advance our understanding of Hopkins's fussy metrics. Meanwhile, Sister Marcella Marie Holloway (*The Prosodic Theory of Gerard Manley Hopkins*) provides an adequate explanation. Hopkins based his metrics upon a rhythmic unit formed by variable numbers of syllables clustering around an accent; he found one model for such practice in the traditional ballad meter; sprung rhythm and ballad measures differ only in degree of emphasis (74-5).

6. Numerous stylistic similarities—common approaches, similar organizations, shared images and language—between Hopkins's writings and his father's writings are examined by Feeney ("His Father's Son").

7. For a compelling summary of the strengths of the *Wreck*, see James Dickey ("Introduction").

INTERCHAPTER 3

1. Nowhere does *crisis* appear in Dante, Boccaccio, Cervantes, Racine, Jean de la Fontaine, or the Baudelaire of *Les Fleurs du Mal*. Nowhere do we encounter it in Horace or Ovid; nowhere in Garcilaso de la Vega, Lorca, or Rimbaud. Among English-language poets, many who wrote after the date of the first *O.E.D.* entry (1543) likewise eschew the word. Chaucer, Spenser, Shakespeare, and Milton ignore it. An extensive list can be compiled: Sir Thomas

Wyatt, Samuel Daniel (sonnets), Sir Phillip Sidney, Michael Drayton (sonnets), Thomas Traherne, John Donne, Ben Jonson, Robert Herrick, Andrew Marvell (English poems), George Herbert, Henry Vaughan, William Collins, Oliver Goldsmith, Alexander Pope, Robert Burns, Samuel Johnson, Thomas Gray (English poems), William Blake, John Keats, Matthew Arnold, A. E. Housman, Alfred Tennyson, William Butler Yeats, James Joyce, and Dylan Thomas. In America, poets who avoid *crisis* include Edward Taylor, Emerson, Lanier, Stephen Crane, Hart Crane, Pound, Marianne Moore, Theodore Roethke, and Langston Hughes. Some poets do use the great noun. Important figures such as Cowper, Coleridge, Byron, Shelley, and D. H. Lawrence did not entirely shrink from it. Even so, and as if to complicate the matter, five poets (Dryden, Wordsworth, Coleridge, Shelley, Eliot) each use it only one single time.

2. A small group of poets who, like Hopkins, regularly eschew *history* includes not only Traherne but also Milton, Shelley, Blake, and Elizabeth Barrett Browning. Consideration of this puzzling phenomenon lies outside my immediate critical task.

CHAPTER 4

1. I cite Sprinker rather than Donald Walhout because Sprinker is much the better critic, but Walhout devotes an entire chapter to "Encagement" (24-48) as symbolizing Hopkins's consciousness. *Encagement* means a "pervasive, spirit-depressing experience, binding confinement or overall containment" (7). The relevance of encagement for late Victorian crisis-consciousness was brought to my attention by my colleague Janet Gabler-Hover.

2. I follow Jeffares in his *New Commentary* on Yeats, except where Jeffares lacks or omits pertinent information, e.g., Yeats's partial ignorance of falconry. In *A Vision*, Yeats defines historical cycles as antithetical moments or patterns: "The approaching *antithetical* influx and that particular *antithetical* dispensation for which the intellectual preparation has begun will reach to complete systematisation at that moment when, as I have already shown, the Great year comes to its intellectual climax" (Jeffares 204). The contrasts between antithetical Yeats and antithetical Hopkins effectively measure some crucial differences between these two great poets. At present, I refer to Yeats only to advance my discussion of Hopkins.

3. The philosopher Jane Duran offers a convincing model of a feminist epistemology that bears, I am arguing in another context, upon Hopkins's dubiously sexed bird and Hopkins himself.

4. The word *falcon* is inherently problematical in English poetry. Among poets who never employ *falcon*: Milton, Donne, Skelton, Jonson, Crashaw, Herbert, Blake, and Coleridge. Poets who do employ *falcon*: Chaucer, Shakespeare, Spenser, Sidney (*Eclogues*), Pope, Wordsworth, Byron, Tennyson, and the Brownings. Curiously, whereas Byron carelessly refers to himself as a falcon, both Pope and Shakespeare carefully indicate that their falcon is female ("When the falcon wings her way above"; "a falcon, towering in her pride of place"). The Brownings are also sexually correct. She refers to "my spirit's falcon," but he writes "my falcon-gentle." Of indirect interest are the sonnet sequences of Daniel, Drayton, Shakespeare, Sidney, and Spenser, which contain not a single instance of *falcon*. Hopkins himself, of course, used *falcon* (actually *Falcon*) only this one single time in his oeuvre.

5. I embed my speculations to some degree in recent historicist theories. Veeser's collection *The New Historicism*—consisting of Veeser's introduction, eighteen essays by various critics, and commentaries on the essays by Hayden White and Stanley Fish—proves useful. One idea has chiefly interested me: "history must disclose and reconstruct the conditions of consciousness and action" (217). Veeser's summary (xi) of New Historical assumptions also proves helpful: every expressive act embeds itself in material practices, every oppositional critique uses the very tools it condemns, literary and non-literary texts circulate inseparably, and no discourse expresses absolute truth. To these propositions, I add Stephen Greenblatt's definition of a work of art: "the product of a negotiation between a creator or class of creators, equipped with a complex, commonly shared repertoire of conventions, and the articulations and practices of society" (12). To historicize a poet, we may need to examine the circulation of materials and discourses at the places of exchange and negotiation between discursive forms, consciousness, and cultural power (13). My antithetical Hopkins is to some degree a poet playing power games against Victorian historiography.

Gerald Graff complains of New Historians' reliance upon certain terms: oppositional, masculinist, logocentric, panoptic, hegemonic, counter-hegemonic, and transgressive (Veeser 175). I find such vocabulary to be rich in meaning and rhetorical power. In deliberately opening my own discourse to such concepts, I am chastened by Brook Thomas's caveat: "knowledge can lead [either] to empowerment [or] domination" (Veeser 201).

6. I have in mind a social-history-of-ideas process such as Erwin Panofsky's concept of *habitus*, i.e., a set of mental habits and a habit-forming cultural force or influence (Chartier 24).

Hopkins's dedication "to Christ Our Lord" (added to the poem seven years after composition and, coming from a priest, a pointless redundancy) comes under Genette's notion of *paratextuality*. An auxiliary discourse subordinate to a text proper, Genette's paratext presents a text to a public. Vestibulary strategies (title, preface, dedication) hover about a printed text and can control a reading by a certain class of reader (261-62). Illocutionary effects (intention, interpretation, plea, promise, threat, permission) delimit a text's possible meanings. Hopkins's epigraph "to Christ our Lord" permits a reader to construe his falcon poem as a pious Christian utterance. The diacritics imposed on "The Windhover" attempt to control such a reader, who is paradoxically being enabled, via sprung rhythm, to enjoy the maximum of freedom.

7. The problem of defining consciousness is complex. How little we know about our own self-consciousness is shown by Daniel Dennet's recent work in the field. See also the Introduction to Hollahan, *Crisis-Consciousness and the Novel*.

8. An irony lurks here. Rhetoricians traditionally relegated the *notari* to the nether regions of the rhetorical pantheon. Isocrates himself started out as a mere law copyist but later concealed that demeaning fact. Hopkins, with his priestly "heart in hiding," could appreciate this irony.

9. Oppenheimer's most technical argument for Giacomo's innovation appears in "The Origin of the Sonnet" (171-90), although he draws no causal connection between Giacomo's invention and *De Arte Venandi*. Hopkins might have known of Frederick's treatise and of Frederick's own sonneteering efforts. A partial manuscript of *De Arte Venandi* resides at Oxford—Bodleian Library MS Digby 152 (Wood and Fyfe lxii), which was a major center of Victorian historical thought. We do not know, in fact, whether Hopkins encountered the book itself, but his early exposure to numerous books (*Hopkins Research Bulletin* 1974-75), and his vast reading, including church history, would almost certainly guarantee his awareness of a controversial Christian statesman such as Frederick II.

Victorians continually searched the past for clues to the present (Culler 284). Hopkins read church history and might well recognize resemblances and differences between Frederick's century and his own. Frederick the skeptic became Holy Roman Emperor in 1216, the year after the death of Innocent III (1198-1215), an effective administrator and jurist. Under Innocent, the pope had become feudal lord over much of Europe. Innocent's fight against heresy used firm but kindly methods. In 1215, he convened the Fourth Lateran Council, whose seventy decrees on the Eucharist and dangerous heresies guided the church for centuries. Innocent laid the groundwork for the Dominican order, the Inquisition, and the flourishing of medieval scholasticism. In Hopkins's own day, Pope Pius IX convened Vatican Council I in 1869. In the face of modern skepticism, the council took the extraordinary step of declaring papal infallibility. Hopkins became a Jesuit novice in 1868 and was ordained a Jesuit priest in 1877, the year of "The Windhover."

10. The Wood and Fyfe edition of *De Arte Venandi cum Avibus* which I consulted provides copious information: a fifty-page translators' introduction; an account of manuscripts and editions; photographs and drawings of Frederick's castles and hunting lodges; and, a 400-page text of *De Arte Venandi*. Appendices by various hands explain mews, diseases, methods of capture, and features of modern falconry. Likewise, photographs: representations on coins and medals; the famous statue of St. Gorgon; Frederick's ancestors both Hohenstaufen and Norman; and, portraits of Frederick and his son Manfred. Further materials list types of birds known to Frederick. Of special use to me was the annotated bibliography of ancient, medieval, and modern falconry, where I found helpful references to Richard Oke and to collections of poetry dealing with falconry. A glossary and index round out the information supplied by Wood and Fyfe. *De Arte Venandi* reads like natural history or scientific historiography. It was as revolutionary as Henry Thomas Buckle's writings in Hopkins's own time and equally as relevant, albeit more obliquely, even abstrusely, to Hopkins's antithetical view of literary history.

11. Hillis Miller depicts this phenomenon under the figure of Ariadne's thread: "This escape can never succeed, since the thread is itself the interminable production of more labyrinth. What would be outside the labyrinth? More labyrinth . . ." (*Theory* 122).

12. An opposite view, to the effect that sprung rhythm aims only to make lyric rhythm not more irregular but merely more precisely mimetic, is proposed by Northrop Frye (*Anatomy* 272).

13. In addition to poems developing an explicit church/house analogy: "In the Valley of the Elwy," "The Starlight Night," "To Oxford (ii)," "The Caged Skylark," "The Lantern Out of Doors," "The Candle Indoors," "Duns Scotus's Oxford," "No worst there is none," "I wake and feel the fell of dark," "Tom's Garland," and "In honour of St. Alphonsus Rodriguez."

14. Just as falconry fuses with sonneteering, Frederick's scientific interest in verbal representation can be read from one experiment. He had a group of children reared, as far as was possible, without exposure to human language, so as to investigate the nature of language. Nothing much came of the crude experiment (Wood and Fyfe xlix).

15. What did Hopkins see from *within* the sonnet form as that form had been influenced by the art of falconry? Nuclear criticism can assist us here. The future which has never been seen must be expressed in an accessible figuration, one which enacts the future's risks and opportunities (Schwenger 251). The *play* of a structure consists of the movement of a presumed circumference around a presumedly empty center. Derrida grounds many of his speculations in an image

which would "orient, balance, and organize" such play: "By orienting and organizing the coherence of the system, the center of a structure permits the play of its elements inside the total form" (278-79). Any part-whole arrangement inscribes a space around an absent but proactive center which anticipates, for example, the multiple conjunctions and distortions of our own global situation at an existential ground zero (Schwenger 258-60).

The falconer stands in the center of an imagined circle, so that the bird knows what to guide on and where to return: "it is to their interest to 'mount up' as high as possible in circles centered on the falconer and his dog" (de Chamberlat 20). The falconry trope looks backwards toward the circle whose center is everywhere but also forward to the nuclear ground zero whose center may prove to be nowhere. In some worst-case scenario, terrors that await man in the rational Frederickian world could dissolve the sternest mettle because ground zero is a "circle around an emptiness" (Schwenger 251-52).

Like Frederick the falconer before him, in "The Windhover" Hopkins would gauge the existential courage that modern life would demand of individuals. They both anticipate Wallace Stevens's image of uncaged modern man: "the listener, who listens in the snow, / And, nothing himself, beholds / Nothing that is not there and the nothing that is." Stevens bodies forth the terrorizing dialectics between the single mind and the limitless universe (Vendler 47-62). Yeats, in "The Second Coming," put it just as apocalyptically: "The falcon cannot hear the falconer; / Things fall apart; the center cannot hold; / Mere anarchy is loosed upon the world." We should perhaps consider that Yeats's threatened "ceremony of innocence" is literally Frederick's discipline, in its seductive ethos. The socially peripheral may be the symbolically central (Leinwand 487); Hopkins would have us believe that the socially central may also be the symbolically central. Viewed from the inside, the falcon's purposive flight may be a playful but centered and disciplined performance. Hopkins never seems more prophetic than in his falcon sonnet, where tropes like "Buckle," "billion," and "gash" explode like the letter bombs described in Peter Schwenger's *Letter Bomb: Nuclear Holocaust and the Exploding Word* (1992).

16. Frederick's sonnet in the original:

> Misura, provedenza e meritanza
> fa esser l'uomo savio e conoscente,
> e ogni nobiltà buon senn'avanza
> e ciascuna riccheza fa prudenta.
>
> Né di riccheze aver grande abundanza
> faria l'omo ch'è vile esser valente,
> ma della ordinata costumanza
> discende gentileza fra la gente.

Omo ch'è posto in alto signoragio
e in riccheze abunda, tosto scende,
credendo fermo stare in signoria.

Unde non salti troppo omo ch'è sagio,
per grandi alteze che ventura prende,
ma tuttora mantegna cortesia.

(Oppenheimer 64)

17. After Frederick's death in 1250, the church nullified until the Renaissance his many innovations. A serious historical irony would obtain if Hopkins the priest uncritically refurbished Frederick's falcon-trope in all of its radical skepticism.

18. One falcon sonnet steers clear of such technical materials: a *duecento* poem, translated by D. G. Rossetti, with the title "A Lady Laments for Her Lost Lover by Similitude of a Falcon" (Wood and Fyfe 1).

CHAPTER 5

1. The year 1889, when Hopkins died, marks the end of a major phase of *Nineteenth-Century Music*. In Dalhaus's terms, 1870-89 is the "Second Age of the Symphony" (263-329). This period introduces "musical historicism," a theory and practice bearing upon Hopkins's historiographical consciousness. During Hopkins's lifetime, musical historicism developed within the contexts of historicism and of universal history. Given the widespread belief that music was a natural, logical, mathematical phenomenon transcending change, musical historicism met fierce resistance. Dalhaus recognizes an antithetical strain.

If we understand by historicism the tendency to take the historical basis of music not simply as a condition of its origin and reception but as a fundamental substance which must guide performers and listeners alike, we can then distinguish two separate issues: the fact of music's historicality (no one would wish to deny that music bears the marks of history), and the by no means obvious, indeed hotly disputed, historicist thesis that these marks of history constitute the essence of each individual work. As readily as the nineteenth century conceded the historicality of music's origins, historicism as an interpretive scheme encountered fierce, and understandable, resistance, both in music theory and in aesthetics. (322)

The writing of musical history involved "hidden motivation," sometimes religious or nationalistic in thrust (328). Polemicists challenged the popular belief that music should serve chiefly as an "aural alternative to reality" (321).

2. Hopkins's claim to hear radical music strumming upon a "secret catgut of the mind" prior to and independent of serious musical training might seem to find support from Marshall Brown's meditation upon unheard melodies: "Listen to the music, unheard by outward ears, which is as a ceaseless and invisible wind, nourishing its everlasting course with strength and swiftness" ("Unheard"). Brown, however, is that rare bird, both professor of literature and professor of music, who has earned the right to such platonic flights. Hopkins, I think, despite his literary genius, never earned that right by seriously studying the technicalities of music.

3. Despite appearances, literature and music are never identical but only analogous. What are the boundaries between literature and music? Where and how do they overlap or violate their distinct confines? What are the typical manifestations of the interaction? What are the concrete manifestations? What are the specific affinities? Which are major areas and common types of comparative study? To what extent can musico-literary study be fruitful for any historicizing literary study?

Again and again, we discover that the seemingly ahistorical Hopkins in fact worked out his unusual literary genius within pressing historiological and historiographical conditions. To advance very far into these thorny ontological perplexities would require authentic musical expertise in tandem with authentic literary expertise, such as we find only rarely, e.g., in Marshall Brown's recent paradoxes: "Music transfigures to the degree that it escapes perceptual fixation" ("Unheard" 465). But perhaps such a logical impossibility is precisely the key to Hopkins's invention of sprung rhythm?

4. Among diverse approaches to music in literature, Scher identifies word music, musical structures and techniques in literary works, and verbal music. With "word music," we construe a familiar poetic practice which verbally imitates acoustics of music. Pure poetry uses onomatopoeic words to evoke auditory musical sensations. Rhythm, stress, pitch, and timbre can create quasi-musical effects. Alliteration, assonance, consonance, and rhyme schemes can also function in this way. No two hearers may agree as to what might actually be the music being imitated (230).

Poets resort to musical forms such as sonata, fugue, rondo, and theme-and-variation. Principles of organization such as repetition, variation, balance, and contrast also link music and literature. The leitmotif, a verbal repetition-formula linking contexts together, has been borrowed from Wagnerian opera and widely used. Even counterpoint—two or more musical lines sounded simultaneously—has been attempted by poets, although Scher thinks that counterpoint can only be a metaphorical way of expressing various contrasts. [Hopkins would agree: "And in fact if you counterpoint throughout, since one only of the counter rhythms is actually heard, the other is really destroyed or cannot come to exist and what is written is one rhythm only and probably Sprung Rhythm, of which I now speak" (*Poetical* 116)].

Since both music and poetry are auditory, temporal, and dynamic, structural correspondences may represent a poem's being inspired by a piece of music (231). With "verbal music," a poet re-presents a musical piece, renders the theme or subject of an actual composition, or characterizes a musical performance or subjective response to music. Verbal music appropriates some intellectual and emotional thrust of music. It usually seems less intrusive than specific sound effects (word music) or approximated musical forms (235). Although prose writers have been successful with verbal music, the poets studied by Calvin Brown in *Tones Into Words* produced only vague effusions and "distinctly minor verse" (142).

Scher describes nonliterary verbalizations of music in program notes, reviews, and technical descriptions of music. He likewise discusses studies treating of musician figures in fictions as well as period influences on individual writers.

Scher lists weaknesses that characterize most musico-literary studies. Many interart comparisons are marred by sheer ignorance of music. Literary critics casually borrow musical terms from musical analysis, applying directly to musico-literary analysis such terms as melody, harmony, counterpoint, cadence, tonality, modulation, and orchestration. Even worse, general terms such as "musical," "musicality," and "music of poetry" are widely abused (241). In literary criticism, the term "musical" carries three basic meanings (acoustic, evocative, structural) but only "structural," signifying arrangement in music-like sequences, may carry any real meaning. Critics should leave "musical" to the poets themselves and instead discuss poetry in terms of acoustics or phonetic qualities. Perhaps, then, they can distinguish between such qualities as euphony and cacophony (242).

5. The difficulty of evaluating Hopkins's musical attainments is shown by the conflicting opinions expressed by three musicologists in 1937, 1960, and 1963. Using Hopkins's letters to Bridges as a source, John Waterhouse lists some contradictory facts: Hopkins experienced music as a boy and loved it throughout his life; he sang airs for his fellow Jesuits; at age thirty-six he studied Stainer on harmony and J. F. Bridge on counterpoint; he was drawn to Henry Purcell's music because it "inscaped" the totality of the self better than any other music; he briefly took violin lessons in 1867; he tried to teach himself to play the piano in 1875 ("to be independent of others"); he frustrated a headful of tunes by his own fumbling fingers; he resented the controls imposed by musical bars; he approved of quarter tones and Greek modes; and, he sought but impertinently rejected the advice of Professor R. P. Stewart.

For Hopkins, music was mainly an escape from intolerable frustrations, particularly during his last years. Despite his "enterprise and enthusiastic impatience" (231), he could not have made steady or solid progress in regular musical study because he wished only to do something new. Rather than condemning Hopkins's ambition as impertinent, Waterhouse judges his mania for originality to be consistent with a poet's ambitions for his writing in and for the real world. Hopkins's musical remains (scores, charts, and the like) exhibit faults of the rank beginner.

Waterhouse thinks that Hopkins's engagement with music was an escape. Hopkins quarrelled with standard concepts such as modulation, dominant key, tonic, diatonic, mode, and the like (233). He did not understand basics of music. Privately, the poet plumed himself on an authentic ear for music. Even so, his musical setting of Collins's "Ode to Spring" in the Gregorian scale of A seems to Waterhouse "very strange and wild and . . . very good" (237). Yet, in studying Greek meters, Hopkins had stumbled upon the original Greek modes and stubbornly preferred them to modern modes. Hopkins's ideas on the subject of modals were not totally devoid of sense; if the poet lived, something "interesting" might have resulted. Hopkins might have become a composer in the peripheral art of the "unaccompanied solo song" (234-35).

In 1959, when C. C. Abbott published Hopkins's journals and papers, Jack Westrup concluded: "There is something pathetic in [Hopkins's] pursuit of an art in which he had no competence." Hopkins's imagination was predominantly visual, even though he was only "an indifferent draughtsman." Hopkins's one setting of a poem of his own—"What shall I do for the land?"—is for Westrup "impossibly banal." Dismissing John Stevens's lament that harsh Jesuits and stern music teachers thwarted a potentially fine musician, Westrup objects that the study of counterpoint never destroyed true melodic inventiveness. Hopkins was insensitive and naively incompetent in handling musical notes; he never could have been other than a clumsy amateur. Just as Norman MacKenzie admonishes Hopkins's admirers not to accept Zaniello's effusive claims about Hopkins's modest scientific expertise ("Review" 106), Westrup admonishes us not to distort Hopkins's true value as a poet by regarding everything the poet did as of equal significance (74-5).

The issue was joined again in 1963 by musicologist William Graves. Given the range of colors, moods, and "distinctive rhythms" in Hopkins's poetry, Graves finds it plausible to imagine Hopkins the poet as a musician and composer.

He acquired most of his technical competency in the rudiments during childhood, beginning with training at home by an aunt. During his early years he learned such skills as solfeggio and musical notation, while absorbing from his entire family a lasting interest in native folksong. His stay at Oxford, although he undertook no specialized study of music, afforded him the opportunities of associating with people with musical interests and of attending concerts. Later, just prior to the beginning of his religious career, *he began the study of the violin on his own initiative*, perhaps because of the influence of John Henry Newman (an amateur violinist and ardent performer of chamber music). Hopkins records having spent an evening listening to a string quartet in which Newman played. A few years later, Hopkins undertook to *teach himself piano*, and pursued the study intermittently as best he could—sometimes with only a sacristy harmonium, sometimes with no instrument at all—for the remainder of his life. Certainly Hopkins possessed taste and cultivation in music—an important fact in the following consideration of his struggles to assert himself as a composer. We can infer much from his references to music and composers—Chopin, Wagner, Berlioz, Beethoven, Purcell, and others. But it is difficult to reconcile his later consuming interest in musical composition with those years in which he *labored by the most tedious of methods, self-instruction*, to further his skill. That he sustained interest through such labor is the *paradox of his musical life*. With scarcely nine years of life remaining, Hopkins *suddenly and intensely felt the desire to compose*. From 1880 on, there are repeated references in his letters to musical inspiration and the spontaneous writing down of melodies. However difficult to explain, there seems no doubt that his concern for music represented a *channeling of his creative energies from poetry*. As a parish priest amid the squalor of industrial Liverpool, he felt walled-in and abandoned by his muse. Life about him was "bleared, smeared," and only occasionally could he find inspiration for a poem. He remarked that all creativity, except for music, had died in him. This period marked the initial appearance of the recurrent *onslaughts of depression* which burdened his last years. (146-47; emphases added)

Music represents an escape from the nightmare of history, both private and public.

Graves thinks that Hopkins's attempts to study counterpoint and harmony did not prosper because he was by turns compliant and rebellious toward customary rules. Hopkins was "caught between the apparently conflicting necessities of basic musical techniques on the one hand and high artistic purposes on the other" (148). Only twenty-seven pieces, all vocal and without any accompaniment, survive. They manifest Hopkins's interest in chant, song, madrigal, and the composer Henry Purcell; they show influences from Latin and Greek theoretical writings; they use quarter tones, an interval abandoned in Western music after the classical period of Greek culture. Presumably anxious to find a musical equivalent for poetical or linguistic sprung rhythm, Hopkins sought a style full of poetical nuance, modally free of restrictive harmonic conventionality, and as archaic and individualistic as possible (148).

Technically, Graves goes beyond Waterhouse and Westrup in examining Hopkins's compositions:

In music, the true counterparts of sprung rhythm are probably best expressed by syncopation, variation of bar length, and the asymmetrical phrase. On the other hand, running rhythm is comparable to regularity of bar length and musical accent, together with balanced phrases comprised of an equal number of bars. As in poetry, the symmetrical principle was ascendant in the music of Hopkins's era. (150)

Sprung rhythm means basically three things: (a) breaking the alternating stresses of running rhythms, (b) varying the syllabic lengths of lines, and (c) juxtaposing accents. Hopkins could have noted, as Graves says, that attributes of sprung rhythm do in fact occur in music, but the poet's own practice in poetry was based mainly on the linguistic principles of symmetry and asymmetry between sprung rhythm and regular (running) rhythm.

Hopkins may have realized that musical rhythm tends to override—Nietzsche would say *erase*—prosodic rhythm (150). This can be seen in his setting of Dixon's "Fallen Rain," with its conventional form of notation combined with certain sprung rhythm effects, a glissando-like group of sixteenth notes adding a touch of tone painting, as well as quarter notes and a strophic structure displaying some "imaginative growth" between the sections. But Hopkins, lacking any knowledge of harmony, provides no accompaniment, even if the setting is marked by vaguely musical considerations rather than prosodic requirements (150-51).

Graves notes that the poet is thought to have set to music three of his own poems: "Hurrahing in Harvest," "Morning, Midday, and Evening Sacrifice," and "Spring and Fall." Such presumed settings do not survive. Three surviving pieces with accompaniments reveal that Hopkins had serious difficulties with harmonization (153).

Graves's final remarks adequately condense the critical problem we face in dealing with Hopkins's curious encounter with music:

> To speculate, as many have done, on the growth of Hopkins' musical talent under favorable conditions underscores the very restrictions which opposed it. He pursued composition through only eight or nine years— under circumstances far from ideal. With little access to the society of trained musicians and to the use of instruments, Hopkins' opportunities to learn more were, to say the least, limited. But the same sensibility of ear which led his interest in the direction of music and, specifically, its melodic virtues, has yielded in his poetry perhaps those very qualities which he had hoped to achieve in an art which remained essentially alien to him through the limitations of time and circumstance. (155)

The poet who would be no poet and the musician who would be no musician happily found his true métier.

6. My speculations draw upon several musico-literary studies: William Freedman's work on Sterne and the lyrical novel, Beryl Gray's work on George Eliot and music, and Robert Wallace's analysis of the musical component in

Emily Brontë and Jane Austen. Yet these interart studies come under Scher's logical strictures. I am left with the sinking feeling that, as Geoffrey Grigson would have it, music and language may be two mutually exclusive contexts (*Notebook* 86).

7. Treitler's *Music and the Historical Imagination* asserts that the sort of antithetical alienation from reality not uncommon to western music may in fact not be a natural phenomenon but rather an induced phenomenon: "It is a product of a psychological dynamic that has received cultural reinforcement and epistemological reinforcement" (11). To understand Hopkins's antithetical reactions to history via music and to music via poetry, we may well begin and end with a view of Hopkins's musical experience as itself inherently conflicted and for some very good reasons.

Hopkins lived during the period that historians of music regard as the English renaissance (Walker 316-43). However, Hopkins managed, as in theology, science, and other areas of intellectual inquiry, to remain at best on the periphery. Hopkins's Victorian crisis-consciousness unfolds between two opinions expressed by music historians, in 1888, the year before his death (Walker 100). Describing an extraordinary increase, a "flood" of people studying music, Henry Fisher noted: "The musical profession is perilously easy to enter, for the simple reason that it does not require the investment of a large capital." Hopkins was unwilling to invest time, energy, and discipline in the study of music; a refusal to invest capital, as it were. Additionally, J. H. Mapleson noted: "Except among the richer classes almost everyone who studies music ends by teaching music to someone else" (Walker 100). Given Hopkins's lifelong annoyance with the demands of teaching, we can easily understand his ambivalence toward music to be in fact, in this and other respects, a response rooted in his firm grasp of a cultural moment in Victorian England.

WORKS CITED

Abrams, M. H. *The Mirror and the Lamp: Romantic Theory and the Critical Tradition.* New York: Norton, 1958.

—. *A Glossary of Literary Terms.* 6th ed. New York: Harcourt Brace Jovanovich, 1985.

Adams, Robert Martin. *The Land and Literature of England: A Historical Account.* New York: Norton, 1983.

—. "A Counter Kind of Book." *The Egoist* by George Meredith. Ed. Robert M. Adams. New York: Norton, 1979. 551-60.

Allan, Keith, and Kate Burridge. *Euphemism and Dysphemism: Language Used as Shield and Weapon.* Oxford: Oxford UP, 1991.

Alter, Robert. *The Pleasures of Reading in an Ideological Age.* New York: Simon and Schuster, 1989.

Amoss, Benjamin McRae, Jr. *Time and Narrative in Stendhal.* Athens: U of Georgia P, 1992.

Anderson, Warren. "A Commentary on the Complete Poems of Gerard Manley Hopkins' 'Never-Eldering Revel': *The Wreck* and the Ode Tradition." Milward and Schoder 131-38.

Anderson, William S. "The Theory and Practice of Poetic Arrangement from Vergil to Ovid." Fraistat, *Place* 44-65.

Arvin, Newton. *Longfellow: His Life and Work.* Boston: Little, Brown, 1963.

Austen-Leigh, James Edward. *A Memoir of Jane Austen.* Ed. R. W. Chapman. Oxford: Clarendon, 1926.

Ayer, A. J. *Wittgenstein.* New York: Random House, 1985.

Baker, William E. *Syntax in English Poetry 1870-1930.* Berkeley: U of California P, 1967.

Ball, Patricia. *The Science of Aspects: The Changing Role of Fact in the Works of Coleridge, Ruskin and Hopkins.* London: Athlone, 1971.

Barry, Kevin. *Language, Music and the Sign: A Study in Aesthetics, Poetics, and Poetic Practice from Collins to Coleridge.* New York: Cambridge UP, 1987.

Barry, Paul J. *Mary in Hopkins' Writings and Life*. Rome: Catholic Book Agency, 1970.

Barthes, Roland. *Mythologies*. Sel. and trans. Annette Lavers. New York: Hill and Wang, 1972.

—. "What is Criticism?" *Critical Essays*. Trans. Richard Howard. Evanston: Northwestern UP, 1972. 255-60.

—. *Sade/Fourier/Loyola*. Trans. Richard Miller. New York: Hill and Wang, 1976.

—. "The Death of the Author." *Image-Music-Text*. Trans. Stephen Heath. New York: Hill and Wang, 1977. 142-49.

Bate, W. Jackson. *The Burden of the Past and the English Poet*. Cambridge: Harvard UP, 1970.

Baudelaire, Charles. *The Flowers of Evil*. Ed. Marthiel and Jackson Mathews. New York: New Directions, 1989.

Beardsley, Monroe C. *Aesthetics: Problems in the Philosophy of Criticism*. New York: Harcourt, 1958.

Bender, Todd K. *Gerard Manley Hopkins: The Classical Background and Critical Reception of His Work*. Baltimore: Johns Hopkins UP, 1966.

Bergonzi, Bernard. *Gerard Manley Hopkins*. New York: Macmillan, 1977.

Bermann, Sandra L. *The Sonnet Over Time: A Study of the Sonnets of Petrarch, Shakespeare, and Baudelaire*. Chapel Hill: U of North Carolina P, 1988.

Bloom, Harold. *The Anxiety of Influence: A Theory of Poetry*. New York:Oxford UP, 1975.

Booth, Wayne. "Metaphor as Rhetoric: The Problem of Evaluation." Sacks 47-70.

Bornstein, George. "The Arrangement of Browning's *Dramatic Lyrics* (1842)." Fraistat, *Place* 272-88.

Boroff, Marie. "Sound Symbolism as Drama in the Poetry of Robert Frost." *PMLA* 107 (1992): 131-44.

Borrello, Alfred, ed. *A Concordance to the Poetry in English of Gerard Manley Hopkins*. Metuchen, N. J.: Scarecrow, 1969.

Boyle, Robert. *Metaphor in Hopkins*. Chapel Hill: U of North Carolina P, 1961.

Braudy, Leo. *The Frenzy of Renown: Fame and Its History*. New York: Oxford UP, 1986.

Breisach, Ernst. *Historiography: Ancient, Medieval, and Modern*. Chicago: U of Chicago P, 1983.

Bridges, Robert. "Preface." *Poems of Gerard Manley Hopkins*. Ed. Robert Bridges. 2nd ed. London: Oxford UP, 1930.

Briggs, Asa. *Victorian Things*. Chicago: U of Chicago P, 1988.

Brodsky, Joseph. "The Keening Muse." Walder 351-57.

Brombert, Victor. "Frisch, Cheever, the Prison Cell." *Rivista di Letterature Moderne e Comparate* 40 (1987): 59-67.

Brooke-Rose, Christine. *A Grammar of Metaphor*. London: Secker & Warburg, 1958.

Brown, Calvin S. *Music and Literature: A Comparison of the Arts*. Athens: U of Georgia P, 1948.

—. *Tones Into Words: Musical Compositions as Subjects of Poetry*. Athens: U of Georgia P, 1953.

Brown, Marshall. "'Errours Endlesse Traine': On Turning Points and the Dialectical Imagination." *PMLA* 99 (1984): 9-25.

—. "Contemplating the Theory of Literary History." *PMLA* 107 (1992): 13-25.

—. "Unheard Melodies: The Force of Form." *PMLA* 107 (1992): 465-81.

Browning, Robert. *The Poetical Works of Robert Browning [,] Complete from 1833 to 1868 and the shorter poems thereafter*. New York: Oxford UP, 1940.

Bücher, Karl. "Work and Rhythm." Bujic 327-33.

Buckle, Henry Thomas. *Introduction to the History of Civilization in England* Ed. John M. Robertson. London: George Routledge, 1904.

—. *The Miscellaneous and Posthumous Works of Henry Thomas Buckle*. 2 vols. Ed. Grant Allen. London: Longmans, Green, 1885.

—. *On Scotland and the Scotch Intellect*. Ed. and intro. H. J. Hanham. Classics of British Historical Literature Series. Chicago: U of Chicago P, 1970.

Bujic, Bojan, ed. *Music in European Thought: 1851-1912*. Cambridge: Cambridge UP, 1988.

Bump, Jerome. "'The Wreck of the Deutschland' and the Dynamic Sublime." *ELH* 41 (1974): 106-29.

—. "Reading Hopkins: Visual vs. Auditory Paradigms." *Bucknell Review* 26 (1982): 119-45.

—. *Gerard Manley Hopkins*. Boston: Twayne, 1982.

—. "Influence and Intertextuality: Hopkins and the School of Dante." *JEGP* 83 (1984): 356-62.

—. "Gerard Manley Hopkins." *Victorian Poetry* 29 (1991): 283-95.

—. "The Hopkins Centenary: The Current State of Criticism." Hollahan, *Hopkins* 7-39.

Bumstead, Lori-Ann. "*The Wreck of the Deutschland* and Inspired Language." *The Hopkins Quarterly* 17 (1990): 69-83.

Burgess, Anthony. *The Clockwork Testament or Enderby's End*. New York: Knopf, 1975.

Bush, Ronald. "Paul de Man, Modernist." *Theoretical Issues in Literary History*. Ed. David Perkins. Cambridge UP, 1991. 35-59.

Buttel, Robert. "Hopkins and Heaney: Debt and Difference." Giles 110-13.

Carlyle, Thomas. *The Life of Friedrich Schiller, Comprehending an Examination of His Works*. 1825. New York: Bedford, Clark, 1872.

Carpenter, Humphrey. *W. H. Auden: A Biography*. Boston: Houghton Mifflin, 1981.

Carretta, Vincent. "'Images Reflect from Art to Art': Alexander Pope's *Collected Works* of 1717." Fraistat, *Place* 195-233.

"Catholic Poets." *Month* 120 (1912): 439-40.

Caws, Mary Ann. *Reading Frames in Modern Fiction*. Princeton: Princeton UP, 1985.

—. *The Art of Interference: Stressed Readings in Verbal and Visual Texts*. Princeton: Princeton UP, 1989.

Chartier, Roger. *Cultural History: Between Practices and Representations*. Trans. Lydia G. Cochrane. Ithaca: Cornell UP, 1988.

Charvat, William, and Michael Kraus, eds. *William Hickling Prescott: Representative Selections*. New York: American Book, 1943.

Christ, Carol T. *The Finer Optic: The Aesthetic of Particularity in Victorian Poetry*. New Haven: Yale UP, 1975.

Cluck, Nancy Anne, ed. *Essays on Form: Literature and Music*. Provo, UT: Brigham Young UP, 1981.

Cockshut, A. O. J. *The Art of Autobiography in Nineteenth and Twentieth Century England*. New Haven: Yale UP, 1984.

Cohen, Paula Marantz. *The Daughter's Dilemma: Family Process and the Nineteenth-Century Domestic Novel*. Ann Arbor: U of Michigan P, 1991.

Cohen, Ted. "Metaphor and the Cultivation of Intimacy." Sacks 1-10.

Collingwood, R. G. *The Idea of History*. 1946. London: Oxford UP, 1956.

Conrad, Peter. *Romantic Opera and Literary Form*. Berkeley: U of California P, 1977.

Conroy, Mark. *Modernism and Authority: Strategies of Legitimation in Flaubert and Conrad*. Baltimore: Johns Hopkins UP, 1985.

Cotter, James Finn. *Inscape: The Christology and Poetry of Gerard Manley Hopkins*. Pittsburgh: U of Pittsburgh P, 1972.

—. "The Mystery of 'It' in *The Wreck of the Deutschland.*" *The Hopkins Quarterly* 17 (1991): 131-38.

Crane, R. S. *Critical and Historical Principles of Literary* History. Fwd. Sheldon Sacks. Chicago: U of Chicago P, 1971.

Culler, A. Dwight. *The Victorian Mirror of History*. New Haven: Yale UP, 1985.

Curran, Stuart. "Multum in Parvo: Wordsworth's *Poems, in Two Volumes* of 1807." Fraistat, *Place* 234-53.

Dale, Peter Allan. *The Victorian Critics and the Idea of History: Carlyle, Arnold, Pater*. Cambridge: Harvard UP, 1977.

Dalhaus, Carl. *Between Romanticism and Modernism: Four Studies in the Music of the Later Nineteenth Century*. Trans. Mary Whitall. Berkeley: U of California P, 1980.

—. *Realism in Nineteenth-Century Music*. Trans. Mary Whitall. New York: Cambridge UP, 1988.

—. *Nineteenth-Century Music*. Trans. J. Bradford Robinson. Berkeley: U of California P, 1989.

Dällenbach, Lucien. *The Mirror in the Text*. Trans. Jeremy Whiteley and Emma Hughes. Chicago: U of Chicago P, 1989.

Dalsimer, Katherine. *Female Adolescence: Psychoanalytic Reflections on Works of Literature*. New Haven: Yale UP, 1986.

Darnell, D. G. *William Hickling Prescott*. Boston: Twayne, 1975.

Davie, George Elder. *The Democratic Intellect: Scotland and Her Universities in the Nineteenth Century*. Edinburgh: Edinburgh UP, 1961.

de Chamberlat, Christian Antoine. *Falconry and Art*. London: Sotheby, 1987.

Dennett, Daniel C. *Consciousness Explained*. New York: Little, Brown, 1991.

Derrida, Jacques. "Structure, Sign, and Play in the Discourse of the Human Sciences." *Writing and Difference*. Trans. Alan Bass. Chicago: U of Chicago P, 1978. 278-93.

Desmond, John F. *Risen Sons: Flannery O'Connor's Vision of History*. Athens: U of Georgia P, 1987.

Dickey, James. "Introduction." *The Wreck of the Deutschland*. Boston: David R. Godine, 1971. [i-iii].

Dilligan, Robert J., and Todd K. Bender. *A Concordance to the English Poetry of Gerard Manley Hopkins*. Madison: U of Wisconsin P, 1970.

Dilthey, Wilhelm. "On Understanding Music." Bujic 370-4.

Dodds, Jerrilynn D. *Architecture and Ideology in Early Medieval Spain*. University Park: Pennsylvania State UP, 1992.

Droysen, Johann Gustav. "The Elevation of History to the Rank of a Science." *Outlines of the Principles of History*. 1893. Trans. E. Benjamin Andrews. New York: Howard Fertig, 1967. 61-89.

Dunham, Michael. "Hopkins' Musical Setting of 'The Battle of the Baltic.'" *The Hopkins Quarterly* 9 (1982): 87-90.

Dunne, Tom. *Gerard Manley Hopkins: A Comprehensive Bibliography*. Oxford: Clarendon, 1976.

Duran, Jane. *Toward a Feminist Epistemology*. Savage, Maryland: Rowman & Littlefield, 1991.

Eagleton, Terry. "Ideology and Scholarship." *Historical Studies and Literary Criticism*. Ed. Jerome J. McGann. Madison: U of Wisconsin P, 1985. 114-25.

Eliot, T. S. "The Music of Poetry." *On Poetry and Poets*. New York: Farrar, Straus and Cudahy, 1957. 17-33.

Ellis, Virginia Ridley. *Gerard Manley Hopkins and the Language of Mystery*. U of Missouri P, 1991.

Ellsberg, Katherine. *Created to Praise: The Language of Gerard Manley Hopkins*. New York: Oxford UP, 1987.

Empson, William. *Using Biography*. Cambridge: Harvard UP, 1984.

Epstein, Julia. "Historiography, Diagnosis, and Poetics." *The Art of the Case History. Literature and Medicine* 11.1 (April 1992).

Ehrlich, Cyril. *The Music Profession in Britain Since the Eighteenth Century: A Social History*. Oxford: Oxford UP, 1985.

Fass, Ekbert. *Retreat into the Mind: Victorian Poetry and the Rise of Psychiatry*. Princeton: Princeton UP, 1988.

Feeney, Joseph J., S.J. "The Gerard Manley Hopkins Archive of the Harry Ransom Humanities Research Center." *Hopkins Lives: An Exhibition and*

Catalogue. Comp. and intro. Carl Sutton; Ed. Dave Oliphant. Austin: Harry Ransom Humanities Research Center [U of Texas], 1989. 11-39.

——. "His Father's Son: Common Traits in the Writing of Manley Hopkins and Gerard Manley Hopkins." Hollahan, *Hopkins* 277-92.

Finnegan, Ruth. *The Hidden Musicians: Music-Making in an English Town*. Cambridge: Cambridge UP, 1989.

Finney, Gretchen Ludke. *Musical Backgrounds for English Literature: 1580-1650*. New Brunswick, New Jersey: Rutgers UP, 1980.

Flieger, Jerry Aline. "The Purloined Punchline: Joke as Textual Paradigm." *Modern Language Notes* 98 (1983): 941-67.

Fogel, Daniel Mark. *Covert Relations: James Joyce, Virginia Woolf, and Henry James*. Charlottesville: U of Virginia P, 1990.

Foltz, William, and Todd K. Bender. *A Concordance to the Sermons of Gerard Manley Hopkins*. New York: Garland, 1989.

Forsyth, R. A. *The Lost Pattern: Essays in the Emergent City Sensibility in Victorian England*. Nedlands: U of West Australia P, 1976.

Foucault, Michel. *Discipline and Punish: The Birth of the Prison*. Trans. Alan Sheridan. New York: Pantheon, 1975.

——. *The Order of Things: An Archaeology of the Human Sciences*. New York: Pantheon Books, 1970.

Fraistat, Neil. *The Poem and the Book: Interpreting Collections of Romantic Poetry*. Chapel Hill: U of North Carolina P, 1985.

——. "The Place of the Book and the Book as Place." Fraistat, *Place* 3-17.

——. *Poems in Their Place: The Intertextuality and Order of Poetic Collections*. Ed. Neil Fraistat. Chapel Hill: U of North Carolina P, 1986.

Freedman, William. *Laurence Sterne and the Origins of the Musical Novel*. Athens: U of Georgia P, 1978.

Froude, James Anthony. *Short Studies on Great Subjects*. 4 vols. London: Longmans, 1867-83.

Fry, Paul H. *The Poet's Calling in the English Ode*. New Haven: Yale UP, 1980.

Frye, Northrop. *Fables of Identity: Studies in Poetic Mythology*. New York: Harcourt, Brace & World, 1963.

——. *Anatomy of Criticism: Four Essays*. New York: Atheneum, 1969.

Fussell, Paul. *Poetic Meter and Poetic Form*. Rev. ed. New York: Random House, 1978.

Fyfe, Gordon, and John Law, eds. *Picturing Power: Visual Depiction and Social Relations*. Sociological Review Monograph 35. New York: Routledge, 1988.

Gabler, Hans Walter, with Wolfhard Steppe and Claus Melchior. *Ulysses: A Critical and Synoptic Edition*. 3 vols. New York: Garland, 1984.

Gabler-Hover, Janet. "The Ethics of Determinism in Henry James's 'In the Cage,'" *Henry James Review* 13 (1992): 253-74.

Gadamer, Hans-Georg. *Truth and Method*. New York: Crossroad, 1984.

—. "The Hermeneutics of Suspicion." *Hermeneutics: Questions and Prospects.* Ed. Gary Shapiro and Alan Sica. Amherst: U of Massachusetts P, 1984. 54-65.

Gagnier, Regenia. *Subjectivities: A History of Self-Representation in Britain, 1832-1920.* Oxford: Oxford UP, 1990.

Gardiner, C. Harvey. *William Hickling Prescott: A Biography.* Intro. Allan Nevins. Austin: U of Texas P, 1969.

Gardner, W. H. *Gerard Manley Hopkins (1844-1889): A Study of Poetic Idiosyncrasy in Relation to Poetic Tradition.* 2 vols. 1949. London: Oxford UP, 1966.

—. "Introduction." *Poems and Prose of Gerard Manley Hopkins.* 1953. Middlesex, England: Penguin, 1975. xiii-xxxvi.

Gates, Barbara T. *Victorian Suicide: Mad Crimes and Sad Histories.* Princeton: Princeton UP, 1988.

Gay, Peter. *Style in History.* New York: Basic, 1974.

Geertz, Clifford. *The Interpretation of Cultures.* New York: Basic, 1973.

Gellrich, Jesse M. *The Idea of the Book in the Middle Ages: Language Theory, Mythology, and Fiction.* Ithaca: Cornell UP, 1985.

Genette, Gérard. "Introduction to the Paratext." *New Literary History* 22.2 (Spring 1991): 262-72.

Georgiades, Thrasybulos. *Music and Language: The Rise of Western Music as Exemplified in Settings of the Mass.* Trans. Marie Louise Göllner. Cambridge: Cambridge UP, 1982.

Giddens, Anthony. *Central Problems in Social Theory.* Berkeley: U of California P, 1979.

Giles, Richard F., ed. *Hopkins Among the Poets: Studies in Response to Gerard Manley Hopkins.* The International Hopkins Association Monograph Series. Monograph #3. Hamilton, Ontario [Canada], 1985.

Gilson, Étienne. "Foreword." *The City of God* by Saint Augustine. Trans. Gerald J. Walsh, S.J., and others. Intro. Vernon J. Bourke. Garden City: Image, 1958. 13-35.

—. *The Philosophy of St. Bonaventure.* New York: Image, 1938.

Glavin, John J. "'The Wreck of the Deutschland' and 'Lycidas': Ubique Naufragium Est." *Texas Studies in Literature and Language* 22 (1980): 522-46.

Gleason, John P. "The Sexual Underthought in Hopkins' 'The Windhover.'" *Victorian Poetry* 27 (1989): 201-06.

Gleason, Robert W. "Introduction to the *Spiritual Exercises.*" Loyola 11-31.

GoGwilt, Chris. "Introduction: A Voice from the World." Hopkins Issue. *Thought* 65 (1990): 475-80.

Goldmann, Lucien. "Structure: Human Reality and Methodological Concept." *The Languages of Criticism and the Sciences of Man: The Structuralist Controversy.* Ed. Richard Macksey and Eugenio Donato. Baltimore: Johns Hopkins UP, 1970. 98-110.

Gorham, Herbert S. *A Victorian American: Henry Wadsworth Longfellow.* New York: Grosset & Dunlap, 1964.

Graves, William L. "Gerard Manley Hopkins as Composer: An Interpretive Postscript." *Victorian Poetry* 1 (1963): 146-55.

Gray, Beryl. *George Eliot and Music.* New York: St. Martin's, 1989.

Greenblatt, Stephen. "Shakespeare and the Exorcists." *Shakespeare and the Question of Theory.* Ed. Patricia Parker and Geoffrey Hartman. New York: Methuen, 1985. 163-87.

Griffiths, Eric. *The Printed Voice of Victorian Poetry.* Oxford: Clarendon, 1989.

Grigson, Geoffrey. *Collected Poems: 1963-1980.* London: Allsion & Busby, 1982.

—. *The Private Art: A Poetry Note-Book.* London: Allison and Busby, 1982.

Habermas, Jürgen. *Knowledge and Human Interests.* Trans. Jeremy J. Shapiro. Boston: Beacon, 1971.

—. *Legitimation Crisis.* Trans. Thomas McCarthy. Boston: Beacon, 1973.

Hagenbüchle, Roland. "Precision and Indeterminacy in the Poetry of Emily Dickinson." *Emerson Society Quarterly* 20 (1974): 33-56.

Hampton, Timothy. *Writing From History: The Rhetoric of Exemplarity in Renaissance Literature.* Ithaca: Cornell UP, 1990.

Hanham, H. J., ed. Introduction. *On Scotland and the Scottish Intellect.* By Henry Thomas Buckle. Chicago: U of Chicago P, 1970. xiii-xxxviii.

Hansen, Harry. *Longfellow's New England.* New York: Hastings House, 1972.

Hardison, O. B, Jr. *Disappearing Through the Skylight: Culture and Technology in the Twentieth Century.* New York: Viking, 1989.

Harries, Karsten. "Metaphor and Transcendence." Sacks 71-88.

Harris, Daniel A. *Inspirations Unbidden: The 'Terrible Sonnets' of Gerard Manley Hopkins.* Berkeley: U of California P, 1982.

Harrison, Antony H. *Victorian Poets and Romantic Poets: Intertextuality and Ideology.* Charlottesville: U of Virginia P, 1990.

Harting, James Edmund. *Hints on the Management of Hawks and Practical Falconry; Chapters Historical and Descriptive.* 1898. Maidenhead: Thames Valley, 1971.

Hassan, Ihab. *The Dismemberment of Orpheus: Toward a Postmodern Literature.* 2nd ed. Madison: U of Wisconsin P, 1982.

Hawkins, Peter S. "Divide and Conquer: Augustine in the *Divine Comedy.*" *PMLA* 106 (1991): 471-82.

Heaney, Seamus. *Station Island.* New York: Farrar, Straus, Giroux, 1985.

Heath-Stubbs, John. *The Ode.* London: Oxford UP, 1969.

Hegel, Georg Wilhelm Friedrich. *Lectures on the Philosophy of World History[:] Introduction: Reason in History.* Trans. H. B. Nisbet; Intro. Duncan Forbes. Cambridge: Cambridge UP, 1975.

Helmecke, Carl Albert. "Buckle's Influence on Strindberg." Diss. U of Pennsylvania (1924).

Heninger, S. K., Jr. "Sequences, Systems, Models: Sidney and the Secularization of Sonnets." Fraistat, *Place* 66-94.

Hertz, David Michael. *The Tuning of the Word: The Musico-Literary Poetics of the Symbolist Movement.* Carbondale: Southern Illinois UP, 1987.

Heuser, Alan. *The Shaping Vision of Gerard Manley Hopkins.* New York: Oxford UP, 1958.

—. "Number, Metre, and Music." *Shaping Vision* 82-87.

Hoagwood, Terence Allan. "Hopkins's Intellectual Framework: Newman, Pater, and the Epistemological Circle." In *Centenary Revaluation of Gerard Manley Hopkins.* Ed. Eugene Hollahan. *Studies in the Literary Imagination* 21 (1988): 23-39.

Hohenstaufen, Frederick II of. *The Art of Falconry[,] being the "De Arte Venandi cum Avibus" of Frederick II of Hohenstaufen.* Trans. and ed. Casey A. Wood and F. Marjorie Fyfe. Stanford: Stanford UP, 1943.

Hollahan, Eugene. "Beguiled Into Action: Silence and Sound in Conrad's *Victory.*" *Texas Studies in Literature and Language* 16 (1974): 349-362.

—. "The Orpheus Allusion in *Evelina* (1778) and *La Peste* (1947): An Essay in Stoffgeschichte." *Comparative Literature Studies* XVI.2 (Spring 1979): 110-120.

—. "An Anxiety of Influence Overcome: Dickey's *Puella* and Hopkins' *The Wreck of the Deutschland.*" *James Dickey Newletter* 1 (1985): 2-12.

—. "Editor's Comment." *Centenary Revaluation of Gerard Manley Hopkins.* Ed. Eugene Hollahan. *Studies in the Literary Imagination* 21 (1988): 1-6.

—. Rev. of *The Mirror in the Text* by Lucien Dällenbach. *Studies in the Novel* 22 (1990): 357-361.

—. "Intertextual Bondings Between 'The Wreck of the Hesperus' and *The Wreck of the Deutschland,*" *Texas Studies in Literature and Language* 33 (1991): 40-63.

—. *Crisis-Consciousness and the Novel.* Newark: U of Delaware P, 1992.

—, ed. *Gerard Manley Hopkins and Critical Discourse.* New York: AMS, 1993.

Holland, Norman N. *The Dynamics of Literary Response.* New York: Norton, 1975.

Holloway, John. *The Slumber of Apollo: Reflections on Recent Art, Literature, Language, and the Individual Consciousness.* Cambridge: Cambridge UP, 1983.

Holloway, Sister Marcella Marie. *The Prosodic Theory of Gerard Manley Hopkins.* Washington, D. C.: Catholic U of America P, 1947.

Holman, C. Hugh, and William Harmon. *A Handbook to Literature.* 5th ed. New York: Macmillan, 1986.

Hopkins, Gerard Manley. *The Note-Books of Gerard Manley Hopkins.* Ed. Humphry House. Oxford: Oxford UP, 1937.

—. *The Letters of Gerard Manley Hopkins to Robert Bridges.* Ed. Claude Colleer Abbott. London: Oxford UP, 1955.

—. *Further Letters of Gerard Manley Hopkins, Including His Correspondence with Coventry Patmore.* Ed. Claude Colleer Abbott. 2nd ed. London: Oxford UP, 1956.
—. *The Correspondence of Gerard Manley Hopkins and Richard Watson Dixon.* Ed. Claude Colleer Abbott. London: Oxford UP, 1955.
—. *The Journals and Papers of Gerard Manley Hopkins.* Ed. Humphry House and Graham Storey. London: Oxford UP, 1959.
—. *The Sermons and Devotional Writings of Gerard Manley Hopkins.* Ed. Christopher Devlin. London: Oxford UP, 1959.
—. *The Poems of Gerard Manley Hopkins.* 4th ed., rev. and enlarged by W. H. Gardner and N. H. MacKenzie. 1967. Oxford: Oxford UP, 1970.
—. *Gerard Manley Hopkins.* Ed. Catherine Phillips. The Oxford Authors. Oxford: Oxford UP, 1986.
—. *The Poetical Works of Gerard Manley Hopkins.* Ed. Norman H. MacKenzie. Oxford English Texts Series. Oxford: Clarendon, 1990.
—. *The Later Poetic Manuscripts of Gerard Manley Hopkins in Facsimile.* Ed. Norman H. MacKenzie. New York: Garland, 1990.
Hopkins Lives: An Exhibition and Catalogue. Comp. and intro. Carl Sutton. Ed. Dave Oliphant. Austin: Harry Ransom Humanities Research Center [U of Texas], 1989.
Houghton, W. E., and G. Robert Stange, eds. *Victorian Poetry and Poetics.* 2nd ed. New York: Houghton Mifflin, 1968.
House, Humphry. *The Dickens World.* 2nd. ed. London: Oxford UP, 1942.
House, Madeline. "Books Belonging to Hopkins and His family." *The Hopkins Research Bulletin* 5 [1974]: 26-41.
Howard, H. Wendell. "The Influence of the Music of Henry Purcell on the Poetry of Gerard Manley Hopkins." *The Hopkins Quarterly* 8 (1982): 137-54.
Hume, Robert D. "Gothic Versus Romantic: A Revaluation of the Gothic Novel." *PMLA* 84 (1969): 282-90.
Humphrey, Nicholas. *Consciousness Regained: Chapters in the Development of Mind.* New York: Oxford UP, 1983.
Husserl, Edmund. *The Crisis of European Sciences and Transcendental Phenomenology.* Trans. with intro. David Carr. Evanston, Illinois: Northwestern UP, 1970.
Isaac, Jeffrey C. *Power and Marxist Theory: A Realist View.* Ithaca: Cornell UP, 1987.
Iser, Wolfgang. *Walter Pater: The Aesthetic Moment.* Trans. David Henry Wilson. Cambridge: Cambridge UP, 1987.
Iyengar, K. R. Sprinivasa. *Gerard Manley Hopkins: The Man and the Poet.* London: Oxford UP, 1948.
Jameson, Fredric. *The Prison-House of Language: A Critical Account of Structuralism and Russian Formalism.* Princeton: Princeton UP, 1972.
—. *The Political Unconscious: Narrative as a Socially Symbolic Act.* Ithaca: Cornell UP, 1981.

Jann, Rosemary. *The Art and Science of Victorian History*. Columbia: Ohio State UP, 1985.

Jansen, Sue Curry. *Censorship: The Knot That Binds Power and Knowledge*. Oxford: Oxford UP, 1988.

Jauss, Hans Robert. *Toward an Aesthetic of Reception*. Trans. Timothy Bahti. Minneapolis: U of Minnesota P, 1982.

Jay, Gregory S. *T. S. Eliot and the Poetics of Literary History*. Baton Rouge: Louisiana State UP, 1983.

Jeffares, A. Norman. *A Commentary on the Collected Poems of W. B. Yeats*. Stanford: Stanford UP, 1968.

Johnson, Carl L. *Professor Longfellow of Harvard*. Eugene: U of Oregon P, 1944.

Johnson, Wendell Stacy. *Gerard Manley Hopkins: The Poet as Victorian*. Ithaca: Cornell UP, 1968.

Johnstone, Robert. "The Impossible Genre: Reading Comprehensive Literary History." *PMLA* 107 (1992): 26-37.

Kahn, Victoria. "Habermas, Machiavelli, and the Humanist Critique of Ideology." *PMLA* 105 (1990): 464-76.

Karl, Frederick R. *A Reader's Guide to Joseph Conrad*. Rev. ed. New York: Farrar, Straus and Giroux, 1969.

Kavanagh, Patrick. *The Green Fool*. New York: Harper, 1939.

Keating, John E. *"The Wreck of the Deutschland": An Essay and Commentary*. Darby, Pennsylvania: Darby, 1963.

Kellner, Hans. *Language and Historical Representation: Getting the Story Crooked*. Madison: U of Wisconsin P, 1989.

Kemp, Anthony. *The Estrangement of the Past: A Study in the Origins of Modern Historical Consciousness*. New York: Oxford UP, 1991.

Kermode, Frank. *History and Value: The Clarendon lectures and the Northcliffe Lectures 1987*. Oxford: Oxford UP, 1988.

Kitchen, Paddy. *Gerard Manley Hopkins*. London: Hamish Hamilton, 1978.

Kivy, Peter. *The Corded Shell: Reflections on Musical Expression*. Princeton: Princeton UP, 1980.

Knapp, Bettina L. *Music, Archetype, and the Writer: A Jungian View*. University Park: Pennsylvania State UP, 1988.

Kramer, Lawrence. *Music and Poetry: The Nineteenth Century and After*. Berkeley: U of California P, 1984.

Kubler, George. *Building the Escorial*. Princeton: Princeton UP, 1982.

Kuhn, Thomas S. *The Structure of Scientific Revolutions*. 2nd ed., enlgd. Chicago: U of Chicago P, 1970.

Lacan, Jacques. "The Mirror Stage as Formative of the Function of the I as Revealed in Psychoanalytic Experience." Trans. Alan Sheridan. *Contemporary Critical Theory*. Ed. Dan Latimer. New York: Harcourt, 1989. 502-09.

Langer, Suzanne K. *Feeling and Form*. New York: Charles Scribner's Sons, 1953.

Larousse Encyclopedia of Mythology. New York: Prometheus, 1960.

Leinwand, Theodore B. "Negotiation and New Historicism." *PMLA* 105 (1990): 477-90.

Leithauser, Brad. "Radical Prosodist." Rev. of *The Poetical Works of Gerard Manley Hopkins*, ed. Norman H. MacKenzie, Oxford English Texts Series (Oxford: Clarendon, 1990) and *Gerard Manley Hopkins: A Very Private Life* by Robert Bernard Martin (New York: Putnam, 1991). *The New Yorker* Oct. 6, 1991: 114-25.

Lentino, Giacomo da. *The Poetry of Giacomo da Lentino: Sicilian Poet of the Thirteenth Century*. Ed. Ernest F. Langley. Cambridge: Harvard UP, 1915.

Lesser, Wayne. "Criticism, Literary History, and the Paradigm: *The Education of Henry Adams*." *PMLA* 97 (1982): 378-94.

Levine, George, ed. *One Culture: Essays in Science and Literature*. Madison: U of Wisconsin P, 1987.

Levine, Philippa. *The Amateur and the Professional: Antiquaries, Historians and Archaeologists in Victorian England, 1838-1886*. Cambridge: Cambridge UP, 1986.

Levinson, Marjorie, et al. *Rethinking Historicism: Critical Readings in Romantic History*. Oxford: Basil Blackwell, 1989.

Lichtmann, Maria R. *The Contemplative Poetry of Gerard Manley Hopkins*. Princeton: Princeton UP, 1989.

Lipking, Lawrence. *The Life of the Poet*. Chicago: U of Chicago P, 1981.

Liu, Alan. *Wordsworth: The Sense of History*. Stanford: Stanford UP, 1989.

Loesberg, Jonathan. *Fictions of Consciousness: Mill, Newman, and the Reading of Victorian Prose*. New Brunswick: Rutgers UP, 1986.

Longfellow, Henry Wadsworth. *The Letters of Henry Wadsworth Longfellow*. Andrew Hillen, ed. 6 vols. Cambridge: Harvard UP, 1966-1982.

—. *The Poetical Works of Longfellow*. Cambridge Edition. Edited, with new introduction, by George Monteiro. Boston: Houghton Mifflin, 1975.

Loomis, Jeffrey B. *Dayspring in Darkness: Sacrament in Hopkins*. Lewisburg: Bucknell UP, 1988.

Loyola, Ignatius. *The Spiritual Exercises of St. Ignatius*. Tr. Anthony Mattola; intro. Robert W. Gleason, S.J. Garden City: Image, 1964.

Ludvigson, Susan. "A Poetry Reading and a Lecture." Georgia State University. 8 April 1991.

MacKenzie, Norman H. *A Reader's Guide to Gerard Manley Hopkins*. Ithaca: Cornell UP, 1981.

—. "From Manuscript to Printed Text: The Hazardous Transmission of the Hopkins Canon." *Hopkins Lives: An Exhibition and Catalogue*. Comp. and intro. Carl Sutton; Ed. Dave Oliphant. Austin: Harry Ransom Humanities Research Center [Univ. of Texas], 1989. 51-73.

—. "Introduction" to Hopkins, *Poetical*. xxv-lxxv.

—. "Review" of Zaniello. *Hopkins Quarterly* 17.3 (1990): 104-7.

McChesney, Donald. *A Hopkins Commentary: An Explanatory Commentary on the Main Poems, 1876-89.* London: U of London P, 1968.

McGann, Jerome J. *The Beauty of Inflections: Literary Investigations in Historical Method and Theory.* Oxford: Oxford UP, 1985.

—, ed. *Historical Studies and Literary Criticism.* Madison: U of Wisconsin P, 1985.

—. "The Third World of Criticism." Levinson 85-107.

—. *Social Values and Poetic Acts: The Historical Judgment of Literary Work.* Cambridge: Harvard UP, 1988.

Mariani, Paul L. *A Commentary on the Complete Poems of Gerard Manley Hopkins.* Ithaca: Cornell UP, 1970.

—. *A Usable Past: Essays on Modern and Contemporary Poetry.* Amherst: U of Massachusetts P, 1984.

Martin, Robert Bernard. *Gerard Manley Hopkins: A Very Private Life.* New York: Putnam, 1991.

Martz, Louis L. *The Poetry of Meditation.* New Haven: Yale UP, 1954.

—. *Poet of Exile: A Study of Milton's Poetry.* New Haven: Yale UP, 1980.

Mellers, Wilfrid. *Harmonious Meeting: A Study of the Relationship between English Music, Poetry and Theatre, c. 1600-1900.* London: Dennis Dobson, 1965.

Merleau-Ponty, Maurice. *Signs.* Trans. and intro. Richard C. McCleary. Chicago: Northwestern UP, 1964.

Mermin, Dorothy. *The Audience in the Poem: Five Victorian Poets.* New Brunswick: Rutgers UP, 1983.

Mill, John Stuart. *On Liberty.* Ed. David Spitz. New York: Norton, 1975.

Miller, James E., Jr. "Whitman's *Leaves* and the American 'Lyric-Epic.'" Fraistat, *Place* 289-307.

Miller, J. Hillis. "The Universal Chiming." *Hopkins: A Collection of Critical Essays.* Edgewood Cliffs, N. J.: Prentice-Hall, 1966. 89-116.

—. *The Disappearance of God: Five Nineteenth-Century Writers.* Cambridge: Harvard UP, 1963.

—. *Theory Then and Now.* Durham: Duke UP, 1991.

Millgate, Michael. *Testamentary Acts: Browning, Tennyson, James, Hardy.* Oxford: Clarendon, 1992.

Milroy, James. "Read with the Ear: Patterns of Sound." *The Language of Gerard Manley Hopkins.* London: Andre Deutsch, 1927. 114-53.

Milward, Peter, S.J. "'On a Pastoral Forehead in Wales': The Composition of Place in *The Wreck.*" Milward and Schoder 68-77.

—. *A Commentary on G. M. Hopkins' "The Wreck of the Deutschland."* Tokyo: Hokuseido, 1968.

Milward, Peter, S.J., and Raymond Schoder, S.J., eds. *Readings of "The Wreck": Essays in Commemoration of the Centenary of G. M. Hopkins' "The Wreck of the Deutschland."* Chicago: Loyola UP, 1976.

Miner, Earl. "Some Issues for Study of Integrated Collections." Fraistat, *Place* 18-43.

Mönch, Walter. *Das Sonett: Gestalt und Geschichte*. Heidelberg: F. H. Kerle, 1955.

Montrose, Louis A. "Professing the Renaissance: The Poetics and Politics of Culture." Veeser 15-36.

Motto, Marylou. *"Mined with a Motion": The Poetry of Gerard Manley Hopkins*. New Brunswick, N. J.: Rutgers UP, 1984.

Murray, John Courtney, S.J. "Foreword." *Freedom and Man*. New York: Kenedy, 1965. 11-15.

Mussalman, Joseph. *Music in the Cultured Generation: A Social History of Music in America, 1870-1900*. Evanston: Northwestern UP, 1971.

Neff, Emery. *The Poetry of History*. New York: Columbia UP, 1947.

Neubauer, John. *The Emancipation of Music from Language: Departure from Mimesis in Eighteenth-Century Aesthetics*. New Haven: Yale UP, 1986.

Nietzsche, Friedrich. *The Will to Power*. Trans. Walter Kaufmann and R. J. Hollingdale. New York: Vintage, 1968.

—. "On Truth and Lie in their Extramoral Sense." *The Portable Nietzsche*. Trans. Walter Kaufman. New York: Penguin, 1976. 42-47.

Nixon, Jude. *Gerard Manley Hopkins and His Contemporaries: Liddon, Newman, Darwin, and Pater*. New York: Garland, 1994.

Noon, William T., S.J. *Poetry and Prayer*. New Brunswick, NJ: Rutgers UP, 1967.

Novick, Peter. *That Noble Dream: The "Objectivity Question" and the American Historical Profession*. Cambridge: Cambridge UP, 1988.

Ong, Walter J., S.J. "The Audience is Always a Fiction." *PMLA* 90 (1975): 9-21.

—. *Hopkins, the Self, and God*. Toronto: U of Toronto P, 1986.

Oppenheimer, Paul. *The Birth of the Modern Mind: Self, Consciousness, and the Invention of the Sonnet*. New York: Oxford UP, 1989.

Ortony, Andrew, ed. *Metaphor and Thought*. Cambridge: Cambridge UP, 1979.

Palmer, Roy. *The Sound of History: Songs and Social Comment*. New York: Oxford UP, 1988.

Pater, Walter. *The Renaissance: Studies in Art and Poetry*. Ed. Donald L. Hill. Berkeley: U of California P, 1980.

Patterson, Annabel. "Jonson, Marvell, and Miscellaneity." Fraistat, *Place* 95-114.

Peck, Harry Thurston. *William Hickling Prescott*. 1905. New York: Greenwood Press, 1969.

Pepper, Stephen. *World Hypotheses: A Study in Evidence*. Berkeley: U of California P, 1942.

—. *Concept and Quality: A World Hypothesis*. La Salle, IL: Open Court, 1967.

Perkins, David. *Is Literary History Possible?* Cambridge: Harvard UP, 1991.

Perloff, Marjorie. "The Two *Ariels*: The (Re)Making of the Sylvia Plath Canon." Fraistat, *Place* 308-33.

Perrin, Norman. *The New Testament: An Introduction*. New York: Harcourt, 1974.

Peters, W. A. M. *Gerard Manley Hopkins: A Critical Essay towards an Understanding of his Poetry*. London: Oxford UP, 1948.

Phillips, C. L. "Robert Bridges and the First Edition of Gerard Manley Hopkins's Poems." *Gerard Manley Hopkins: The Centenary Revaluation*. Ed. Eugene Hollahan. *Studies in the Literary Imagination* 21 (1988): 7-21.

Pick, John, ed. *Gerard Manley Hopkins: "The Windhover."* Columbus, Ohio: Merrill, 1969.

Plotkin, Cary Price. *The Tenth Muse: Victorian Philology and the Genesis of the Poetic Language of Gerard Manley Hopkins*. Carbondale: Southern Illinois UP, 1989.

Price, Derek J. de Solla. *Little Science, Big Science . . . and Beyond*. New York: Columbia UP, 1986.

Quinones, Ricardo J. *Mapping Literary Modernism: Time and Development*. Princeton: Princeton UP, 1985.

Rajan, Balachandra. *The Form of the Unfinished: English Poetics from Spenser to Pound*. Princeton: Princeton UP, 1985.

Ransom, John Crowe. *The World's Body*. New York: Charles Scribner's Sons, 1938.

Ricks, Christopher, ed. "The order of the poems." *The Poems of Tennyson*. London: Longmans, 1969. Xxi-xxiii.

Riddle, Florence K. "Allusions of Job in *The Wreck of the Deutschland*." *Cithara* 13 (1974): 57-68.

Riffaterre, Michael. "Compulsory reader response: the intertextual drive." *Intertextuality: Theories and practices*. Ed. Michael Worton and Judith Still. New York: Manchester UP, 1990. 56-78.

Robertson, John M. Introduction. *Introduction to the History of Civilization in England*. By Henry Thomas Buckle. iii-xv.

—. *Buckle and His Critics: A Study in Sociology*. London: Swan, Sonnenschein, 1895.

Robinson, John. *In Extremity: A Study of Gerard Manley Hopkins*. New York: Cambridge UP, 1978.

Rodden, John. *The Politics of Literary Reputation: The Making and Claiming of 'St. George' Orwell*. New York: Oxford UP, 1989.

Rosenthal, M. L., and Sally M. Gall. *The Modern Poetic Sequence: The Genius of Modern Poetry*. Oxford UP, 1983.

Ruggles, Eleanor. *Gerard Manley Hopkins: A Life*. New York: Norton, 1944.

Ruskin, John. *The Works of John Ruskin*. 39 volumes. Ed. E. T. Cook and Alexander Wedderburn. London: George Allen, 1912.

Ruthven, K. K. *Critical Assumptions*. Cambridge: Cambridge UP, 1979.

Sacks, Sheldon, ed. *On Metaphor*. Chicago: U of Chicago P, 1979.

Said, Edward W. *Beginnings: Intention and Method*. New York: Basic Books, 1975.

—. *The World, the Text, and the Critic.* Cambridge: Harvard UP, 1983.

Salvin, Francis Henry, and William Brodrick. *Falconry in the British Isles.* London: John Van Voorst, 1855.

Scher, Steven Paul. "Literature and Music." *Interrelations of Literature.* Ed. Jean-Pierre Barricelli and Joseph Gibaldi. New York: Modern Language Association, 1982. 225-50.

Schnapp, Jeffrey T. *The Transfiguration of History at the Center of Dante's "Paradise."* Princeton: Princeton UP, 1986.

Schneider, Elisabeth W. "*The Wreck of the Deutschland*: A New Reading." *PMLA* 81 (1966): 110-22.

—. *The Dragon in the Gate: Studies in the Poetry of G. M. Hopkins.* Berkeley: U of California P, 1968.

Schwenger, Peter. "Circling Ground Zero." *PMLA* 106 (1991): 251-61.

Seelhammer, Ruth. *Hopkins Collected at Gonzaga.* Chicago: Loyola UP, 1970.

Shafer, Robert Jones, ed. *A Guide to Historical Method.* Rev. ed. Homeward, IL: Dorsey, 1974.

Shawcross, John T. "The Arrangement and Order of John Donne's Poems." Fraistat, *Place* 119-63.

Shimone, Kunio. "'Speech Framed To Be Heard': The Function and Value of Sound Effects in The Wreck." Milward and Schoder 142-53.

Simpson, Lewis P. *The Brazen Face of History: Studies in the Literary Consciousness of America.* Baton Rouge: Louisiana State UP, 1980.

Sitterson, Joseph C., Jr. "The Genre and Place of the Intimations Ode." *PMLA* 101 (1986): 24-37.

Smeaton, Oliphant. *Longfellow and His Poetry.* 1913. New York: AMS, 1971.

Smith, Barbara Herrnstein. *Poetic Closure: A Study of How Poems End.* Chicago: U of Chicago P, 1968.

Smulders, Sharon. "'A Form That Differences': Vocational Metaphors in the Poetry of Christina Rossetti and Gerard Manley Hopkins." *Victorian Poetry* 29 (1991): 161-73.

Sprinker, Michael. *"A Counterpoint of Dissonance" The Aesthetics and Poetry of Gerard Manley Hopkins.* Baltimore: Johns Hopkins UP, 1989.

St. Aubyn, Giles. *A Victorian Eminence: The Life and Works of Henry Thomas Buckle.* London: Barrie, 1958.

Stephenson, Edward. *What Sprung Rhythm Really Is.* Alma, Ontario: International Hopkins Association, 1987.

Stevens, John. "Gerard Manley Hopkins as Musician." *The Journals and Papers of Gerard Manley Hopkins.* Ed. Humphry House and Graham Storey. London: Oxford UP, 1954. 457-97.

Stevens, Wallace. *The Palm at the End of the Mind: Selected Poems and a Play.* Ed. Holly Stevens. New York: Knopf, 1971.

Stocks, Kenneth. *Emily Dickinson and the Modern Consciousness: A Poet of Our Time.* New York: St. Martin's, 1988.

Stonum, Gary Lee. *The Dickinson Sublime.* Madison: U of Wisconsin P, 1990.

Storey, Graham. "Introduction." *Hopkins: Selections*. London: Oxford UP, 1967.

—. "Hopkins as a Mannerist." Hollahan, *Centenary* 77-89.

Sulloway, Alison G. *Gerard Manley Hopkins and the Victorian Temper*. New York: Columbia UP, 1972.

Tennyson, G. B. *Victorian Devotional Poetry: The Tractarian Mode*. Cambridge: Harvard UP, 1981.

Thomas, Alfred, S.J. *Hopkins the Jesuit: The Years of Training*. London: Oxford UP, 1969.

Thompson, James Westfall. *A History of Historical Writing*. 2 vols. New York: Macmillan, 1942.

Thompson, Lawrence. *Young Longfellow: (1807-1843)*. 1938. New York: Longman, Green, 1955.

Thornton, R. K. R., ed. *All My Eyes See: The Visual World of Gerard Manley Hopkins*. Tyne and Wiser: Ceolfrith, 1975.

Ticknor, George. *Life of William Hickling Prescott*. Boston: Ticknor and Fields, 1864.

Treitler, Leo. *Music and the Historical Imagination*. Cambridge: Harvard UP, 1989.

Turkheimer, David. "The Deus Ex Machina in Literature: The Poetry of Gerard Manley Hopkins as a Test Case." M. A. thesis (Georgia State University, 1985).

Turner, Paul. "Hopkins." *English Literature 1832-1890 Excluding the Novel*. Oxford: Clarendon, 1989. 140-58.

Updike, John. *Hugging the Shore: Essays and Criticism*. New York: Vintage, 1984.

Veeser, H. Aram, ed. *The New Historicism*. New York: Routledge, 1989.

Vendler, Helen. *Wallace Stevens: Words Chosen Out of Desire*. Knoxville: U of Tennessee P, 1984.

Wagenknecht, Edward. *Longfellow: A Full-Length Portrait*. New York: Longman, Green, 1955.

Walder, Dennis, ed. *Literature and the Modern World: Critical Essays and Documents*. Oxford: Oxford UP, 1990.

Walhout, Donald. *"Send My Roots Rain": A Study of Religious Experience in the Poetry of Gerard Manley Hopkins*. Athens: Ohio UP, 1981.

Walker, Ernest. *A History of Music in England*. [1952]. 3rd. ed. Rvsd. and enlgd. J. A. Westrup. New York: Da Capo, 1978.

Wallace, Robert K. *Jane Austen and Mozart: Classical Equilibrium in Fiction and Music*. Athens: U of Georgia P, 1983.

—. *Emily Brontë and Beethoven: Romantic Equilibrium in Fiction and Music*. Athens: U of Georgia P, 1986.

Warner, Rex, ed. *Gerard Manley Hopkins: Look up at the Skies: Poems and Prose Chosen by Rex Warner*. London: Bodley Head, 1972.

Warton, Thomas. *History of English Poetry in Four Volumes*. 1774. Facsimile ed. New York: Johnson Reprint, 1968.

Waterhouse, John F. "Gerard Manley Hopkins and Music." *Music and Letters* 18 (1937): 227-35.

Weatherby, Harold L. *The Keen Delight: The Christian Poet in the Modern World*. Athens: U of Georgia P, 1975.

Wellek, René, and Alvaro Ribeiro, eds. *Evidence in Literary Scholarship: Essays in Memory of James Marshall Osborn*. Oxford: Clarendon, 1979.

Welsh, Alexander. *George Eliot and Blackmail*. Cambridge: Harvard UP, 1985.

Westrup, Jack A. Rev. of *The Journals and Papers of Gerard Manley Hopkins*, ed. Humphry House and Graham Storey. *Music and Letters* 41 (1960): 74-5.

Weyand, Norman, S.J., and Raymond Schoder, S.J., eds. *Immortal Diamond: Studies in Gerard Manley Hopkins*. New York: Sheed and Ward, 1949.

Whitaker, Thomas R. *Swan and Shadow: Yeats's Dialogue with History*. 1964. Critical Studies in Irish Literature, vol. 1. Washington: U of America P, 1989.

White, Hayden. *Metahistory: The Historical Imagination in Nineteenth-Century Europe*. Baltimore: Johns Hopkins UP, 1973.

—. *Tropics of Discourse: Essays in Cultural Criticism*. Baltimore: Johns Hopkins UP, 1978.

—. *The Content of the Form: Narrative Discourse and Historical Representation*. Baltimore: Johns Hopkins UP, 1987.

White, Norman. *Hopkins: A Literary Biography*. New York: Oxford UP, 1992.

Williams, Carolyn. *Transfigured World: Walter Pater's Aesthetic Historicism*. Ithaca: Cornell UP, 1989.

Williams, Cecil B. *Henry Wadsworth Longfellow*. New York: Grosset & Dunlap, 1964.

Wimsatt, William A., Jr., and Cleanth Brooks. *Literary Criticism: A Short History*. New York: Alfred A. Knopf, 1957.

Winks, Robin, ed. *The Historian as Detective*. New York: Harper & Row, 1968.

Wisenthal, J. L. *Shaw's Sense of History*. Oxford: Oxford UP, 1988.

Wittreich, Joseph Anthony, Jr. "'Strange Text!': 'Paradise Regain'd . . . To which is added *Samson Agonistes*.'" Fraistat, *Place* 164-94.

Wood, Casey A., and F. Marjorie Fyfe. "Translators' Introduction." Hohenstaufen xxxv-l.

Woolford, John. *Browning the Revisionary*. New York: St. Martin's, 1988.

Zaniello, Tom. *Hopkins in the Age of Darwin*. Iowa City: U of Iowa P, 1988.

INDEX

Oedipus Complex, 11, 12, 14, 99,
    102, 132
Ong, Walter, S.J., 4, 58, 64, 67,
    68, 71, 77, 79, 86, 100,
    116
Oppenheimer, Paul, 18, 68, 127,
    131-136, 143, 145, 146;
    *The Birth of the Modern
    Mind*, 68
Ovid, 17, 57, 59, 60, 66, 118
Oxford University, 4, 7, 13, 28,
    29, 39, 53, 64, 73, 82, 84,
    135, 142, 162, 169, 177

Palmer, Roy, 170
Paratextuality, 132, 206 n. 6
Parmenides, 51
Parnassian Poetry, 49
Pascal, Blaise, 49, 50, 167
Pater, Walter, 15, 16, 38, 39, 54,
    77, 124, 132, 157
Patmore, Coventry, 63, 96
Patterson, Annabel, 60
Pepper, Stephen, 69
Perkins, David, 3
Perloff, Marjorie, 62
Petrarch, 60, 61, 68
Pick, John, 22, 25
Pindar, 103
Plath, Sylvia, 62; *Ariel*, 62
Plato, 132
Plotkin, Cary, xix, 4, 15, 28
Poe, Edgar Allan, 97
Pope, Alexander, 7, 57, 61, 69,
    78, 118, 119, 121, 131,
    135, 136
Prescott, William Hickling, 45-
    46, 52, 154
Price, Derek J. de Solla, 19, 36
Progress, 26-29, 33, 34, 55, 159
Prosody, xvii, 2, 51, 104, 109,
    116, 141, 161, 162
Psychiatry, 73, 144

Psychoanalysis, 7, 8, 18, 34, 52,
    72-74
Purcell, Henry, 67, 125, 157, 159,
    162, 168, 172, 177-181,
    187
Pusey, E. B., 13

Rajan, Balachandra, 28, 49, 58,
    73, 75
Ransom, John Crowe, 54
Real Presence, 13, 84
Red Letter (Hopkins's), 14
Renan, Ernst, 15, 124
Renunciation (of speech), 77
Rio, A. F., 13
Robertson, John M., 26, 28-30,
    37, 41
Rodden, John, 78
Roman Catholic Church, 12, 84,
    100
Romanticism, 177
Rossetti, Dante Gabriel, 48, 55,
    144
Ruskin, John, 4, 20, 25, 34, 41
Russell, Bertrand, 38
Russian revolution, 15

Sacks, Sheldon, 7
Said, Edward, xix, xx, 3, 11, 23,
    28, 31, 55, 57, 71, 76, 77,
    91, 97, 120, 123, 141,
    150, 153, 181; *Begin-
    nings*, xix, 3, 55-57, 71,
    73, 88, 120, 141, 150,
    153
St. Aubyn, Giles, 22, 34, 37, 38
Scher, Steven, 160, 161, 163, 216
    n. 6
Schneider, Elisabeth W., 63, 87
Science, xviii, 4, 19, 25, 28, 30,
    31, 37, 38, 71, 76, 121,
    135, 136, 141, 143, 144,
    146, 171, 189
Scotland Yard, 16